Topics in
Management Accounting

Topics in
Management Accounting

Edited by
JOHN ARNOLD,
BRYAN CARSBERG &
ROBERT SCAPENS

University of Manchester

Philip Allan

First published 1980 by

PHILIP ALLAN PUBLISHERS LIMITED
MARKET PLACE
DEDDINGTON
OXFORD OX5 4SE

0 86003 508 5 hbk
0 86003 609 X pbk

Reprinted 1981, 1983

British Library Cataloguing in Publication Data

Topics in management accounting
   1. Managerial accounting
   I. Arnold, John, *b. 1944*
   II. Carsberg, Bryan Victor
   III. Scapens, Robert William
   658.1'511   HF5635

ISBN 0–86003–508–5

ISBN 0–86003–609–X Pbk

Set by MHL Typesetting Limited, Coventry
Printed in Great Britain at The Camelot Press Limited, Southampton

Contents

Preface

British writers have contributed substantially to the development of the literature on management accounting. In this book we have attempted to bring together contributions from a number of leading British academics, many of whom have been involved in the advancement of the literature. The book is intended to complement introductory and intermediate level text books in management accounting. It is aimed primarily at students taking undergraduate university courses, or other courses of a similar level. The book should give such students some insights into the scope and methods of the subject and an appreciation of its more exciting and challenging aspects. It is also suitable for managers who are interested in a relatively non-mathematical account of the state of management accounting in British universities.

The particular contribution of the book is that it brings together original writings by authors who are experts in the topics covered. All of the authors are, or have been, based at UK universities and, in consequence, the book illustrates current UK academic thinking in management accounting. Each chapter contains an explanation of the topic covered at a fairly basic level and a discussion of possible applications. Where appropriate, simple numerical examples are used to illustrate the main points. Inevitably, in a book of this size, it has not been possible to deal with all topics which are currently thought to be within the management accounting area. To those readers who rue the omission of, for example, contributions in the area of capital budgeting, we apologise.

The chapters that are included fall into six main categories. The first four chapters examine topics which are prerequisites for a study of almost any aspect of accounting, and which provide a framework for the remainder of the book. Chapter

5 deals particularly with problems involved in, and methods available for, forecasting. This is an activity which is central to much of management accounting. In Chapters 6 to 9 various aspects of (short-term) decision making are discussed; in particular the measurement and application of relevant costs for decisions. Chapters 10 to 12 are concerned with the control of the implementation of plans arising from the decision making process, and with the ways in which control information might be used to develop future plans. Chapter 13 provides an historical perspective of management accounting and explains the current state of the subject. We believe that an understanding of the historical development of management accounting methods is of great importance in evaluating their usefulness. Chapter 14 summarises and provides a synthesis of previous chapters, and suggests certain areas in which future research could be conducted.

We extend our thanks to all those who have contributed chapters. No-one refused our invitation and everyone accepted our often unreasonable deadlines with good grace. Our thanks go also to the anonymous (to us) secretaries who typed the first drafts of the chapters by authors not from our department. We owe a particular debt to Imelda Welsby and Colette White who typed the chapters emanating from our department and re-typed several of the others, frequently working to deadlines even more unreasonable than those we imposed on the authors!

John Arnold
Bryan Carsberg
Robert Scapens

Department of Accounting and Business Finance,
University of Manchester

May 1980

1

Introduction

BRYAN CARSBERG

Professor of Accounting,
University of Manchester

The purpose of this book is to provide a review of some of the most important topics in management accounting. It is hoped that the book will serve to stimulate the reader's interest in further study by illustrating the methods of thought that are contributing to the development of the subject and by offering glimpses into some of the problems that are being investigated in current research. In this introductory chapter, we shall discuss the nature of management accounting. We shall discuss its purposes and some of the procedures that it involves. A convenient focus for the discussion is a comparison of management accounting with financial accounting.

Management Accounting versus Financial Accounting

All branches of accounting are concerned with systems for providing information that will be useful to people who take decisions. The primary focus of accounting is on financial information, but the system may also deal with related statistics. Accounting systems are potentially useful in any situation in which financial decisions have to be taken and the relevant considerations are too complex to be dealt with informally. However, an accounting system will actually be established only if the benefits from its use, in terms of improved decisions, are expected to exceed the costs of establishing and operating it. Most businesses and government organisations have accounting systems, because the complexity of their affairs makes it impossible to carry out their legal obligations without one. An individual might also benefit from an accounting system — for example, one that records expenditures on different commodities and prices at different shops. Some individuals do keep such records, but most do not because of the effort (cost) involved.

Many types of decision, taken by people in various roles, are based on accounting information. In some cases, the people who arrange for the information to be collected are also its main users. For example, the managers of a business require a system to provide information which they can use for decisions about which products should be manufactured by the business. Such systems are classified as management accounting systems.

In other cases, the people who arrange for the information to be collected are not the people who use it. In those cases, the systems are usually regarded as part of financial accounting. Examples of the decisions that are based on financial accounting information include:

(a) Decisions by people who have invested in a business about whether they should invest more or try to sell their investment to someone else.
(b) Decisions about extending credit to a business.
(c) Decisions by prospective employees about job offers.
(d) Decisions by government officials about the amount of tax to be demanded from a business.

The dividing line between financial accounting and management accounting is not clear cut. Financial accounting reports normally deal with a business at an aggregate level — for example, the statement of assets and liabilities and the income statement that are prepared for the owners of a business are regarded as financial accounting statements. That type of report is also important to managers, even if they have no interest as owners. The managers as a group know that owners will assess their performance on the basis of income and net assets; consequently, the managers will use the financial accounting statements when they establish plans and assess whether progress has been satisfactory. Managers in overall charge of an organisation may also use an income statement and statement of net assets to monitor the performance of their colleagues who are responsible for part of the organisation, for example a separate division.

However, in spite of those managerial uses of the financial accounting statements, the focus of management accounting systems is usually on information at a more detailed level, on results for individual products or groups of products and on costs for particular productive operations. Even at that level, management accounting normally is not separate from financial accounting. Part of the information required for management accounting often represents a detailed analysis of the financial accounting information. It is usually economical, in terms of cost, to use an integrated system for both kinds of information, even though that procedure may sometimes involve compromises in the acceptance of information that is not the best for the purposes at hand.

Standard-Setting in Accounting

Financial accounting is now subject to a great deal of regulation. Various bodies, some of them government agencies, others organised by the accounting profession, have drawn up rules that specify standard accounting practices. Those rules are normally followed in the preparation of financial accounting statements because of direct or indirect legal sanctions. The standards have been developed because of a widespread belief that businesses would not produce satisfactory statements without the guidance of standards. Before the advent of standards, it was common for different businesses to treat a given type of transaction in different ways. For example, some businesses would treat research and development expenditures as a deduction from income when they were incurred; others would treat the expenditures as assets on the ground that they were expected to bring future benefits. Accounting standards have reduced the frequency of occurrence of that kind of difference.

The level of importance that should be attached to the avoidance of variations in accounting practice is largely a matter of subjective judgment. Some people argue that such variations are relatively unimportant and that market mechanisms would lead to the disappearance of undesirable practices. They believe that a business that provided too little information or that used unacceptable methods of measurement would find itself unable to obtain capital at a normal cost and would therefore be forced to change its ways. However, most people take a different view. They believe that market competition cannot be relied upon to provide sufficient incentives to avoid the use of inferior accounting practices: the identification of inferior practices might take too long; incentives might be too remote; and, even if superior practices prevailed in the long term, many people might suffer damage in the meantime. The majority view, though it is unsupported by firm evidence, has been encouraged by the observation that minority accounting practices have often been used by firms which have failed or which have received unfavourable publicity for other reasons.

Management accounting has few standard-setting bodies and few standard practices. In the following pages we shall discuss the need for standards of management accounting and then consider what standards we might promulgate if we were in a position to do so. The Financial Accounting Standards Board (FASB), the body mainly responsible for the development of financial accounting standards in the United States, has been working on a project to develop a conceptual framework for financial accounting and reporting. The conceptual framework comprises a body of concepts that can be used to guide decisions on individual standards. It deals with general issues and is intended to promote consistency in standard-setting. We shall focus our attention on the selection of topics that might be included in a conceptual framework for management accounting.

The Need for Management Accounting Standards

At first sight, it may seem strange to suggest that there is a need for standards of management accounting. As noted above, management accounting systems are normally operated by managers for their own use in decision taking. If managers think that some particular information would be useful, they can arrange for its collection and there is no need for outside interference. Moreover, it would be difficult to make management accounting standards effective. It might be possible to compel businesses to collect specified kinds of information in specified ways, but it would not be possible to compel the managers to use the information for decision-taking purposes.

However, a case can be developed for the formulation of management accounting standards. The case is linked to the needs of financial accounting. In essence, it is that investors and creditors need information about the management accounting system of a firm as a means of assessing the performance of managers in making effective use of shareholders' resources. Management accounting standards could help to meet that need by providing a basis for reports by independent assessors (the auditors) about deviations between actual practice and standard practice. A good system does not guarantee a good performance, but it is a contributory factor.

Let us consider these arguments for management accounting standards in greater detail. Much of the literature on the design of management accounting systems rests on the implicit or explicit assumption that the main objective of managers is to maximise the wealth of people who have invested in the business. That assumption is unrealistic. It is much more likely that the primary goal of managers is to maximise their own wealth and other aspects of the satisfaction they get from their employment. To some extent, the behaviour required to achieve managers' own goals may be the same as the behaviour required to maximise the wealth of shareholders: high levels of business profit may enable managers to obtain correspondingly high rewards. However, the interests of managers and investors are not identical. Managers may, for example, be more interested than investors in increasing the size of the business and in avoiding ventures that are potentially profitable but risky. A report to investors on the management accounting system of a business may give them some minimal assurance of the extent to which their interests are the focus of managerial behaviour, because such a report would provide information about whether the system deals with financial indicators that reflect investors' objectives.

A second advantage of reporting on deviations between actual management accounting practices and standard practices may be stronger. Efficient managers are likely to have better management accounting systems than inefficient managers. Reporting on those systems would provide investors with information that would contribute to their assessments of managerial efficiency.

We shall not attempt to reach a firm conclusion regarding the need for standards of management accounting. The arguments are too numerous to be considered in detail in this chapter. Instead, we turn our attention to the issues that would have to be resolved if we were to prepare an authoritative statement of management accounting concepts. The following are some of the main steps that would be involved:

(a) Specify the main purpose(s) of a management accounting system.
(b) Identify the decisions that depend on management accounting information.
(c) Describe the principles that determine the selection of information for inclusion in the system.
(d) Describe the main types of information that should be provided.

Financial Accounting Concepts

The fundamental objectives of financial accounting were described in the FASB Statement, *Objectives of Financial Reporting by Business Enterprises*. That Statement emphasises that financial reports should be useful to users in making business and economic decisions. It identifies investors and creditors as the main users, but refers also to the needs of other users. The main decisions discussed by the Statement are decisions on investment (for exampie, the purchase and sale of shares) and on granting credit. The most important conclusion is, perhaps, that users require a basis for assessing the amounts, timing and uncertainty of future cash flows. That conclusion is based on the models of individual behaviour, developed in the literatures of economics and finance, in which individuals are assumed to wish to maximise the satisfaction that they obtain from the contemplation of future consumption. In those models, personal satisfaction depends on the amounts, timing and uncertainty of cash flows; consequently, individuals will wish to invest in businesses that seem to be likely to generate favourable cash flows — and assessment of future cash flows is an important part of the investment decision.

It is beyond the scope of the FASB Statement on Objectives to reach detailed conclusions about the means for satisfying the objectives; that goal will be pursued in other statements. The Objectives Statement simply observes that there is a need for certain types of information, for example, information on economic resources and obligations; it asserts also that the primary focus of financial reporting is information on earnings.

The Purpose of Management Accounting

There is not likely to be much controversy about the first steps in our exercise to develop a statement on the concepts of management accounting. It should be readily agreed that management accounting, like financial accounting, must be useful for taking decisions. More specifically, it may be stated that management accounting must provide information that is useful to the managers of an organisation in taking decisions within the scope of their managerial responsibility.

The next step in the development of our concepts statement is to identify the types of decision with which the management accounting system is expected to help. It would be impracticable to develop a complete list, reflecting all the peculiarities of different types of business. It is sufficient for our purposes to note the main types:

> *Output Decisions.* These are decisions on what types of goods and services should be supplied, at what prices and in what quantities.

Input Decisions. These are decisions on how the outputs should be produced, i.e. what quantities should be used of different materials, labour and other resources.

Input and output decisions are related: the cost of resources required to produce goods and services is relevant to decisions on the best quantities to produce and the best prices to charge. Moreover, each broad decision category leads into many subsidiary types of decision. For example, decisions on outputs involve consideration of sales promotion strategies. Decisions on inputs often involve trade-offs between different mixes of materials, labour and machinery; those decisions involve investment decisions that lead in turn to decisions on how investments are to be financed. Decisions on the allocation of people to particular jobs, resting on judgments of their efficiency, may also be regarded as decisions on inputs.

The Identification of Useful Information

Now that we have described some of the main decisions that have to be taken by managers, we come to more difficult questions about the types of information that should be provided by the management accounting system. In order to make progress in dealing with such questions, we need to have a good understanding of what the business managers are trying to achieve. As noted above, the traditional view is that managers are trying to obtain the best possible results for people who have invested in the business. Moreover, investors are assumed to wish to maximise the satisfaction they obtain from contemplating the uses of cash provided by the business. This line of thought suggests that managers will wish to maximise the net present value of cash flows available to investors. Now, cash flows available to investors are derived from cash flows to the business: consequently, the managers should attempt to maximise the net present value of cash flows to the business.

The above argument has been greatly simplified and it rests on the questionable assumption that managers do actually try to act in the best interests of shareholders. However, it can probably be accepted as a reasonable basis for the development of management accounting concepts. No alternative statement of business objectives commands general acceptance; and any alternative would be likely to attach considerable weight to the maximisation of the present value of future cash flows to the business.

If we do accept the above statement of business objectives, we must infer that managers will attempt to choose, from among the available alternatives, the course of action that is expected to result in future cash flows having the highest possible net present value. Management accounting, if it is to be useful for managers' decisions, must help with the estimation of the future cash flows that will be earned under each alternative. We are now ready to formulate a key concept for our statement on management accounting: *The management accounting system should provide the best information for assessments of the amounts, timing and uncertainty of cash flows to the business from each alternative course of action available to the business.*

The Characteristics of Useful Information

The next question that must be addressed in our concepts statement on management accounting concerns the meaning of the word 'best' in the above conclusion: what guidance can be given for the identification of the best information for the assessment of future cash flows?

Identification of the best information for predictive purposes depends mainly on empirical research. The best indication of the usefulness of information is in statistical evidence about some consistent relationship between the information and the future cash flows that are the object of prediction.

However, it is possible to give some additional guidelines for the identification of useful information. A first guideline is that the information should be relevant: it must be possible to demonstrate some relationship between the information and future cash flows. Secondly, the information should be reliable. Any prediction of the future will be subject to some uncertainty, because the relationship between past events and future events is never completely fixed. It will depend on some chance factors. However, the uncertainty of a prediction may be larger than necessary, because of unreliability in the measurement of the past event that forms the basis for the prediction. Unreliability does not necessarily preclude use of the information. Sometimes, all relevant information is unreliable; but reliable information will be preferred over unreliable information, other things being equal.

It would be possible to develop a long list of desirable qualities for information. However, we limit ourselves to discussion of one further consideration: the evaluation of costs and benefits. The collection of information will be worthwhile, only if it is expected to have benefits that exceed its costs. The benefits of useful information arise because it increases the chances of taking good decisions and, consequently, the value of future cash flows available to the business. However, those benefits must be weighed against the costs of collecting and analysing the information. Some information may be relevant to the assessment of future cash flows and yet be so costly that its collection is not worthwhile.

The Components of a Management Accounting System

Our description of some of the characteristics of useful information has been in general terms. The reader of our concepts statement will be impatient for more specific guidance. There is a limit to the amount of help we can provide. The detailed specification of the information that should be collected and provided to managers must be determined by each business for itself, partly from a process of experimentation. However, we can give some additional guidelines.

Important clues to the design of a management accounting system may be obtained from a study of the factors that are relevant for decisions in the business concerned. For example, decisions on the optimal output of various products depend partly on estimates of the change in total costs for each extra unit produced. If it is believed that the past relationship between total costs and output quantities is relevant to the prediction of future relationships, it follows that records should be kept in a form that facilitates the estimation of past relationships. Similarly, future price changes are relevant to the assessment of future cash flows. If it is believed that a knowledge of past price changes is relevant to the prediction of future price changes (a belief that may be justified for some resources and not for others), it follows that information about past price changes should be recorded. These examples suggest that there may be a principle of management accounting that requires records of actual transactions to be kept in a form that corresponds to the estimates that were made at the time of the decision to undertake the transactions.

It is natural to assume that the main focus of management accounting systems should be a record of past activities of the business; and, as suggested above, such a record is likely to be useful. However, it should not be supposed that information about past activities of the business is sufficient in itself. The advantages and disadvantages of alternative courses of action available to a business will depend critically on external factors, and various external statistics may be helpful for predictions of those advantages and disadvantages. For example, it may be important for a business to collect statistics about general economic trends (indices of national income and of price levels) and about trends in their industry (trends in sales and prices), because those statistics give information about changes in demand for various products. Another example is the usefulness of information about the results of competitors. That information may be useful for the evaluation of business performance. The management accounting system should make explicit provision for the collection of those types of information from external sources.

Another important property of a management accounting system would merit discussion in our concepts statement. The above discussion has suggested a rather static approach to the design of the system: business activity has been depicted as a sequence of decisions in which there is no study of relationships between actual results and expected results. In fact, it is widely accepted that a system of budgetary control should be integrated with the management accounting system.

The essence of a budgetary control system is that the estimates of future results, made for decision-taking purposes, should be reviewed to ensure that they are the best attainable and then recorded; subsequently, actual results should be compared with the corresponding estimates and differences should be analysed to discover their causes. Such a system has two main advantages. First, the identification of reasons for errors in past estimates may promote a learning process that will lead to improvements in future estimates. Second, the comparison of actual and estimated results may provide information that is useful for the assessment of individual performance — for differences may be attributable to superior or inferior performance as well as 'unrealistic' estimates.

We can now see management accounting as a key part of what is essentially an iterative decision-taking process:

(a) Alternative courses of action are identified.
(b) Estimates are made of the results of each alternative.
(c) Preferred courses of action are chosen (in terms of business objectives).
(d) Actual results are compared with corresponding estimates.
(e) New courses of action are identified.

The process is repeated continuously.

Our concepts statement on management accounting would need also to deal with the principles of communication. System design must consider more than the collection of information. The information will not be used effectively unless it is communicated effectively. Thought must be given to the problem of information overload — the provision of so much information that none of it can be used well. People have a limited capacity to process information and system design must make sure that they do not receive more material than they can absorb. An approach that is likely to be fruitful is the provision of summarised information, perhaps using key indicators (a top manager may use a report of rate of return on capital employed in much the same way that an aeroplane pilot uses his altimeter), with provision for the supply of additional information when it is required.

The subject of communication in accounting and other

issues related to the concepts of management accounting
could be discussed at much greater length. However, we shall
not attempt to reach firm conclusions at this stage. The rest
of this book will provide much greater understanding of the
concepts that are relevant to the design of a management
accounting system and the purpose of this chapter is only to
introduce the main ideas. In the remainder of this introduction,
we shall give a short preview of the contents of the other
chapters.

Preview of the Book

Most modern subjects that involve the application of theory
to the solution of real problems draw on many different
disciplines, with the result that traditional subject boundaries
have become blurred. This book indicates that management
accounting exhibits that characteristic.

Management accounting has grown out of the subject
known as cost accounting. Both forms of accounting are
intended to assist with decision taking in business (and other
similar) enterprises. Cost accounting was based on the rather
unsophisticated assumption that almost the only requirement
for decisions on selling prices and similar decisions was
information about the cost of the item concerned in the
recent past; and cost would be measured by spreading costs
that could not be identified with individual items over all the
items produced by the enterprise.

A key step in the development of the subject took place
when certain firms started to introduce systems of budgetary
control. The importance of such systems was discussed above.
The incorporation of budgets into the internal accounting
system is perhaps the key to distinctions between management
accounting and cost accounting. Several chapters in the book
discuss aspects of the methods and usefulness of budgets and
in doing so they illustrate the contribution made to management accounting by other disciplines. Chapter 5 explains how
various statistical methods can be used to make the forecasts
required for preparation of budgets. Chapter 6 shows how
budgets can be used to assist decisions by analysing estimates

of the key differences between results of alternative courses of action; in doing so, it demonstrates the extent to which the methods of economics may be useful in accounting. Chapters 10 and 12 show how budgetary systems can provide vehicles for the control of business operations; they also draw on the methods of economics. Chapter 11 discusses budgetary systems from a different perspective — that of behavioural science. It reminds us that an effective approach to planning and control must take account of the impact of the system on the behaviour of the people who run a business.

A substantial change in the range of topics studied in management accounting has taken place in the last twenty years or so. Some of the new topics have been methodological. They have dealt with questions such as: How should people take decisions? How do people take decisions? How much information do they need for the purpose? Chapter 2 discusses the extent to which the methods of the natural sciences can illuminate decision-taking processes. Chapter 3 reviews our knowledge of decision taking in theory and practice, drawing on ideas developed in both economics and behavioural science. Chapter 4 addresses the main business of management accounting — the provision of information. It provides an introduction to a branch of economics that deals with questions related to judgments of the 'best' amount of information.

It is possible to argue that the topics discussed in Chapters 2, 3 and 4 are not 'part of' management accounting. However, such territorial disputes are of little interest. It seems hard to dispute the usefulness of the topics to anyone who wishes to design and operate management accounting systems — and that is sufficient justification for their inclusion in this book.

If someone who is familiar with the literature of management accounting were to be asked to name the most far-reaching development in the subject in recent years, the choice would probably be the development of quantitative decision models. Those models first took root in the work of operational researchers. Their influence in accounting has been more apparent in contributions to the development of concepts than in actual practice. Nevertheless, they are important. Various types of mathematical model building for decision purposes (without the use of advanced mathematics) are described in Chapters 7, 8 and 9.

The purpose of a mathematical model is to analyse information of the type provided by a management accounting system in a manner that is helpful to people who have to take decisions. No mathematical system can take account of all relevant factors. Nearly all decisions depend to some extent on subjective judgment of strategic factors that cannot readily be measured.

However, the usefulness of mathematical methods stems from the large number of alternative courses of action available in most business situations, and the complexity of relationships between the various factors that influence results. Ordinary methods of decision taking could not possibly evaluate all of the most promising alternatives to identify the best. The mathematical analyses incorporate methods for identifying, from a large number of alternatives, the courses of action that are worthy of further investigation.

Some writers would argue that mathematical model building, like the subjects of the first few chapters, is beyond the scope of management accounting. They would distinguish between the system for gathering information and methods of using it for decision purposes. However, a knowledge of the type of information needed for use in mathematical models is one important factor to be taken into account in decisions about what information should be produced by an accounting system. The management accountant cannot function efficiently without some broad understanding of mathematical methods.

The two remaining chapters look backwards at the history of accounting for decisions and forward to prospects for future developments. A knowledge of the history of developments in a subject is often the only way to understand the reasons for current practices. Applied subjects like accounting evolve in response to demands made by those who use them — and those demands reflect changing business and social conditions. Management accounting still encompasses practices which evolved to meet the needs of the last century; like most applied subjects it has never been designed afresh, without regard to inheritances from the past.

The only safe prediction that can be made about the future development of management accounting is that it will involve attempts to solve problems that are apparent today. A study of history is the best starting point for speculation; and history makes it seem likely that management accounting will make increasing use of research developments in both behavioural science and mathematics.

2

Scientific Method

ROBERT J RYAN

Lecturer in Accounting,
University of Manchester

Introduction

A brief examination of the modern accounting literature reveals a wide diversity of modes of analysis and thought. This book is no exception. Within its pages ideas from psychology, decision theory, economics and even accounting are discussed. However, it is pertinent to ask what it is about all of these different disciplines which qualifies them for inclusion in an accounting text? One answer is that they all, in some way or other, claim to aid the scientific analysis of decision making. But this begs the question as to what we regard as scientific — the question which we attempt to answer in this chapter. It is an important question, because in modern Western society, science is viewed as a highly efficient means of progressing towards the solution of particular 'real-world' problems. The success of scientific method is a question for historians. Our concern is with the problem of understanding the nature of science and what distinguishes it from other forms of human activity.

The first question we consider is whether scientific activity is concerned with a range of subject areas or with method. This discussion is followed by an examination of the problem of demarcation, or how we distinguish between scientific and pseudo-scientific activities. We then examine whether a methodological distinction exists between the so-called 'hard' and 'soft' sciences.

Our aim is not to present a crash course in philosophy, but rather to consider the *power* of philosophical analysis when faced with competing approaches to problems.

Science: Subject or Method?

Many widely different disciplines claim to be scientific. Subjects such as polymer science, catering science, communication science now stand side by side in many college prospectuses with the time-honoured disciplines of chemistry, physics and biology. It would appear, in the minds of the authors of these new titles at least, that the word 'science' represents a particular and presumably desirable way of studying the subject matter under investigation. It is pointless to argue whether these new and novel subjects are sciences *per se*; the word science is a label denoting the *intention* of the participants in the particular discipline concerned. What is important at the philosophical level is to determine whether different users of the word 'science' are referring to the same thing and, if so, to analyse what this thing called science is all about.

One thing which is clear when talking to individual scientists about their disciplines is that, with the notable exception of quantum physicists, all believe the world to be made up of a time series of contingent events. Everything happening in the world must have been *caused* by some preceding event and sufficient care in observation will lead the investigator to general conclusions about how the world behaves.

Quantum physics is the exception in that the founders of the subject found it necessary to abandon the principle of causality in order to achieve a greater understanding of sub-atomic processes. Instead of accepting causality as the fundamental principle governing atomic processes Werner Heisenberg proposed that it is impossible to identify uniquely at the same time the position and the momentum of a sub-atomic particle. If this is true, it is impossible to say precisely what brought the particle in question to its current position and where it will be at a given instant in the future. Einstein vigorously resisted the quantum approach as he could not accept the lack of determinism at such a fundamental level in nature. However, as a view of its own particular reality, the quantum approach proved very successful, and is today the dominant approach in sub-atomic physics.[1]

The importance of the above discussion is that scientific belief in causality is a methodological decision. As David Hume, the famous Scottish philosopher argued, causality is a matter of faith based upon the psychological propensity of human beings to superimpose rationality upon reality. But there is no ultimate guarantee that reality is rational.[2]

The only criterion generally accepted about the subject matter of science is that it must have some empirical basis.[3] The scientist has to believe that events do not occur arbitrarily, but that there is some feasible means whereby events can be connected to their causes. Consequently, an analysis of the spectral properties of angels' wings or even medical analysis of miracles (as such) would be unscientific!

Scientific method is, then, applicable to any empirical phenomena which can be shown to exist or be created. The scientist attempts, often with great difficulty, to view the reality of his discipline as objective experience, i.e. to seek the truth about empirical behaviour as it is. There is a school of thought which believes that the subjective element in human rationality precludes the objective understanding of real behaviour. Man is a being of the world and cannot stand back from the empirical world and view it as objective reality. This of course becomes an even more difficult problem when we attempt the scientific analysis of human behaviour and psychology itself.

However, in an important sense the subjectivist—objectivist debate is meaningless, as it is the intention and commitment of the participants in scientific activity which is important. If

1. For a lively exposition of Einstein's view see Banesh Hoffman, *Einstein*, Paladin Books 1973.
2. D. Hume, *Treatise on Human Nature*, Dent 1939.
3. By 'empirical basis' we mean that the subject matter of a given science must, at least in the minds of the scientists concerned, represent some real phenomena which are capable of being observed or generated by experiment.

an individual attempts to understand objectively and analyse
the experience of interest to him, he is being scientific. In
order to pursue objective knowledge, the scientist often views
himself as a member of a selective, critical peer group. Indeed,
the peer group rather than the individual can be regarded as
the instrument of scientific activity. The individual may discover new empirical evidence or create new theories, but it is
the scientific community which initially assesses the validity
of the work and ensures its scientific status.

Our discussion so far has characterised science as a sociological phenomenon where the individual scientist acts within
a group which has made a methodological commitment to
objectivity in the study of its discipline. We now turn to the
nature of the methodology employed and in particular to
the nature of theories.

The Nature of Theories

Scientists express their ideas through the medium of theoretical statements with a view to achieving one of two ends:

- either to *explain* a particular phenomenon by finding a
  general proposition which covers it (a general proposition
  is one of the form 'all *x*'s are *y*'s'), or
- to *predict* a particular phenomenon from some general
  proposition.

In so far as theories are language statements of some sort
or other (for example, in verbal, mathematical or some other
symbolic form), they do not have an existence outside the
human intellect. They are purely mental artifacts. This raises
an interesting and difficult problem which has vexed philosophers throughout the centuries. There is one school of thought
which argues that theories are simply 'instruments' or 'tools'
which can aid in the prediction of future events. Theories, as
such, are valueless except in as far as they aid us in making
connections between observable events. It is interesting to
note that much of positive economics is based upon this
instrumentalist position. For example, Friedman argues that
even though the assumptions underlying a theoretical argument may be completely unrealistic, what determines whether

the theory is good or bad is whether it can generate useful implications (i.e. predictions).[4]

In opposition to the instrumentalist view, 'realists' would argue that theories should actually attempt to describe processes which exist in the real world. In other words, theoretical statements are attempts at directly reflecting objective reality. The realist—instrumentalist debate is an old one. Indeed, fundamentally it was the issue which separated Galileo from the Inquisition. Theologically, the Inquisition was quite content with the Copernican system as a means of enabling better predictions about planetary motion. What it would not accept was that the Copernican system represented 'real' physical processes. But Galileo, even when forced to recant, looked at the earth beneath his feet and whispered 'yet it moves'.

In recent years the same argument has re-emerged in the economics literature as the Samuelson—Friedman debate.[5] Even though neither side has been forced to recant (as yet!), it is the same issue which separates the way different individuals view the world of theories.

Few philosophers now accept the instrumentalist position, mainly because it generates more problems than it solves. If a theory were simply a 'calculating tool' we would not expect it to be particularly useful for more than it was intended. Yet many theories in the past have generated new and novel predictions unanticipated by the theory's original creator.

A more substantial criticism of the instrumentalist approach is that it is exceedingly difficult to differentiate between objective observation and the connections provided by theory. Think about any observation you care to make and you will see that it is bounded by certain conceptions and theories about the world. For instance, the observation of an individual buying goods would seem straightforward. But when making such an observation we subsume concepts of individuality, exchange, the role of money and so forth. It is not possible to view theories as artifacts linking observations. The observations themselves are 'theory-laden' and subject

4.   M. Friedman, The methodology of positive economics, in *Essays in Positive Economics*, Chicago University Press 1953.
5.   This debate was conducted in the *American Economic Review*, 1963—1965 (vols. 53—55).

to the world-view held by the observer. Consequently, it is impossible to identify uniquely any single test which will clearly reject or confirm a given implication. This is a vitally important idea because, as we shall see in the next section, the demarcation between scientific and non-scientific theories is fundamentally dependent upon the *intention* of the theorist rather than upon some objectively verifiable distinction.

Science versus Pseudo-Science (the Problem of Demarcation)

Before examining the problem of demarcation in more detail, some groundwork is necessary on the nature of statements. As indicated in the previous section, statements are the building blocks with which theories are constructed. It is through the nature of the statements incorporated in a theory that we gain insight into the meaning which can be attached to the theoretical 'superstructure'. As we have argued, scientists are characterised by a methodological commitment to the empirical verification of ideas. Consequently, our aim should now be to narrow down the range of statements (and the theories derived from them) to those which can be said to have some empirical base. We will concern ourselves with three basic classifications of statements which have been of central importance in the theory of knowledge. The first distinction to be discussed is an attempt to demarcate between statements of values (which are often loosely described as 'metaphysical' i.e., *beyond* physical reality) and statements of empirical significance. The second and third distinctions relate to the subtle, but none the less important, issue of the logical status of statements.

(i) *The prescriptive (normative)/descriptive (empirical) distinction*

David Hume argued in his *Treatise on Human Nature* that it is logically impossible (in order to construct a deductively valid argument) to connect a statement using the word 'ought' (a prescriptive statement) to a statement concerning the word 'is' (an empirical statement). A moment's reflection will show why this is so. A statement using the word 'ought' expresses an individual's desire, based upon his or her own set of personal values, for the world to operate in a particular way. For instance, if we assert that accounting information ought to be prepared in order to be useful to the user of that information, we are making a value judgement about the purpose of accounting activity. Now it may be possible, by logical means, to extend and explore the ramifications of this value judgement which may be a very useful and salutary exercise in itself. But no amount of mathematics or logic *would alter the facts* if accounting information were not prepared using the usefulness criterion.

The normative—empirical distinction demonstrates the importance of the intention of the individual. Individuals have their own predilections and values which will, inevitably, motivate and direct their perceptions. It might be that an individual has some particular value (x) which he thinks everyone should accept. If he proposes the generalisation that all individuals hold value (x) and tests it, then he is undertaking scientific research. However, if he proposes that all individuals ought to hold value (x), he is making an assertion of a different order, which is untestable in that it *transcends* the need for empirical verification.

Danger lies in the situation where the researcher proposes that all individuals *ought* to hold value (x) and advances further theories to discover how they could, in practice, be forced to *adopt* value (x). The untutored reader could be lured into the belief that the scientific aspect of such research in some way validates the original value judgement. It is for this reason that many scientists insist that empirical science should be clearly divorced from any question of values — although this is far easier said than done!

(ii) *The analytic/synthetic distinction*

Statements can be further categorised into those which are analytic and those which are synthetic. Analytic statements are true or false by definition (e.g. all husbands are male; $2 + 2 = 4$). Synthetic statements are dependent upon the way the world is (e.g. this table is made of wood). Clearly a logical argument consisting entirely of analytic statements will not advance our knowledge of the world. All such arguments do is to extend the range and capabilities of the definitions we employ. If we are told that 'X' is a husband, we know 'X' must be male; no test is required to establish the husband—male connection. Similarly, if we can distinguish a singular property in some physical objects and can count two sets, each containing two such objects, then our number system, based on Peono's postulates, guarantees that four such objects will be present. Again, no further testing is required. Much of modern mathematics is analytic in the sense that it is a deductive extension of some analytically true proposition.

(iii) *The* a priori/a posteriori *distinction*

This distinction is particularly subtle and its relation to the synthetic—analytic distinction has provided the power-house for centuries of fierce philosophical debate. The distinction rests fundamentally on the way we gain knowledge about the world. An *a priori* statement is one which can be discerned to be true of false *before* experience, i.e. certain knowledge about the world is innate. *A posteriori* statements are ones which can be verified only by resort to experience.[6] Now you might argue that this is no more than the analytic—synthetic distinction put another way; and if you believed that you would be an 'empiricist'. However, some philosophers whom we will call 'rationalists' (this being a label rather than a slight on empiricists) believe that it is possible to possess knowledge *a priori* which is synthetically true. Putting it crudely, rationalists argue that it is possible to know something to be true about the world without ever having experienced, or ever needing to experience, it. Space prohibits a full discussion of the empiricist—rationalist debate. The empiricist position remains safe until someone can offer a statement which is clearly *a priori* whilst being synthetic. No-one has done that as yet, so the onus remains with the rationalists to prove their

6.   For example, 'if A precedes B and B precedes C, then A precedes C' is an example of a statement which we know to be true *a priori* — that is, before experience.

case. To be an empiricist is a respectable philosophical position; it does not entail a commitment to mindless 'data-dredging' as has sometimes been supposed. All the empiricist asserts is that to gain true (synthetic) knowledge about the world, one must look for it!

So far we have divided statements into various categories. Is it now possible to decide what distinguishes theories, which are bundles of statements, into the scientific and non-scientific? Theories based upon presuppositions about what ought to be (normative theories) are not open to empirical testing, although the analysis of normative propositions by logical methods can be an important step in understanding the ramifications of such propositions. Similarly, purely analytical statements cannot be 'tested' because they represent logical truths, which cannot be disproved without logical contradiction. This leaves us with the range of statements which make propositions about the real world.

One important characteristic of the historical development of science has been the temporary nature of its theories. The most significant example of this was the overturning of Newton's mechanics by Einstein's theories of general and special relativity. Other examples can easily be found where a well-established theory has been found wanting and replaced by a new one. This has led some philosophers to argue that scientific theories are not created as generalisations from repeated observational experiment (the inductivist view), but rather are conjectured and subjected to rigid and critical testing. According to this view, a good theory is one in which deduction is used to generate a number of falsifiable assertions.[7]

Popper has argued that a theory can be regarded as scientific only if it yields certain implications that are capable of refutation. A theory which cannot be refuted is unscientific. At first sight this may seem counter-intuitive, as common sense suggests that science should attempt to prove theories rather than disprove them. However, it is easy to see that no matter how many different tests are applied to a theory,

7.   Deduction is the process of constructing logically valid arguments. The importance of deduction is that it permits the transmission of *truth value* through an argument.

one test cannot demonstrate its universal validity (the next
test to be undertaken may disprove the theory); whereas a
single instance where the theory fails demonstrates that it is
not universally true.

One major problem with the falsificationist[8] approach is
how to decide, given that all observations are concept-
bound,[9] that a particular observation refutes a theory.
Returning to Galileo for a moment, telescopic observation
clearly demonstrated as incorrect the popular view that
planetary bodies were perfect spheres. Or did it? At the time
the science of optics was poorly developed, and some argued
that telescopic observation was unreliable. The same problem
arises in economics, where theories are often constructed
utilising *ceteris paribus* conditions. If an economic theory is
refuted by experiment, the question remains whether it is the
theory or the *ceteris paribus* conditions that are being refuted.

As Lakatos has pointed out, *ceteris paribus* type clauses
are a feature of all science. This being so, it is difficult to
visualise any observational statements capable of refuting the
basic premises of a theory. This leads to his important conclusion:

> . . . some scientific theories are normally interpreted as containing
> a *ceteris paribus* clause: in such cases it is always a specific theory
> *together* with this clause which may be refuted. But such a
> refutation is inconsequential for the specific theory under test
> because by replacing the *ceteris paribus* clause by a different one
> the specific theory can always be retained whatever the tests say
> . . . Moreover, one can easily argue that *ceteris paribus* clauses
> are not the exception, but the rule in science. . . Scientific theories
> are not only equally unprovable, and equally improbable, but
> they are also equally undisprovable.[10]

The failure to find a general principle of demarcation

8.   'Falsificationism' is that approach where philosophers attempt to
       demarcate between scientific and non-scientific arguments
       (theories) on the basis of their ability to generate falsifiable
       assertions.

9.   Any observation is *bound* by the particular set of concepts the
       observer has of the real world.

10.   I. Lakatos, Falsificationism and the methodology of research
       programmes, in I. Lakatos and A. Musgrove (eds), *Criticism and
       the Growth of Knowledge*, Cambridge University Press 1970,
       p. 101.

between scientific and non-scientific theories led Popper, and later Lakatos, to develop a philosophical position called 'methodological falsificationism'. This approach shifted attention away from single theories and towards the concept of a 'research programme'. Theories are regarded as structures consisting of certain fundamental assumptions, and an array of supporting (auxiliary) hypotheses specifically designed to protect the core of the theory from falsification. Scientists supporting a theory must make a methodological *decision* not to reject or alter these basic fundamental assumptions. These assumptions remain inviolate and may contain critical concepts which are undefinable except within the terms of the theoretical structure itself.

Newton for instance, proposed the concept of momentum which takes on a precise meaning only within the context of his theories of motion. Similarly, in economics a central concept is that of 'utility'. Classical economists such as Marshall, Hicks and others proposed a concept of utility which, as many subsequent writers have pointed out, is undefinable. But to the methodological falsificationist the fact that utility is undefinable is irrelevant. Utility as a core concept within positive microeconomic theory assumes a meaning only within the context of the theory itself. Microeconomists in their work make a decision to accept the central concepts of their subject as given. The theoretical economist's task is, as far as possible, to create or modify the auxiliary hypotheses in order to bring the theory into line with experimental evidence.

The methodological decision by scientists to accept the core concepts of their theories represents what is termed the *negative heuristic* of the research programme. Any scientist who modifies these core concepts has opted out of that particular research programme and started anew. On the other hand a *positive heuristic* for any research programme represents a research programme's ability to open up new implications and new opportunities for further research.

A further characteristic of methodological falsificationism is that a theory can never be disproved. Rather, it degenerates as new implications fail to arise or refuting evidence accumulates. But a theory is never quite dead. For example monetarism as a theory of economic control was replaced in the

1940's by the emergence of the apparently more fruitful Keynesian economics. The failure of Keynesian economics in the 1970's has led to a revival of monetarism both at the academic and political level.

But what has all this to do with the problem of demarcation? Lakatos argued that a research programme must possess two characteristics to render it scientific:[11]

(i) A positive heuristic — i.e. the ability to generate new research opportunities.

(ii) The occasional discovery of new phenomena.

The significant point embodied in methodological falsificationism is that it clearly focuses attention upon the *decisions* required of the individual scientist. First, the individual scientist must commit himself to the pursuit of objectivity in collaboration with other scientists within, or who may join, the research programme. Second, scientists within the research programme must decide to accept the core principles of that research programme.

Not all philosophers, by any means, accept this position. Indeed there are some who dispute the possibility of ever establishing any methodological principles governing scientific activity. A notable criticism of all attempts to establish a methodology of science has been offered by Feyerbend. He regards science as an ideology which happens to have taken hold of Western man, perhaps in the same way that witchcraft took hold of primitive peoples and religion captures the minds and hearts of many millions today. But like all other ideologies, science is ultimately irrational. Feyerbend argues that the history of science reveals clear examples to refute even the most sophisticated methodology and states:

> there is only one principle that can be defended under all circumstances, and in all stages of human development — it is the principle: anything goes.[12]

11.   I. Lakatos, *op. cit.*
12.   P. Feyerbend, *Against Method*, Verso 1978, p. 28.

Social Science and Scientific Method

We have argued that the general problems of science are ones of methodology rather than of subject matter. However, the view is commonly expressed (often by natural scientists) that the social sciences are not really sciences at all. Various reasons for this view are often given which can usually be condensed to three main arguments:

(i) Social science is concerned with human beings who are not inert objects but possess a rationality of their own. Thus, it is impossible to predict individual human behaviour (the 'indeterminacy' argument).

(ii) Because the subjects of social science enquiry are responsive the scientist must of necessity react with his subject causing change by virtue of his activity (the 'interactive' argument).

(iii) Because the scientist is bound by his own set of norms and prejudices he can view the actions of his subject only in the context of those values (the 'independence' argument).

Other arguments are occasionally offered such as the impossibility of laboratory experiments in the social sciences. But a moment's thought reveals that many natural sciences are subject to the same problem. For example, few would argue that astronomy is not a natural science, although laboratory experimentation is impossible. This example clearly demonstrates our problem. In order to establish a clear distinction between the social and natural sciences, it is necessary to identify some feature of either natural or social science which is not present in the other.

At the risk of being charged with setting up straw men to knock down, let us examine the three arguments proposed above:

(i) The indeterminacy problem is not unique to the social sciences. Most social sciences seek to understand and generalise about the behaviour of individuals, either as groups or through some process of aggregation and abstraction. In this respect, social science has much in common with quantum physics. As we noted earlier, the position or momentum of individual particles is indeterminate. It is just as difficult to guess where a particle's next position will be, as it is to predict an individual's future action. Nevertheless, atomic physics is made possible by studying the behaviour of large numbers of particles where probabilities can be better calculated. Similarly, it is possible to make generalisations about the probabilities of human behaviour by observing large numbers of individuals. On this score then, no fundamental difference exists between the social and natural sciences.

(ii) In laboratory experiments the mere monitoring of system performance entails some intervention in the process. The more sensitive the experiment, the more difficult the problem becomes. For instance, the major source of temperature gain in low-temperature physics is often caused by the measurement transducers. At the other extreme, standing on a snow-covered mountain and predicting an avalanche in a loud voice can often result in a self-fulfilling prophecy! So no fundamental difference exists between the social and natural systems through interactive effects, although in the social sciences the problems are often more difficult to handle.

(iii) We discussed the independence argument in more detail earlier. If, for instance, the argument can be sustained that the natural sciences are completely value free, whereas the social sciences are not, then a definite distinction between the two can be made. Our earlier discussion suggests that such a distinction is unlikely.

Conclusion: the Status of Accounting as a Social Science

Accounting as a practical discipline owes much to its roots as a craft. Indeed, the 'artisan' mentality behind the pronouncements of leading practitioners of the subject is often too clearly demonstrated. But it is not the practical level which concerns us in deciding about the scientific status of accounting. Rather, it is at the level of development and innovation that the role of scientific method is of critical importance.

If accounting theoreticians regard their function as discovering the effects of information systems upon the users of information, then a scientific approach is more likely to be useful than mere metaphysical speculation. It is important to understand, to explain and to predict how individuals respond to and act upon the information content of accounting reports, because, in the final analysis, users will respond to new information (new in terms of its preparation and presentation) only if it corresponds to their own particular needs. Resort to the types of normative speculation and prescriptive methodologies advocated by some accounting academics is an abrogation of the scientific commitment to understanding *real* accounting issues.

It may be that in the long run, discoveries made through the analysis of the needs of users (the 'scientific' aspect of accounting) could have application in the development of more useful accounting systems (the 'technology' of accounting). However, this application of scientific results to the technology of accounting should not be regarded as the principle motivation for scientific research. The example of the natural sciences is clear to see. It was only when the rigid orthodox social structures of the middle ages began to break down that science began to develop.[13] It flourished because new ideas would be tolerated irrespective of their pragmatic value or theological implication. Brilliant advances could be made without the incessant questioning of their potential applicability. It is likely that Rutherford had no idea where splitting the atom would lead. Similarly, to be useful, accounting science should be as unfettered as resources will allow.

The empirical domain of accounting lies at the level of the individual user of accounting information — whether he or she acts alone or as a member of some social group. Only through a study of human behaviour can the purpose of accounting information be understood.

13.   See M.N. Richter, *Science as a Cultural Process*, Frederick Muller 1973.

Further Reading

A.F. Chalmer, *What is This Thing Called Science?* Open University Press 1976. A superb little book; easy to read, with a thoroughly good review of the major schools of thought in the philosophy of science.

I.M. Copi, *Symbolic Logic*, 4th edn, Collier Macmillan 1973. Clear and well written; a good self-study text.

J. Hospers, *An Introduction to Philosophical Analysis*, Routledge & Kegan Paul 1967. A bit dated, but gives an excellent coverage of the more general problems of philosophy.

T.S. Kuhn, *The Structure of Scientific Revolutions*, Chicago University Press 1970. This book caused quite a stir when it was first published. Kuhn's views are regarded as too sociological for many philosophers' tastes and there are some serious weaknesses with his ideas. But he did introduce the concept of a 'paradigm'. A good read!

I. Lakatos and A. Musgrove (eds), *Criterion and the Growth of Knowledge*, Cambridge University Press 1970. One of the best books of readings available. Important contributions by Lakatos and Feyerbend.

K. Popper, *The Logic of Scientific Discovery*, Hutchinson 1959. 'One of the most important documents of the twentieth century', Sir Peter Medawar, *New Scientist*. 'The results of this book appear to me completely untenable . . .', H. Reichenbach, *Erkenntnis*. Two views expressing the disagreement this book provoked. The most commonly held view is the first one.

K. Popper, *Conjectures and Refutations*, 4th edn, Routledge & Kegan Paul 1974. The first reading beautifully encapsulates Popper's position.

3

Models for Personal Choice

DAVID COOPER

Lecturer in Accounting,
University of Manchester

Introduction

Frequently, decisions that you make in your life can be made without a lot of fuss. Either the best choice is clear without much analysis, or the decision is not important enough to warrant conscious attention. Occasionally, however, there are situations where it is worth spending time to make a choice between alternative courses of action. For example, you may not wish to spend too much time considering which side of the bed you should get up from each morning, but you may wish systematically to choose between alternative job opportunities, alternative house purchases, or alternative pension plans.

This chapter introduces a framework, referred to as decision analysis, that may be helpful in making the latter type of choices. Following this introduction, the basic building blocks of a model of personal choice are introduced.

Taken together, the three building blocks of action, environment and preference, underlie most theories of personal choice. We will introduce a simple example to illustrate the argument. The discussion will be developed by considering the most commonly used formal model of personal choice: the model that suggests that individuals try to maximise their subjective expected utility (SEU).

The SEU model of personal choice was chosen because of its pervasive influence in management science (and management accounting). The influence and use of formal decision analysis will be outlined. The SEU model underlies many of the economic models which form the basis of much of the material in this book. For example, in chapter 4 the value of information is explained in terms of changes in the expected utility of the decision maker. In chapter 7 the technique of linear programming is discussed, in part, in terms of optimal allocation of resources. The idea of optimality is equivalent to the maximisation of the decision maker's subjective expected utility.

The analysis and discussion in the majority of the chapters in this book assume the validity of the SEU model. We therefore outline some difficulties with that model. The difficulties and problems with formal decision analysis have led to the development of alternative models of personal choice that emphasise the process of choosing rather than the outcome (i.e. the choice). We shall introduce this alternative, process orientated model.

Before presenting the models for personal choice, it is important to recognise that the argument is intended to be decidedly practical. The use of theoretical terminology and the notion of a 'model' often suggest sterile academic theorising. The perspective of this chapter is that there is nothing more practical than a good theory. Theory is a guide to action: it provides a generalisation of real-life experiences. The emphasis on *models* for personal choice is an attempt to base decision making on a framework that is practical and applicable to accounting.

To be practical and applicable, a model must possess some descriptive validity. In other words the model must be based on how people make decisions. A model must also possess some normative quality; that is to say, the model should provide some guidelines about how people should make decisions. It thereby provides a standard to which decision makers might aspire. The standard which we utilise will be the notion that people aspire to rationality. We will observe, however, that the notion of rationality means different things to different people.

The Subjective Expected Utility Model

Since this is a chapter about personal choice, let us illustrate the concepts we are about to introduce by considering a choice. This choice will be analysed through the framework of the subjective expected utility model. The reason the model is referred to as the subjective expected utility model will become clear by the end of this section.

Let us suppose that the introduction to this chapter has finally convinced you of one thing: you must leave your studies (and this book) and express yourself in some other way. You are considered to be a rather good singer. You now wish to pursue your singing career and forget about accounting (or whatever). Let us analyse your choice in detail.

Actions

The first element in your decision is a consideration of alternative actions. Action is the essence of decision making. A decision situation can only exist when we recognise that we must choose between alternative courses of action. Given that you have already decided to be a singer, your choice is now between alternative singing opportunities. On a scrap of paper you wrote down the following alternatives: you could sing in an 'angry' rock group, you could sing in a 'lyrical' rock group, or you could become a soloist. In the language of decision analysis, you have, thereby, specified your alternative actions.

The next step is to consider the outcomes that are associated with each action. The prediction of the outcomes associated with each action is clearly a major task. It is, however, an essential task, since it is the consequences or outcomes of an action, rather than the action itself, that are of value.

Let us assume for the moment that only monetary outcomes are of interest; the choice of singing career will be based on the monetary values of the consequences of the specified alternative actions. Later in the chapter we will relax this assumption, but in the meantime it should be recognised that the simplification we are making still represents an important class of decisions — particularly in business organisations.

The scrap of paper may now look something like the following:

Sing in Angry Group	£150 per month income
Sing in Lyrical Group	£900 per month income
Sing Solo	£700 per month income

This information would probably be sufficient for you to make a choice with regard to your singing career, if you are convinced about the certain nature of the outcomes. In most choice situations, however, the outcomes of a choice are unlikely to be determinate; the outcomes are usually contingent or dependent on some actions outside the control of the decision maker. The analysis thus far would be sufficient if actions leads to certain outcomes.

Many of the techniques discussed in introductory management accounting assume a world of certainty. For example, the discussion of opportunity costs and alternative budgets in chapter 6 assumes a certain world; consequences of alternative actions are known with certainty. Although this representation of the world is clearly inaccurate, the 'model' may nevertheless prove to be a useful first approximation for a decision maker. To return to our singing example, the information on the scrap of paper may be sufficient to make a choice.

Environment

You may, however, feel uncomfortable with the certainty in your model. Perhaps you wish formally to incorporate uncertainty into your decision making. Uncertainty refers to the variety of outcomes that could be associated with your action. This variety, it is assumed, is due to factors in your decision making environment that are beyond your control. It is crucial to recognise that whilst any actions that are within the decision maker's control can be included in the 'actions' category, actions that are not within the decision maker's control are in the 'environment' category. Notice that this categorisation is quite common in economics. In models of perfect competition, the individual market agent (a consumer or a firm) may take actions (e.g. purchase goods or produce output), but is unable to influence the environment. The individual consumer and firm is said to be a 'price taker'.

The recognition of uncertainty about the consequences of action means that the decision maker identifies various states of the world (his environment) that may influence the outcomes from any given action. In particular, the decision maker must identify his (or her) attitudes towards the environment. Two of these attitudes are particularly important in the SEU model of decision making.

The first attitude concerns the way in which the environment is divided; the decision maker must partition the states of the world to capture those environmental factors that are likely to affect differentially the outcomes of his (or her) actions. In the singing example, you may decide that the state of the national economy will be a major influence on the outcome of your acts. Of course, other factors in the world may also influence the outcomes, but the exclusion of these factors would suggest that you regard their impact as being minor or that the state of the national economy sufficiently captures the impact of the other factors. The classification or partitioning of the states of the world into categories should be exhaustive and exclusive. That is, each category must be uniquely defined so that any particular state of the world can be unambiguously classified into only one of the categories. In our example we define the two states 'national economic growth' and 'national economic decline'. But we must do so with sufficient precision so that every possible situation can be assigned into one or other of these two categories.

The second attitude to the environment that a decision maker must consider is the likelihood of each state occurring. Since we have previously classified states in a complete fashion, it must be certain that one or other of the states will occur. If a particular state is certain to occur, we can say that the probability of that state occurring is 1.0. A state that is certain not to occur has an associated probability of 0.0.

When analysing the decision environment, the decision maker must specify possible alternative states of nature and assign a probability of each state occurring. But where do these probabilities come from?

We may identify two sources of information about probabilities. The classical approach is to say that probabilities can
be determined by the observation of events. Probabilities are
objective frequencies. In many decision making situations,
however, there is little opportunity to observe frequencies.
Consider the statement: the probability that Cooper will be
elected Prime Minister is 0.1. We cannot repeat the election
many times to see if the number of times I am elected
approaches 0.1. In this example probabilities cannot be determined from observation. Instead, the probabilities may be
regarded as beliefs about the likelihood of an event occurring.
Clearly different people may, entirely reasonably, arrive at
very different assessments. The subjectivist approach regards
probabilities as a personal statement of belief. Conveniently,
the subjectivist and classical approaches to probability would
seem equally appropriate in models for *personal* choice.[1]

In the context of our singing example, we might decide
that the original prediction of outcomes associated with our
three choices reflected an implicit assumption about the state
of the world. Now, as shown in table 3.1, we might predict
the outcomes for each of our alternative actions. Each
outcome is contingent on the environment being in a specific
state, namely that of economic growth or economic decline.
In this chapter we do not consider in any detail how the
predictions (or payoffs) were made. Chapter 5 provides some
indication of how this may be done. We might suggest the
following prediction model, however. If the economy is
growing, people are likely to be happier and hence responsive
to a lyrical group or soloist. An angry group will make little
impact in such conditions. In times of economic decline you
assess that an angry group is likely to reflect the mood of the
times and, therefore, achieve popularity. The lyrical group
will now only appeal to optimists. As a soloist your style
would be quite adaptable and you could expect to be somewhat successful.

Table 3.1 also indicates your personal assessment of the

1.   Most modern decision theory utilises subjective probability assess-
     ments. L.J. Savage, *The Foundations of Statistics*, John Wiley
     1954, provides a rigorous axiomatic development of subjective
     probabilities in decision making.

Table 3.1 Payoff Table using Monetary Values

		States of the world		Expected monetary value
		Economic growth	Economic decline	
Actions	Angry group	150	1,000	660
	Lyrical group	900	450	630
	Soloist	700	600	640
Probability of state		0.4	0.6	

likelihood of the economy being in decline or in growth. Those beliefs may be based on so-called objective data (e.g. economic statistics or econometric forecasts) or represent subjective assessments. In either case, the crucial point is that reasonable people could arrive at different beliefs. It seems entirely sensible to base your choice on your beliefs about the future.

Preferences

Table 3.1 provides the basic information — your alternative actions and their associated payoffs, dependent on specified states of the world with specified probabilities of occurrence — from which you may make the choice about your singing career.

But how do you choose? In many repetitive decision making situations the way you might choose seems reasonably clear. Based on the simple behavioural assumption that you prefer more money to less, you would, other things being equal, choose to maximise your income (and wealth). The problem for you is that the payoffs of each action depend on the state which actually occurs. You might choose the angry group over the other two alternatives if the economy were to decline, but the lyrical group in an economy experiencing economic growth. If we have to make a decision in advance of knowledge of the actual states (perhaps we cannot defer the decision because the action opportunities will disappear), then we may calculate what would happen if each action were chosen repeatedly. In this repetitive decision, table 3.1

can be interpreted to mean that for 40 per cent of the months you expect to receive £150 and for the remaining 60 per cent of the months, you expect £1000 per month. In other words you might assess the average long-run outcome of your action to join an angry group at £660, calculated as follows:

$$0.4 \ (150) + 0.6 \ (1000) = 660$$

This mathematical expectation, calculated by multiplying each outcome by its associated probability of occurrence and adding all the resultant products, is referred to as the expected monetary value (EMV) of the action. The EMV of each action is indicated in the right hand column of table 3.1.

As EMV reflects the long-run average result, it would seem reasonable that actions should be ranked on the basis of this calculation. The action with the highest EMV would then be chosen; by choosing to join the angry group you might say that you are maximising your expected monetary gain.

The preceding argument might be fine if you were making a repetitive decision. You could say that your long-run average monthly income would be maximised by choosing to join an angry group.

It is more likely, however, that the choice of a singing career is a more permanent decision that commits you to an action over the next few years. In such a case, the decision can be regarded as 'one-off' or unique. The states in table 3.1 would then refer to the long-run state of the economy and the payoffs are to be interpreted as the average monthly income over the next few years if the specified state occurs. You may, in this one-off choice, still decide to join the angry group, but now the long-run average monthly income will be either £150 or it will be £1,000.

Inspection of table 3.1 might lead you to doubt the wisdom of choosing to join an angry group if this represents a one-time, irrevocable decision. The outcomes associated with your choice look rather variable compared to some of the alternative choices. Doubts about the wisdom of choosing on the basis of maximising expected monetary gain have been recognised for a long time. It was recognised that monetary values (in particular, wealth) must be converted into an index of satisfaction in order to produce a normative model which is consistent with observed choice behaviour. The need for this is based on the recognition that money and satisfaction may not be linearly related. Many people seem to display diminishing marginal satisfaction for money: an extra £1 provides more satisfaction if your wealth is zero than if it is one million pounds.[2]

Preferences may thus be expressed in terms of satisfaction (or utility) rather than money. The problem, then, is to derive a utility function of an individual so that we may replace the monetary outcomes in the payoff matrix of table 3.1 with a measure of preference. We will consider how to derive utility functions in both certain and uncertain situations. In certain situations we only require an ordinal utility function. In uncertain situations, a cardinal utility function is useful.

(a) *Ordinal utility*: In conditions of certainty, outcomes only need to be ranked in order of preference so that you might say that you prefer £900 to £700 to £150. We may assign a utility measure (perhaps referred to as a 'utile') of 3 utiles to £900, of 2 utiles to £700 and of 1 utile to £150. This assignment would give us the ranking feature we are concerned with; 3 utiles is preferred to 2 utiles, which is preferred to 1 utile. Notice that we could have chosen to assign utility measures of 10.23 utiles to £900, of 0 utiles to £700 and of -193.1 utiles to £150. The actual utility numbers are unimportant; in conditions of certainty, all that is required is that the utility numbers display ordinal properties.

There are at least two, not entirely innocuous, assumptions that underlie ordinal utility functions. The first assumption is often referred to as the axiom of transitivity.[3] This assumption is frequently regarded as the essence of rationality and

2. M. Friedman and L.J. Savage, The utility analysis of choices involving risk, *Journal of Political Economy*, April 1948, pp. 279–304; F. Mosteller and P. Nogee, An empirical measurement of utility, *Journal of Political Economy*, October 1951, pp. 371–404; and C.J. Grayson, *Decisions Under Uncertainty*, Harvard Business School 1960, all provide examples and explanations for the general tendency of diminishing marginal utility for wealth. They also all find (and explain) that utility functions with convex portions are quite common.

3. For a discussion of the axioms of utility theory see R.D. Luce and H. Raiffa, *Games and Decisions*, John Wiley 1964. W. Baumol, *Economic Theory and Operations Analysis*, Prentice Hall 1977, provides a simpler introduction.

represents a normative concern for consistency. Transitivity means that if you prefer outcome A to outcome B and you prefer outcome B to outcome C, then you would prefer outcome A to outcome C. If your preferences, as represented by your utility function, do not display transitivity, then you may behave inconsistently (choosing A over B and B over C, but preferring C to A!).

The second assumption guarantees the existence of a continuous utility function. This continuity axiom means that you can rank your preferences. Perhaps not surprisingly in a model of choice, indecision is not acceptable, although indifference between alternative outcomes is allowed.

With these two axioms, it is possible to derive an ordinal utility function from preferences made in a certain world.

(b) *Cardinal utility:* The simple ranking of preferences that is achieved with ordinal utility functions is insufficient to aid choice in an uncertain world. For most decision making we need to know the strength of our preferences. Cardinal utility functions provide not only an indication of order, but also enable the prediction which of two uncertain alternatives a person will prefer.[4] This prediction of preference can be made by numerical calculation, based merely on a ranking of two alternatives.

Let us see how this calculation is performed in our singing example. Referring back to table 3.1, we wish to calculate the utility associated with each of the monetary outcomes in that table. Table 3.2 presents the results of some calculations.

We start by choosing two extreme outcomes and assigning any measure of utility to them. So we arbitrarily assign the numeral 100 to £1,000 and the numeral 0 to £0. We may then proceed by constructing a series of gambles (or 'lotteries') with these two monetary outcomes being uncertain. For example, we can construct a lottery that in 75% of occasions will pay out £1,000 and on the other 25% of occasions will pay nothing. Then we can ask the decision maker the maximum

---

4.   This particular notion of cardinal utility was developed by John von Neumann and Oskar Morgenstern, in their seminal work *Theory of Games and Economic Behaviour*, Princeton University Press 1947.

Table 3.2 Questions and Hypothetical Answers to Elicit a Utility Function

Question (lottery)	Hypothetical answer	Implied utility*
(1) 0.75, £1,000; 0.25, £0	£450	75
(2) 0.45, £450; 0.55, £0	£150	33.75
(3) 0.9, £1,000; 0.1, £450	£900	97.5
(4) 0.5, £900; 0.5, £450	£600	86.25
(5) 0.35, £1,000; 0.65, £600	£700	91.06

* Assuming that the utility of £1,000 is 100 and that the utility of £0 is 0.

price he would bid for such a lottery. Let us assume that £450 is the answer given. The answer suggests that the decision maker would value £450 as 75 utiles, given a scale that sets £1,000 at 100 utiles and £0 as 0 utiles. Our evaluation is derived from the following calculation:

Utility of £1,000 = 100 utiles; Utility of £0 = 0 utiles
Utility of lottery:
$(0.75 \times £1,000 + 0.25 \times £0)$
$= 0.75 \,(100 \text{ utiles}) + 0.25 \,(0 \text{ utiles})$
$= 75 \text{ utiles.}$

We could, also, have derived this utility of £450 by offering the lottery of £1,000 or £0 and asking the probability that would yield indifference between the certainty of £450 and the uncertain lottery (uncertain, that is, in terms of the respective likelihoods of the two component outcomes). Given that £1,000 is assigned a utility of 100 utiles and £0 is assigned 0 utiles, we now know that the decision maker would assign 75 utiles to £450. We can continue by asking for the probabilities which would make the decision maker indifferent between a certain sum of £150 or a lottery with a chance of receiving either £1,000 or £0.

The calculations in table 3.2, however, are based on asking the decision maker the maximum price he is willing to pay (known as the certainty equivalent) for a specified uncertain lottery. If he answers that he would be willing to pay up to £150 for a lottery with a 45% chance of winning £450 and (by implication) a 55% chance of winning £0, then the answer implies a utility of 33.75 utiles for £150:

Utility of £450 = 75 utiles; Utility of £0 = 0 utiles
(0.45 × £450 + 0.55 × £0)
$$= 0.45 \ (75 \ \text{utiles}) \ + \ 0.55 \ (0 \ \text{utiles})$$
$$= 33.75 \ \text{utiles}$$

We leave it to the reader to check the remaining calculations of implied utility in table 3.2, given the specified lotteries.

We could plot the utilities calculated in table 3.2 against their equivalent monetary value. Such a plot would provide a visual representation of the decision maker's utility function. For the data in table 3.2 we would observe a concave curve, indicating the common tendency of risk aversion. A linear function is referred to as risk neutrality; and a convex function, indicating that the decision maker is willing to pay for the privilege of being faced with uncertain outcomes, reflects an attitude of risk seeking.

If the continuity assumption holds, we can assign a utility to any monetary value between £1,000 and £0. Indeed, we could determine an algebraic expression of the utility function. With a mathematical expression it would then be possible to assign a utility value to any monetary outcome.

With table 3.2 completed, the decision maker could delegate his or her choice to an agent. For example, a decision analyst could replace the monetary outcomes of table 3.1 with the implied utility calculated in table 3.2. This has been done in table 3.3. With such a replacement, the analyst could calculate your expected utility of the alternative actions. Joining an 'angry' group would result in an expected utility score of 73.5 (i.e. 33.75 utiles × 0.4 + 100 utiles × 0.6). The third column of table 3.3 indicates that a solo career is the action alternative which will lead to the greatest expected utility (88.17 utiles = 91.06 utiles × 0.4 + 86.25 utiles × 0.6). This personal choice of career was determined by multiplying the utility of outcomes by the subjective probability of each state occurring, to yield an expected utility. The action chosen by the decision analyst on behalf of the decision maker maximises the decision maker's subjective expected utility. From the vantage point in time before the actions are made, the career as a soloist will lead to the greatest expected utility.

Table 3.3 Payoff Table using Utilities of Outcomes

		States of the world		Expected utility
		Economic growth	Economic decline	
	Angry group	33.75	100	73.5
Actions	Lyrical group	97.5	75	84
	Soloist	91.06	86.25	88.17
Probability of state		0.4	0.6	

Two additional assumptions are implicit in the above calculations of the von Neumann–Morgenstern cardinal utility function. The assumption of independence is concerned to rule out any utility attached to gambling. If a person is indifferent between two certain outcomes A and B, then he is assumed to be indifferent between two gambles that are identical in all respects except that one gamble offers A as an outcome and the other offers outcome B. The second assumption, concerning compound probability arithmetic, is designed to ensure that only ultimate outcomes are of interest to a decision maker. If a person is offered a gamble whose outcomes are other gambles, then his attitude to this 'compound' gamble will be the same as if he went through all the probability calculations to determine the ultimate odds this compound gamble was offering. This assumption of compound probability calculation is required since many decision situations are more complex than our singing example. We could develop the singing example and suggest that the outcomes would be affected by the relative popularity of male or female singers as well as the state of the national economy. We would then need the assumption of compound probability calculation for consistent choices to be made.[5]

We have now reached the point where the building blocks of models of personal choice have been introduced. A table, or payoff matrix (exemplified by tables 3.1 and 3.3), can be constructed to formalise choice activity. One dimension of

5. For a particularly well written introduction to the method of calculating compound probabilities see Howard Raiffa, *Decision Analysis*, Addison Wesley 1968, Chapter 2. Indeed, the whole book is an excellent non-mathematical introduction to formal models for personal choice.

the table indicates the alternative actions which the decision maker wishes to evaluate. The second dimension of the table indicates the possible nature of the environment — the states of nature — that are identified by the decision maker as likely to affect the outcome of any action considered. And the elements in the payoff matrix represent the preferences for the identified outcomes associated with each action—environment combination.

Uses of the Subjective Expected Utility Model

The simple singing example — although it provides an illustration of the SEU model — does not suggest the range of uses of the model. In this section we briefly consider five such uses or benefits of formal decision analysis using the SEU model.

Problem Decomposition

A typical reaction of someone first introduced to formal decision making is that the fancy analysis merely reflects what the decision maker already knew. For example, in the choice of singing career problem, you (the potential singer) provided the probability assessments for each state and the utility assessments for each outcome. The model for personal choice merely reflects what the decision maker already knows.

This reaction, whilst undoubtedly accurate, masks the fundamental importance of knowing the appropriate questions to ask. By utilising a formal model of personal choice, an individual is encouraged to split his problem into a number of parts. Each of these parts can be considered separately. The problem can be decomposed into its component parts: identification of conditions that can affect the outcomes, assessment of the likelihood of such conditions occurring, prediction of the outcomes associated with each condition and action combination, and valuing these outcomes. After each component part of the problem has been considered, then the problem can be re-structured again and a choice made.

This process of decomposing and then re-structuring a decision problem provides a framework for making any important decision, no matter how complex. The SEU model suggests that the constituent elements can be considered in terms of actions, states and preferences. The strategy of decomposition and re-structuring has been used in a wide range of cases — many of them considerably more complex than the personal choices most of us will ever have to consider. The earliest applications seem to have been in oil exploration and other business investment decision making.[6] More recent applications, using complex extensions of the SEU model, have included public or social choice. Decision analysis has been performed on the treatment of car pollution, means to reduce the destructive potential of hurricanes, nuclear plant location, medical and legal decision making and airport location.[7] In short, the general strategy of making choices by decomposing a complex decision problem, considering each part carefully and then re-composing the parts to make the final choice, has proved to be a highly beneficial procedure in both business and public choice. As we shall see in the next section, however, this strategy has its limitations.

Consistent Choice

Whereas problem decomposition refers to a general strategy

6. C.J. Grayson, *op cit.*, 1960, applied utility analysis to US oil and gas operators. Part Two of G.M. Kaufman and H. Thomas (eds), *Modern Decision Analysis*, Penguin Books 1977, provides other examples of business applications of decision analysis, including new product development, space programme planning, investment decision making, credit decisions, marketing, and bidding strategies. For a summary of the work done at Unilever Ltd see W.G. Byrnes and B.K. Chesterton, *Decisions, Strategies and New Ventures*, Allen and Unwin 1973.

7. Details of the first three applications are found in Part Three of G.M. Kaufman and H. Thomas (eds), *op cit.*, 1977. Ron Howard's review, Social decision analysis, *Proceedings of the IEEE*, March 1975, pp. 359--71 (reprinted in G.M. Kaufman and H. Thomas (eds), *op cit.*, 1977), is particularly recommended. The Mexico Airport decision, as well as some other recent applications, is discussed in R.L. Keeney and H. Raiffa, *Decisions with Multiple Objectives: Preferences and Value Tradeoffs*, Wiley 1976.

for making choices, a major benefit of the SEU model is its prescriptive element. If a decision maker wants to make choices that conform to the assumptions of the model, then the model provides a guide for action. The SEU model indicates how an individual who wants to make a choice that is consistent with his personal judgements (e.g. beliefs about the likelihood of events occurring) and his preferences (in terms of a utility function) should go about choosing.

As we shall see in the next section, people have considerable difficulty in making choices that are consistent with their own expressed or revealed beliefs and preferences! Using a formal model has the benefit of policing both the consistency of these beliefs and preferences and the calculation of their implications for action. If a decision maker wants to make choices that display transitivity, continuity, compound probability arithmetic and independence, then the SEU model provides an outline of how the choice can be made. And, to reduce any tendency to deviate from this ideal, a variety of decision aids can be produced. Examples of such aids include consistency checks in probability and utility assessments and computational checks in probability arithmetic and expectation calculations.

Foundations of Economics

One of the most important uses of the SEU model has been as the behavioural foundation of much economic theory. Although much of economic theory has been constructed on the assumption of certainty, the economic actor (whether it be consumer or producer) is assumed to maximise his (or her) own utility. When risk is incorporated into the economic world, than an individual is assumed to act as an expected utility maximiser. No economist would suggest that this assumption is descriptively valid for all consumers or producers. Rather, there exist some individuals who aim to maximise their utility and it is these individuals who set the limits of market transactions. Market survival, it is argued, ensures that others follow. As a simple and concise statement about human behaviour, the SEU model also serves as the basis of many accounting prescriptions.

Although it is clear that people do not behave as the model suggests they should, many economists regard such descriptive niceties as comparatively unimportant. For these economists, the predictions of their model are all that matter; and many of them are content with the predictive accuracy of the SEU model.

Foundation of Information System Design and Evaluation

If the SEU model is a representation of how people should make decisions, it follows that the model provides guidelines as to the type of information which is relevant and the manner in which it can be used to make a rational choice. This is considered in greater detail in the next chapter. It is sufficient for the present to say that the design of information systems has been influenced by the SEU model of choice.[8] In a well-defined situation, where a decision maker is able to construct a payoff table, then information only has a place in the revision of beliefs about the possible states of the world. In a less-well-defined choice situation (where there is doubt about the construction of the payoff table), information can also be used to help structure the problem and provide feedback as to the quality of prediction of the outcomes.

Extensions to More Complex Decision Situations

The decision making situations that have been considered can be extended, whilst still working within the framework of formal decision analysis and with individuals making choices in relation to the maximisation of their expected utility. Two such extensions seem important and have been well researched: the introduction of multi-attribute utility functions and the introduction of gaming situations.

Most people obtain satisfaction from more than one source. In our singing example, the choice was made on the basis of

8.   The literature on information system design is immense. Joel Demski's *Information Analysis*, Addison Wesley 1972, is an example that is solidly based on the SEU model. An alternative, more applied, approach is summarised in P. Keen and M. Scott Morton, *Decision Support Systems*, Addison Wesley 1978.

financial outcomes. Other variables, perhaps including status, nature of job, independence and self respect may also influence the choice.[9] In formal terms, attributes other than wealth may enter into an individual's utility function. The extension of SEU theory into multi-attribute utility analysis is an attempt to incorporate more than one variable into formal decision analysis.[10] Although the inclusion of multiple objectives in formal decision making can, at present, only be handled by making further assumptions (e.g. the independence of each objective), multi-attribute decision making techniques are being applied increasingly frequently, particularly in the area of public choice.

Many decisions made are based on the belief that the environment will respond to the action choices. In the singing example, the environment (states of the world) is quite reasonably assumed to be independent of, and unaffected by, the choice of singing career. Yet, in many instances a decision maker may not wish to assume the environment to be passive. Game theory is designed to model such situations and ulti-mately provide a strategy for the decision maker (known in this context as a 'player') that will maximise his expected utility.[11] Game theory treats the environment as an opponent, who simultaneously wants to maximise his or her utility. The decision maker determines the opponent's optimal counter-strategy to the decision maker's own optimal strategy and consequently incorporates the appropriate defensive measures into that optimal strategy. These gaming strategies, although seemingly complex, are typical of many decision situations.

9. There is a well developed tradition in psychology that is concerned to identify man's needs and the factors that yield utility; a classic statement is found in A.H. Maslow, A theory of human motiva-tion, *Psychological Review*, vol. 53, 1943.

10. A useful summary is K.R. MacCrimmon, An overview of multiple objective decision making, in J.L. Cochrane and M. Zeleny (eds), *Multiple Criteria Decision Making*, University of Southern Carolina Press 1973. Some recent developments are considered in R. Keeney and H. Raiffa, *op cit.*, 1976.

11. The classic work in this area is J. von Neumann and O. Morgenstern, *op cit.*, 1947. Thomas Schelling's, *The Strategy of Conflict*, Oxford University Press 1963, presents a delightful non-mathematical discussion of gaming strategies.

A worker may assess his or her best strategy about effort expended at work after considering the strategies that the foreman (or boss) might optimally adopt. Similarly, a firm may consider its optimal pricing strategy in relation to the actions of its rivals. Indeed a major development in accounting, auditing and finance has been the introduction of gaming models in decision making involving two or more inter-dependent parties (owner and manager, auditor and auditee, superior and subordinate).

Some Limitations of the SEU Model

The SEU model (and its variants and extensions) suffers from a number of problems that can be classified into broad types. One class of limitation relates to things the model intends to deal with, but appears not to do very adequately. The second type of limitation refers to aspects of decision making that the SEU model does not cover.

Inadequacies

Psychological studies of decision making have increasingly shown that there are difficulties with the SEU model, both as a normative standard and as a descriptive statement of how people make decisions.[12]

Perhaps the most well documented limitation relates to man's inability to act as an intuitive statistician. The SEU model, and indeed all formal decision analysis, assumes an ability to use probabilistic information. In laboratory experiments and in real-life situations, whether the decision maker is rewarded or not for appropriate use of probabilistic information about uncertain events, the evidence is remarkably consistent. Although early research showed that people were conservative in the inferences they made from available

12. There have been several reviews of decision theory that have sum-marised the essentially psychological studies of decision making. A good recent one is P. Slovic, B. Fischhoff and B. Lichtenstein, Behavioural decision theory, *Annual Review of Psychology*, vol. 23, 1977.

information, later psychological studies have shown that, in
some tasks, people's inferences are too extreme. Examples of
the biases include a belief in the law of small numbers (under-
estimating the unreliability of small samples of data), a failure
to distinguish association from causality, and a failure to consider base rates (alternatively referred to as prior probabilities)
in assessing the likelihood of events.[13] Whatever the direction,
it is apparent that people intuitively cannot act as the SEU
model assumes. Instead we use a variety of heuristics — rules
of thumb — that work well most of the time, but can lead to
systematic and consistent bias on occasion. The existing
studies do not adequately indicate when the heuristics are
appropriate and when they are inappropriate, although it
would seem that anxiety and stress are associated with more
bias. Of course, stress is likely to be present when important
decisions have to be made.

A second inadequacy is that the assumptions or axioms of
the SEU model are consistently violated. Recall that there
were four axioms required for the construction of a cardinal
utility function. Decision makers have been found, in one
instance or another, to violate all four of the assumptions.
But once these violations were shown to the decision makers
('Do you really want to act inconsistently?'), they could be
led to see the error of their ways. However, recent work has
suggested that people often feel there is a good reason to
violate the assumptions — especially the independence
axiom — and *choose* to act in violation of so-called rational
principles.[14]

One response to the vast amount of evidence about the
poor descriptive validity of the SEU model is to emphasise its
normative uses: as a (micro) theory of individual behaviour

13.   A most influential and persuasive explanation for the biases can
       be found in A. Tversky and D. Kahneman, Judgment under
       uncertainty: heuristics and biases, *Science*, vol. 185, 1974. Details
       of the biases can be found in a variety of sources; perhaps the
       most readable is P. Slovic, From Shakespeare to Simon: specula-
       tions — and some evidence — about man's ability to process
       information, *Oregon Research Institute Research Monograph*,
       vol. 12, 1972.
14.   P. Slovic and A. Tversky, Who accepts Savage's axioms?, *Be-
       havioural Science*, vol. 19, 1974.

for (macro) economics; as a provider of insights for information system design; and as a guide, perhaps through a decomposition strategy, for consistent decision making. In many respects, then, the descriptive limitations are recognised, but dismissed as irrelevant. Unaided, many people may be unable to act as the model suggests. Perhaps they do not want to act in accordance with the particular notion of rationality that emphasises, for example, consistency between choices and the irrelevance of the mode of presentation of a decision problem. But for individuals who do wish to act in accordance with the assumptions of rationality in the SEU model, the model can provide an ideal to aim at. The basic problem with this attitude is that the descriptive studies of decision making also suggest that techniques to aid decision making often do not work either! For example, the strategy of decomposing and re-composing a problem has itself been found to be intellectually difficult; some people are better able to make decisions using a more global or holistic approach which does not involve sub-dividing a problem into actions, states and preferences.

Another response to the SEU model's limitations has been to try and produce a model that is structurally similar (i.e. made up of actions, states and preferences), but descriptively more accurate. I will not describe these recent developments,[15] for although they overcome some of the descriptive weaknesses, they still suffer from the same errors of omission that the SEU model displays.

Omissions

Neither the SEU model itself, nor more recent developments, attempt to deal with all features of decision making. Omissions involve three themes: how decisions are structured, the relationship between action and preferences, and the nature of group decision making.

Formal analysis of decision making assumes that structuring a decision problem is straightforward. The decision maker is

15. A notable recent alternative model is found in D. Kahnemann and A. Tversky, Prospect theory: an analysis of decision under risk, *Econometrica*, 47, March 1979.

assumed to have an exhaustive list of alternatives available
for a problem that is well defined. In many decision situations,
however, problems may not be recognised, the definition of
the problem is unclear and the generation of alternatives is a
major concern.

How and why a situation is viewed as a problem (and hence
in need of a decision) is not well understood. Perhaps a problem
is recognised when a potential decision maker perceives a gap
between a desired state of affairs and the existing state.[16]
The source of such perceptions is unclear. It has been suggested
that our own historic models of how things ought to be, or
our use of other people's models of how things ought to be,
may be influential in stimulating the original perception.[17]
But the whole issue of problem recognition and definition,
although crucial in decision making, is only poorly understood.
In terms of our singing example, the SEU model is silent on
why we choose to consider singing as a solution to the problem
of how to express ourselves.

The SEU model is silent on the way the decision problem
is structured in terms of alternatives identified and states of
the world regarded as important. The specification of states
and alternatives would seem to be the product of a combination of standard responses and creative solutions. There is
considerable evidence that individuals try initially to use
standard procedures to structure and ultimately solve a
problem. The use of such procedures would be easiest for
well-defined and frequently occurring problems.[18] In novel
or unusual situations creative responses are required since, by
definition, the problem has rarely been faced before and
standard procedures may be inappropriate. Their inappro-
priateness does not, of course, mean that standard procedures

16.   A. Newall, J.C. Shaw and H.A.Simon, Elements of a theory of
      human problem solving, *Psychological Review*, vol. 65, 1958,
      and J.G. March and H.A. Simon, *Organisations*, Wiley 1958,
      present similar models of search based on levels of satisfaction.

17.   W.F. Pounds, The process of problem finding, *Industrial Manage-
      ment Review*, vol. 11, 1969.

18.   H.A. Simon, *The New Science of Management Decision*, Prentice-
      Hall 1976, distinguishes between programmed and non-program-
      med decision making, a distinction that has subsequently both
      proved valuable and been widely adopted.

are ignored. Indeed they may be part of the explanation for the biases in the use of probabilistic information that we have already considered (see footnote 13).

The role of creativity in decision making is not well understood, although there exist several techniques designed to stimulate creativity.[19] In our singing decision example, it is never clear why the alternative careers are either the only feasible ones, or how they are related to the original problem of expressing yourself. The SEU model does not consider such issues, but takes them for granted.

Similarly, the SEU model takes for granted the ability of the decision maker to identify factors in his environment that may influence the outcomes of the alternative actions specified. This is an enormous demand. When considering the choice of singing career, it would seem particularly difficult to identify those factors that will influence the outcomes. The state of the economy may be important, but the decision maker has thereby decided to exclude consideration of other factors which may be influential, but about which he is ignorant. The identification of influential states involves a predictive task; the decision maker may have little experience in such situations.

Indeed, we are left with the uncomfortable feeling that the SEU model omits from consideration some really fundamental aspects of choice behaviour. It is a model of alternative selection, which ignores the design of decision problems and the identification of decisions.

A second omission of the SEU model is a concern for the relationship between actions and preferences. Choice involves action and the presumption of formal analysis of choice is that preferences are an input to the choice process. Recently it has been suggested that preferences may be an outcome of action.[20] In other words, individuals discover their preferences through choice. A problem may demand action, and from that

19. There are several notable exceptions to the failure to consider creativity in decision making. Ken MacCrimmon's *Developing Alternatives*, University of British Columbia 1976, is an excellent review of imaginative decision analysis — particularly in problem formulation and alternative specification.

20. J.G. March, Bounded rationality, ambiguity and the engineering of choice, *Bell Journal of Economics*, vol. 9, 1978.

action preferences may be inferred. This suggestion is not a technical criticism; it suggests that the normative orientation of most formal analysis is misguided. There may be no link between the process of rational consideration of a problem and the decision made. Actions made may represent a set of behaviours that the decision maker wanted to carry out. A particular problem may then represent an opportunity — or excuse — for the action. This view of choice is provocative and appealing, in that it questions the notions of consistency as a fundamental rationale in personal choice. Yet it is not without its problems. How, for example, is the decision maker 'protected' from the problem that provided the excuse for an irrelevant action?

The third omission from formal decision analysis, and the SEU model in particular, is a concern for group decision making. This chapter is concerned with models for personal choice, yet we must recognise two organisational aspects of decision making. Firstly, many personal choices are made in an organisation and this organisational context influences the personal choices made. Secondly, decision making in organisations often attempts to solve organisational (rather than specifically personal) problems. The SEU model is not really a model of organisational decision making, although there have been some attempts to extend it in that direction.[21] Crucial elements in organisational decision making are conflicts about the best means to achieve any given end, and difficulties of estimating and communicating those estimates to the appropriate decision maker(s).[22] The SEU model, because of

21.   Perhaps K. Arrow, *Social Choice and Individual Values*, Wiley 1951, has discouraged formal analysis of group preference functions. He showed, from seemingly innocuous assumptions, that it is logically impossible to create a group preference structure from differing individual preferences. J. Marschak and R. Radner, *Economic Theory of Teams*, Yale University Press 1972, discuss the problems of coordination in the absence of conflict (over preferences).

22.   R.M. Cyert and J.G. March, *A Behavioural Theory of the Firm*, Prentice-Hall 1963, and J.G. March and J.P. Olsen, *Ambiguity and Choice in Organisation*, Universitetsforlaget 1976, present alternative models of decision making in organisations that reflect differing views of organisational preferences — ill-defined in the former case and ambiguous in the latter model.

its individual focus and its assumptions of well-defined problems, preferences and beliefs, does not seem to represent an adequate model for organisational choice. This is particularly unfortunate for management accounting, since most 'management' decision making occurs in organisational settings!

A Process Model of Personal Choice

A recognition of the limitations of the SEU model and formal decision analysis has led to an alternative model of personal choice. This model is descriptively based, reflecting observation of how decisions are produced and what decision makers do. Observation of decision making has led to a belief that the process of decision making comprises three phases.[23] The first phase may be referred to as intelligence activity. It involves finding occasions which require a decision — the recognition of problems. The second involves the analysis of the problem, the specification of alternative solutions and the prediction of the outcomes. The third phase, which seems to correspond with the emphasis of formal decision analysis, is concerned with choice. A particular action is selected which reflects the decision maker's preferences.

The process of decision making tends to be sequential: intelligence activity precedes design, and design activity precedes choice. The sequence of activity can be more complex than this, and, as was suggested above, choice may precede design activity.

The stages in the process of decision making are intended to incorporate many of the omissions in formal decision analysis. The descriptive limitations of the SEU model — notably, its failure to recognise man's limited ability as an intuitive statistician — form the basis of how these stages are

23.   Herbert Simon has been the dominant influence in this approach to decision making. A good introduction to his ideas can be found in H.A. Simon, *Administrative Behaviour*, Free Press, 3rd edn, 1976, first published in 1947, and *The New Science of Management Decision*, Prentice-Hall 1976, first published in 1960. His talk when he received the Nobel Prize for economics summarises all his work; see *American Economic Review*, vol. 69, 1979.

carried out. Limited capacity to make complex choices means that individuals tend to use simplified models of choice. Essentially, the process of decision making is carried out by people who intend to be rational. That intention, however, is limited by the complexity of their environment. As the complexity cannot be fully handled, the model is referred to as a model of bounded rationality.

The process model of decision making is intended to reflect an expanded view of the stages of decision making and recognise human limitations in processing information and making choices. These two features suggest a particular characterisation of models of bounded rationality.

The intelligence phase is the least well understood phase of decision activity. There is some evidence that people, and organisations, systematically scan their environments both for threats and opportunities.[24] A large proportion of the time, however, people respond to challenges or threats from their environment. Problem definition often involves dealing with a perceived threat from the environment. The environment — which may be a threat and thus a stimulus for choice activity — is both objective and subjective. It has been demonstrated that individuals perceive only a limited aspect of their environment. For example, accountants see problems as accounting and finance orientated, production managers see problems as production orientated and sales managers see problems as related to sales matters. Indeed, social psychologists have shown how social group and organisational features tend to lead to shared views of the world that may be incomplete or fundamentally in error. The continual interchange and modification between what is perceived and what is indeed in the environment, means that a theory of bounded rationality incorporates man as a learning and adaptive

24.   F. Aguilar, *Scanning the Business Environment*, Harvard University Press 1967; H.I. Ansoff, *Corporate Strategy*, Penguin 1969; E.E. Carter, The behavioural theory of the firm and top level corporate decision, *Administrative Science Quarterly*, vol. 16, 1971; and H.L. Wilensky, *Organisational Intelligence*, Basic Books 1967, either describe or prescribe how organisations search for problems. There is little about how individuals scan their environment, although Stafford Beer's *Brain of the Firm*, Penguin 1972, is suggestive — especially the discussion of arousal filters.

organism trying to acquire knowledge about an ever-changing environment. The formation of expectations about the environment, and how these expectations are modified in the light of experience, is a fundamental part of a descriptive theory of decision making.[25]

The search for solutions to a perceived problem tends to be biased and simple minded. It often focuses on the problem that has been identified, not on the basic cause of that problem. In other words, the search is problem orientated and tends to follow a process of incrementalism or marginalism. Starting from the existing state of affairs, it focuses on changes which are only slightly removed from existing activities. There is a tendency for individuals, when facing a problem that requires a choice, to settle on 'the' solution before they have considered alternative solutions. The problem acts as an excuse to embark on a particular course of action. It has been suggested that, in some decision contexts, the favoured choice may be deliberately and favourably compared with an alternative — selected for such a comparison specifically because it was seen as the 'least good' alternative! Although this observation about the comparison between favoured and least favoured alternatives is still very preliminary, there is clear and consistent evidence that only one or two solutions are systematically considered in complex choice situations.[26]

Estimating or predicting the consequences of the limited number of alternatives considered seems to be a most difficult, time consuming and (in organisations) contentious activity. Not only is estimating difficult, but the communication of estimates between individuals and sections within organisations can itself lead to both intentional and unintentional systematic bias. This area is of particular interest to the accounting function, which provides and communicates financial information within organisations. Some of the formal methods of forecasting are indicated in chapter 5. These methods, however, rely on systematic collection of relevant past data that can validly be used to make predictions. The process of

25. H.A. Simon, Theories of decision making in economics and behavioural science, *American Economic Review*, vol. 49, 1959.
26. R.M. Cyert, H.A. Simon and D.B. Trow, Observations of a business decision, *Journal of Business*, vol. 29, 1956.

prediction in unstructured and data-scarce situations is not well understood.

Perhaps the most important aspect of decision making that has been found from the observation of how people make choices is that people do not attempt to maximise or optimise any clear objective. Instead, individuals aim to achieve a satisfactory level of performance rather than pursue optimising performance. Furthermore, both individuals and organisations have a series of objectives, some of which are mutually inconsistent. It would seem that both individuals and organisations would prefer not to confront the possibility of conflict over objectives. So various strategies are adopted to avoid conflict. Consistency, a central principle of formal decision analysis, is not paramount. Inconsistency (and even some hypocrisy) is acceptable, given the costs of conflict resolution. Attention is focused on one goal at a time and once an acceptable level of performance is achieved (which may be described in terms of meeting the constraint that the goal represents), then attention is switched to another activity.

The descriptive theory of decision making emphasises the process of choosing, not the outcome itself. Rather than provide detailed guidelines for making choices (as does, for example, the SEU model), the theory seeks to explain choice behaviour. To achieve adequate explanations, the descriptive, process-orientated model views individuals and firms as adaptive, intendedly rational people who cannot fully handle the complexity of their environment.

Conclusion

This chapter has reviewed models for choice. We find that the SEU model of choice, which dominates much of managerial accounting, provides detailed prescriptions of how we may best go about making choices. If a problem and decision making situation are well understood by a decision maker, then the SEU model can serve as a useful mechanism to ensure consistency between a decision maker's choices and his beliefs and preferences. Further, we can use the model to help develop aids to overcome individuals' cognitive and information processing limitations. If problems and a decision making situation are not well understood by the decision maker, then the SEU model has little to offer. A process-orientated model of choice provides not only an explanation of how decisions are made in such situations, but provides some guidelines (in terms of learning what should be done) on how to produce a decision. Indeed, the descriptive model suggests that we might consider allocating our decision making resources to earlier stages in the process of decision making. Management accounting has not contributed much to helping decision makers to recognise and formulate problems. Nor has it been concerned with identifying alternatives that might be considered as solutions to a problem. These are fertile areas for management accounting, since major decisions are typically ill-structured.

4

Value of Information

J R MACE

Senior Lecturer in Accounting and Finance,
University of Lancaster

Introduction

Accounting is not an end in itself, but a means for the provision
of information for taking decisions. Opinions differ as to the
information which can be, is, or ought to be conveyed by
accounting reports, but there is no serious dispute that
accounting reports which are more useful to their users are to
be preferred to those which are less useful.

This chapter is concerned with some of the ways in which
information from accounting reports can be useful to users in
management, and with ways by which the usefulness of
information may be assessed. Usefulness is a difficult concept
to pin down and describe precisely. We shall suggest that
information is only useful as part of a wider system and that
it is the value of this wider system which should be examined
when we attempt to evaluate the information within it. We
shall seek to demonstrate that information, like any other
economic good, should be produced to the point at which its
marginal cost is equivalent to the marginal revenue derived
from its use, and we shall emphasise that the viewpoint of
the evaluator of information is critical in determining what
information should be produced.

Lev's comment on the problem is as follows:

> The design and selection of information systems obviously require a criterion to indicate the relative usefulness of the various possible systems, and to guide the (systems) analyst in choosing the optimal one. In principle this criterion is straightforward . . . the optimal information system is the one that when used by the decision maker maximises his expected utility. The information value of a system thus depends on the specific model used by the decision maker.[1]

The Usefulness of Information

We cannot avoid the ultimate conclusion that information is or will be produced because people want it, or want to produce it. Nevertheless, an examination of the reasons for which information is wanted may help those who make decisions concerned with the supply of, or with the demand for, information.

At one extreme, some information is undoubtedly produced just for its intrinsic interest or its entertainment value. Unless such information is produced for sale in a market, its usefulness can be assessed only in terms of the subjective utility functions of each of its users. Further analysis in this case is unlikely to be constructive.

At the other extreme, some information will be requested and produced purely for a decision taking purpose. In such cases the intrinsic interest or entertainment value of the information may be ignored and the usefulness or potential usefulness of the information may be analysed solely in relation to the decision at hand. It is this type of information upon which we shall concentrate.

Useful information may be derived in some cases from a measurement process. Some of the attributes of a useful measurement are:

(i) Relevance to the needs of its user
(ii) Reliability (freedom from bias and verifiability which means, for example, that erroneous action should not be encouraged)

---

1. B. Lev. *Financial Statement Analysis: A New Approach*, Prentice-Hall 1974, pp. 105–7.

(iii) Understandability (consistency with user concepts, comparability and simplicity)
(iv) Significance (i.e. whether it will materially affect the user's decision)
 (v) Sufficiency (i.e. whether additional information from other sources will be needed for the user to take his decision)
(vi) Practicality (i.e. whether the measurement is timely and worth more than its cost).[2]

Similar characteristics of 'useful' reports were outlined in 'The Corporate Report'. The Inflation Accounting Committee listed the desirable characteristics of accounting information as objectivity, realism, prudence, comparability, consistency, intelligibility and ease and economy of preparation. The comments of the Committee referred primarily to external reporting, but similar desirable characteristics may be listed for internal accounting reports in circumstances where any imprecision remains as to the nature of the decision for which the information may be used.[3] The difficulty in using these characteristics as a guide in information system design is that they are mutually inconsistent.

The Systems Approach

The systems approach is a help in achieving a satisfactory compromise in matters of information system design, because it recognises explicitly that decisions about the production of information cannot be made in isolation from the context. Detailed analysis of a system requires the examination of the activities and goals of the parts of the system and a determination of measures of their performance. It also requires an examination of the methods of control adopted by the system to monitor its own performance and coordinate its parts and

2.   H.J. Snavely, Accounting information criteria, *Accounting Review*, April 1967, p. 231.
3.   Report of the Inflation Accounting Committee (The Sandilands Report), Cmnd 6225, HMSO, September 1975, pp. 62–6.

their activities towards the accomplishment of the objectives of the system as a whole.[4]

Analysis of systems using accounting information as a method of control would proceed as follows:

(i) Define the perimeter of the system to be considered and schedule the resources and decision takers which it contains.

(ii) Identify the people whose interest will be affected by the design and operation of the system.

(iii) Specify the value systems of the people identified in (ii) above and show how they would rank the various stimuli which they may receive from the system.

(iv) Specify the objectives of the decision takers within the system in relation to the people identified in (ii) above.

(v) Examine the constraints upon the design and operation of the system which are imposed by the physical and sentient environment of the system.

If decision takers in a system are explicitly assumed to be perfect receptors and processors of accounting messages, the most useful accounting system may be one which is oriented toward the production of information for decision models. Accounts designed in this way may be appropriate for systems containing a uniformly perfect group of information processors, who are taking programmable decisions using homogeneous value systems and no alternative information sources. Such systems are mechanistic and are likely to have a greater stability than systems in which the information processors are imperfect and have conflicting value systems, multiple information sources and heuristic decision methods to determine their choices and actions.

In this latter case, the most useful accounting system would be one which catered for the perceptions and perceptiveness of individual users of accounts and for the interaction between accounting information and information from other sources in creating images in their minds. In a constructed system in which it is assumed that the other sources of information are

4. C.W. Churchman, *The Systems Approach*, Dell Publishing Company 1968, pp. 28–47.

fixed, the adaptive development of accounting may be towards the support and supplementation of these other sources in meeting the requirements of decision takers. If, on the other hand, information sources are competitive, each may view the perimeter of its sphere of activity as flexible and vie with the others to be more useful to users.

Value as a Summary of Usefulness

Provision of one kind of accounting information is likely to involve more expense than provision of another kind, and it is clear that this must be borne in mind in considering the comparative advantages of different information sources. In the absence of an analytical means of comparing the utilities experienced by different individuals, we are reduced to assessing information sources by the net value they confer to the larger system of which they are part. The principles of the process are well established. We evaluate the consequences of taking each decision within the system in the absence of the information; we re-evaluate the consequences of taking each decision when the extra information is available; and we use the difference between these two figures as a measure of the value of the extra information.

The consequences of making a particular choice as an output from a decision process, and acting upon that choice, will be unaffected by the information available to the decision taker at the time of making his choice. In other words, the information affects the perceptions of the decision taker, but does not affect the outturns of his alternative actions. It follows that information only has value attributable to it when the decision taker's optimal action using the information differs from his optimal action in its absence. This incremental value may be termed the 'gross' value of the extra information and it is only when the gross value exceeds the cost that there will be a positive net value for the extra information, and a consequent justification for its production.

The actual value of a piece of information can only be determined on completion of the consequences of all actions arising from its use. Decisions about the production of information cannot wait until after the value of the information is known: they must be based on expected values and costs.

A decision taker's uncertainty about various factors relevant to the context of a particular decision may be expressed in terms of the probabilities which he allocates to different states or events. The primary role of information is that it changes the probabilities which had been assigned to various states or events. If all possible outcomes of an event are fully specified and mutually exclusive, the sum of the allocated probabilities will be one. Perfect information in relation to such an event will be that which removes, in each instance, the uncertainty about the outcome of the event by substituting a probability of one, for one of the possible outcomes, and zero for all the others. Imperfect information will be that which revises the probability allocation without going so far as to substitute one for the probability of any of the possible outcomes of the event.

Morris writes that:

> To apply statistical decision theory to information decisions, it is necessary to be able to enumerate the possible outcomes of future data collection efforts, and further, to compute the probabilities of these outcomes. In addition, it must be possible to indicate just how the information will quantitatively change the decision maker's view of his choice.[5]

A definition of 'the decision maker's view of his choice' is critical to the evaluation problem. To determine the incremental value of information of different types, we need to know:

(i) the prior information states of decision takers within the system

(ii) the interpretations given by those decision takers to those information states

(iii) the decision taker's views of their objectives and of the matters in relation to which they are prepared (i.e. willing) to take decisions

5. W.T. Morris, *The Analysis of Management Decisions*, Revised Edition, Irwin 1964.

  (iv) the decision processes presently used and the appro-
       priateness of those decision processes to existing
       information states
   (v) the expected delay before decision processes would
       have adapted to the new information state
  (vi) the effectiveness of the process by which actual or
       potential users detect signals in reports and interpret
       messages from the signals they have detected
 (vii) the processes by which such messages are merged into
       the image structure of decision takers and affect their
       actions
(viii) the varying abilities of decision takers to detect signals,
       interpret messages and assimilate information
  (ix) the varying willingness and ability of each individual
       user to act in response to changes in his mental image.

Accuracy and Value of Information

Perfectly specified decision models are often discussed in the
literature, though they are infrequently to be found in
practice. The reason why normative decision models are incompletely specified in economic or social matters is that the
information inputs for such models are predictions about
states of affairs in the future which cannot be obtained by
observation in natural systems.[6] Predictions must be clearly
derived from observations, but the method of transformation
is not part of the model and in most cases it remains obscure.

When decision models are perfectly specified, actions,
outcomes and utilities are by definition unaffected by information systems, and the only purpose of the information system
is to provide the decision taker with the set of probabilities
associated with the various outcomes, or to modify his existing
probabilities. Perfect information indicates to the decision
taker exactly which action to take. It enables him to guarantee
that his selected action will be the appropriate one in every
instance and it will ensure that he does not incur irrecoverable

6.   The Markowitz portfolio selection model is an example of a model
      of this type. H. Markowitz, Portfolio selection, *Journal of Finance*,
      7 March 1952, pp. 77–91.

costs. Imperfect information, on the other hand, will still leave the decision taker to determine his optimal action in each instance on the basis of the specific information available to him. On such occasions, his optimal action may be the same as without the imperfect information, but the extra information (if it has value) will allow him to discriminate between instances that he would otherwise have treated identically. Sometimes events will show him to have been right to discriminate and at other times he will be shown to have been wrong.

The costs and values of information for a perfectly specified decision model may often be calculated to have the relationships shown in figure 4.1. The degree of imperfection in the information may be described as its percentage inaccuracy. It is likely that the cost of information increases as greater accuracy or precision is produced, and that the marginal cost of greater accuracy will increase the nearer one approaches to achieving perfect information. On the other hand, the gross value of information usually increases only linearly with

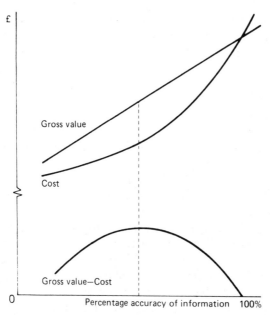

Figure 4.1 *Cost and Revenue from Increased Accuracy of Information*

improved accuracy. The consequence of this is as shown in the diagram, namely that the net value of information may reach a maximum at a level of accuracy which is less than 100%. In mathematical terms, the maximum expected net value of information is achieved when the marginal cost of additional accuracy equals the expected marginal revenue from additional accuracy. The preference between competing sources of information of different accuracy levels will depend upon their relative costs, and it is not always the case that the most accurate information source should be the one selected.

Other factors which influence the value of decisions resulting from the use of information include the frequency with which reports are produced by the system and the speed of processing of the information. In the first case, it is found, for example, that reporting frequency will alter the ability of decision takers to control the progress and development of a system in accordance with a predetermined plan. Very frequent reporting will be expensive and will tend to over-emphasise short-run variations from the plan to the detriment of effective control. As the reporting interval increases, the cost of the reporting system will fall and the effectiveness of control will increase; but after a point of optimum overall efficiency the effectiveness of overall control will again decline, because performance trend changes will be unrecognised until after the system has strayed for some longer time from its intended path.

In the case of the speed of information processing, we may note that, for a given technology, rapid information processing is likely to be more costly than slow systems of information processing. Faster systems are likely to cost disproportionately more than slower ones, as the processing time is reduced — though switches in information technology are likely to produce great changes in processing speed at little extra cost as, for example, when a computer system replaces a manually operated information system. If gross benefits from more timely information are linearly related to processing time, as may be the case for a process control operation, or only indirectly related to processing time, we may be able to determine that there is an optimal information processing time which is somewhat more, when cost is considered, than the minimum processing time which may be technologically achievable.[7]

An Example of Information Evaluation when Some of the Assumptions of the Perfectly Specified Decision Model are Relaxed

Consider an example of the information evaluation process, as it might apply within a simple closed system. We shall assume that the system contains, and is valued by, a person, whose sole objective is the maximisation of long-run expected value from the sale of hot meat pies as crowds leave the local football ground after matches. We shall assume that the standard of local football may be graded and the grades plotted as a time series in which any reasonably long sample is typical of the whole series. Pies are bought at 40 pence each and sold at £1.00 each. Pies must be bought before a match and, if not sold, we shall assume that they must be scrapped, since it would be contrary to health regulations for them to be re-heated for sale after a subsequent match.

The pie vendor has no informal memory for football and his decisions are based solely on formal records available to him concerning the demand for meat pies after matches, and upon certain knowledge that 30 pies will be demanded after a top grade match, 20 after a middle grade match and 10 after a low grade match. Consider some possible mutually exclusive perceptions which the pie vendor may have from his formal records. *One* of the following perceptions will provide the background for the adoption of a decision rule:

(a) He may perceive only that 'middle grade' is a close estimate of the average standard to be expected from local football.

(b) He may perceive that relative frequencies of standards

7. For further discussion of matters raised in this subsection, see J.R. Mace, *Management Information and the Computer*, Prentice-Hall 1974, and Gerald A. Feltham, *Information Evaluation*, American Accounting Association 1972.

in a reasonably long sample of football matches are as follows:

Top Grade	50%
Middle Grade	30%
Low Grade	20%

(c) He may perceive sufficient information about the time series of grades of football match to predict exactly the standard of any particular match in advance of purchasing meat pies.

A mathematically precise view of some perceptions of the payoffs to the pie vendor from selected possible actions is given in table 4.1.

Each figure in the columns of table 4.1 headed 'Top Grade', 'Middle Grade', or 'Low Grade' is calculated by multiplying the quantity sold by the selling price (of £1) and subtracting the total cost of the number of pies bought (at 40 pence each). For example, when 30 pies are bought and the standard of match is 'middle grade' the payoff to the pie vendor is $(20 \times 100) - (30 \times 0.40) = 20 - 12 = 8$. The column of table 4.1 headed 'Expected payoff' is the weighted average of the entries in the three preceding columns using the corresponding probabilities as weights. For example, when 30 pies are bought, the expected payoff is $0.5(18) + 0.3(8) - 0.2(2) = 9 + 2.4 - 0.4 = 11$.

The pie vendor's view of his decision situation may be less comprehensive than this. In perception state (a) above, he will decide to make regular purchases of 20 pies and this will give him an average achieved payoff of 10 (see the 'Expected payoff' column of table 4.1 opposite the action of buying 20 pies). In perception state (b) above, it is highly likely that he will calculate an expected demand for pies as follows

$$0.5(30) + 0.3(20) + 0.2(10) = 23 \text{ pies}$$

If he falsely interprets this long-run expectation as equivalent to a short-run certainty, he will decide to purchase 23 pies in advance of each match. He may justify this decision by calculating that the optimal purchase decision is 23 pies when he views his problem as one of maximising payoff, where payoff is expected sales revenue minus cost of purchases (as

Table 4.1 Payoff Table for Pie Vendor

Actions	Standard of Match			
	Top Grade probability 0.5	Middle Grade probability 0.3	Low Grade probability 0.2	Expected payoff
Buy 10 pies	6	6	6	6
Buy 20 pies	12	12	2	10
Buy 23 pies	13.8	10.8	0.8	10.3
Buy 30 pies	18	8	−2	11
Buy 31 pies	17.6	7.6	−2.4	10.6

before), subject to the constraints that the quantity sold may not exceed the quantity purchased or the quantity demanded (namely 23). The payoff he will expect from this decision will be $(23 \times 1.00) - (23 \times 0.40) = 13.80$ per match, but his long-run achievement will only be 10.3 per match (see the 'Expected payoff' column of table 4.1 opposite the action of buying 23 pies).

An optimal decision process in state (b) will show that expected payoff is maximised at 11 when 30 pies are regularly purchased (see table 4.1 again) and experience will confirm over a reasonably long sample that the expected payoff has been achieved. In state (c) the pie vendor will maximise expected payoff by varying his purchases so as to match each purchase to the corresponding (correct) prediction of demand. He will expect $0.5(18) + 0.3(12) + 0.2(6) = 13.8$ per period and his expectation will be achieved over a reasonably long sample.

A question similar to this example was used in tutorial work at the University of Manchester for some six years, during which time a majority of students made the false interpretation of perception state (b) which was outlined above. They failed to see without assistance that their expectation in state (b) would not be achieved and that the optimal action in state (b) is to make the regular purchase of 30 pies (since this action corresponds to the maximum value in the 'Expected payoff' column in table 4.1).

Almost all the students reacted correctly to the perception of certainty available under state (c) and adapted their decision processes correctly to state (c), whether or not they had

Table 4.2 Estimates of Information Values

Change of information state	Interpretation of perception state (b)	Value of information based on maximisation of expected value	Value of information based on maximisation of average achievement
a–c	–	$13.8 - 12 = 1.8$	$13.8 - 10 = 3.8$
a–b	true	$11 - 12 = -1$	$11 - 10 = 1$
b–c	true	$13.8 - 11 = \dfrac{2.8}{1.8}$	$13.8 - 11 = \dfrac{2.8}{3.8}$
a–b	false	$13.8 - 12 = 1.8$	$10.3 - 10 = 0.3$
b–c	false	$13.8 - 13.8 = \dfrac{0.0}{1.8}$	$13.8 - 10.3 = \dfrac{3.5}{3.8}$
a–b	false	(as above) 1.8	(as above) 0.3
b–b	false–true	$11 - 13.8 = -2.8$	$11 - 10.3 = 0.7$
b–c	true	(as above) $\dfrac{2.8}{1.8}$	(as above) $\dfrac{2.8}{3.8}$

made best use of the information available in state (b). We may use the figures taken from table 4.1 to demonstrate information values in terms of the payoffs from decisions based on its use. The minority of students who had interpreted their perceptions in state (b) correctly could see their expectation improve from 11 to 13.8, when their perceptions changed from state (b) to state (c) and would pay up to 2.8 per match for their change to state (c). On the other hand, the majority who had concluded while in state (b) that their expected payoff was 13.8 were able to see no improvement in that expectation from a conversion to state (c) and in consequence would pay nothing for it. These figures are set out in table 4.2 in the column headed 'Value of information based on maximisation of expected value'.

The Consequences of Feedback

Consider some of the possible consequences for the pie vendor in our example if he collects information on his achieved profit performances. If he were in perception state (b) (falsely interpreted) and regularly purchased 23 pies per match, he would expect 13.8 payoff per match. Feedback on his achieved profit performance would show him, for a reasonably large number of matches, that his average payoff had been 10.3 (see table 4.1 and explanations given above). We cannot be sure how we will interpret this signal from the feedback device, that his actual performance represents an under-achievement of $13.8 - 10.3 = 3.5$ per match (by comparison with his expectations). It is possible, if his predictions are empirically based and not analytically based, that he may revise the predictions of his performance downwards from 13.8 towards (or to) 10.3. It is unlikely, however, that the feedback signal will produce in him the considerable leap of understanding which is required before he will accept *the reason* for the error in his original prediction.

Feedback on actual performance may sometimes aid the decision taker in the formulation of his objective. The pie vendor may be made aware, for example, that maximisation of expected value is a satisfactory objective only when expectations are soundly based. If he adapts the specification of his objective to reflect that his true interests lie in maximisation of *achievement* rather than in maximisation of expectation, this may assist him in making more effective use of available mathematical techniques for decision taking, and in understanding the relevance of the feedback loop between performance measurement and decision taking.

If the existence of the feedback loop converts the pie vendor from his false interpretation of perceptions in state (b) to the true interpretation of perceptions in state (b), and he continues to act optimally (with respect to the state of his information), the feedback loop may be said to have an information value equal to the change in average achievement. Thus he would respond to the uncertainty by consistent purchases of 30 pies per match (see table 4.1) and he would achieve an average payoff of 11 per match, instead of the 10.3 he previously achieved when purchasing 23 pies per match, giving a gain of 0.7 per match in terms of long-run average achievement. This gain from the existence of the feedback loop is a 'once-only' gain, and after the change has occurred there is no further scope for improvement in achievement from continued feedback on actual performance unless perception state (c) is achieved. Movement to perception state (c) would increase his expected payoff to 13.8 and he would value such conversion at $13.8 - 11 = 2.8$ per match for all future matches (these and other figures are shown in the column headed 'Value of information based on maximisation of average achievement' in table 4.2). His feedback system on achieved payoff will again have no value in terms of helping him to improve his achievement once he is in state (c).

Only when information valuation is based on maximisation of average achievement will it be possible for the pie vendor to observe that the adaptation of his interpretation of state (b) from falsehood to truth has resulted in extra value for him of 0.7 per match from the time of his change to a policy of regular purchase of 30 pies. Without feedback, he could not have appreciated that true interpretation of state (b) had any advantage for him over his false interpretation. Indeed, there is nothing in the signal of 'under-achievement by 3.5' to indicate that his error lies in the interpretation of the perceptions in state (b), rather than in some aspect of the performance itself, and in practice this may make it difficult for him to make appropriate adaptations to his mental image.

If the feedback information on achieved payoff had been sufficient to make his expectation (from the action of buying 23 pies) fall from 13.8 to the true (realistic) level of 10.3 but insufficient to cause the change in action (to one of buying 30 pies), it could have bizarre side effects. First, it may cause him to doubt his other predictions, which may have been valid; and second, if he came to believe that 13.8 would really be achievable under perception state (c), it would cause him to value a conversion from state (b) to perception state (c) at $13.8 - 10.3 = 3.5$ per match. *He* would achieve the extra 3.5, whereas someone already acting optimally in state (b) would (as shown in table 4.2) value the conversion at 2.8 per match and would achieve the extra 2.8.

Some Tentative Conclusions

Our example has shown a situation in which the provision of (feedback) information is valued at different prices by different users. The price which a purchaser of information (or an investor in an accounting system) is willing to pay has been shown to depend upon the purchasers' view of the context of his decision. It depends *inter alia* upon the decision model he uses and the information available to him for deciding upon whether or not to invest in the information (or accounting system) under consideration for purchase.

Tentative conclusions from the example are as follows:

1. A user whose present decision model is sub-optimal may be prepared to pay more for new information than would a user whose decision methods are ideally matched to currently available information. Selection of new information to be produced must be based upon the cost of producing the new information (cost was ignored in our example) and upon some view of the incremental value likely to accrue from its use. The incremental value is not easily assessed, if at all (either by the user himself or by

any outside observer), because of the variety of prior states in which the potential users of the new information may be found and the inadequacy (based on our example) of any assumption that potential users are making optimal use of their prior information state. The consequence of making the assumption that the decision taker always employs an optimal decision process in relation to the state of his information is that the component of value which may accrue from any improvement in the relative optimality of the decision process which is applied will be ignored.

2. Our example shows that the use of an optimal decision model in combination with a valid objective and a realistic interpretation of available information made feedback valueless in the absence of change in the statistical structure of the observations to be recorded. In other words, a major part of the total value from feedback may derive from a once-for-all shift in the behaviour of the decision taker. It follows that the optimal life of a feedback system may be quite short (in the absence of change in the statistical structure of the observed variable). Short sequences of feedback information would normally be adequate to confirm that there had been no change in the statistical characteristics of the observed variable and continuous monitoring may be unnecessarily costly.

3. The materiality of information as evidenced by its value is dependent upon context. A single item of data, regularly produced, may never have value in a given system; it may at some time produce a once-for-all shift in the behaviour of the system; it may be valuable as one of the specified inputs for all operating decisions of a given type; or it may have value only in relation to the decisions of a wider system.

Practical Problems in Information Evaluation

A number of practical problems arise in attempting to evaluate information by the method we have been discussing. First, an economic system has abstract or intangible characteristics which affect its performance just as much as do its real and tangible characteristics. The tension and stress under which individuals are working, and their states of mind, are believed to affect their readiness to respond to changing circumstances and the effectiveness of their responses. The objective is to keep managers from extremes of frustration or of boredom and occasional messages of reassurance may have the effect of providing a stimulus to them for further effort. If messages reaching a manager did nothing but confirm his probability distributions about factors and events relevant to his decisions, they would not change the decisions he would otherwise make, and our evelution method would lead to them being discarded, since they would not be costless to produce. Indeed, some attempts to increase management efficiency have proceeded precisely along this path. The summarisation of information has removed much 'redundant' detail from reports to managers, and the use of standard costing and the analysis of variance has eliminated many messages of reassurance and has concentrated attention instead upon the techniques of 'management by exception'.

A second practical problem is that information has an effect in aggregate which may differ from the separate effects of its components. Thus the value of a single component of the information reaching a decision taker cannot validly be assessed in isolation from the totality of information at his disposal. Some of the benefits from information will be joint benefits arising only from the conjunction of a number of pieces of information from various sources. Our evaluation method would allocate the whole benefit to each component in turn, so it follows that the values attributed by our method to the separate components of total information could not validly be aggregated to give a total value for all the available information.

The problem of jointness in the assessment of information value is illustrated in the saying that it is the *last* straw which breaks the camel's back. Items of data may rarely be material to the decision taker's image or to the choice made in a specific decision when considered *on their own*; but in combination with other items, from accounting sources or elsewhere, they may be material. We cannot identify the last of the straws from any of the others in order to label it and help the camel to avoid it. Similarly, we cannot determine in advance which item of information will be the one which actually alters the choice of a decision taker in order that we should pay special attention to it. Our assessment of the value of items must therefore consider the likelihood that an item of information alone *or with others* will alter the choice to be made by a decision taker.

A third practical problem is that the evaluation process has assumed neutrality to risk on the part of the evaluators of information, in that it has based its calculated values on long-run averages. The truth of the matter is that many business decisions are 'one-off' affairs, where long-run average values do not adequately reflect the attitudes taken by the decision takers. Many decision takers are averse to risk and such people are likely to pay more for information than its expected value, simply so that they may gain the benefit from operating under conditions in which their uncertainty is reduced. To that extent, the expected value understates the 'market' value of the information.

A fourth practical problem, which has been touched upon in our example, is that the decision models for which accounting information may be used are incompletely specified. Where information is being provided as input for a specific decision model, it is increasingly likely that the decision process will be incorporated within the information system, so that the output from the information system is a decision for implementation and the role of the decision taker is pre-empted by the information system. It follows that the circumstances in which information evaluation is most required as a guide to information production will be precisely those in which it is least possible, namely those circumstanes in which structured (and programmable decisions) simply do not exist. Attempts to evaluate information are no less important, however, just because of the enormity of the practical difficulties which arise. We cannot record everything, so it will always be necessary to be selective on economic grounds in the general purpose information that we choose to record.

Summary and Conclusion

Signals contained in accounting reports can motivate and possibly direct (i) changes in decision rules (towards optimal decision taking within an assumed context), (ii) changes in the assumed context including changes in objectives followed by the decision taker, and (iii) changes in his perceptions of the extent and operations of the system within which he is taking his decisions. Thus, for example, the availability of new types of data will define a new area for a decision taker to pay attention to, and cause him to create new goals specifying his objectives in regard to the control of the new variable.[8]

The importance of information is often unpredictable, because most decision situations are simplified by the decision taker on grounds of economy and for lack of knowledge of optimal prediction methods for transforming firm variables into the inputs for normative decision models.

> For example, the decision maker will usually avoid the enumeration of all possible actions open to him and will consider instead a smaller subset of actions; he will also ignore many outcomes or states and focus on a few plausible outcomes; he will simplify the probability assignment to outcomes by applying a convenient function, such as the normal distribution; and he will similarly simplify the utility assignment to each action-outcome by using a general utility function, such as the quadratic or logarithmic functions, or even equate utilities with monetary values.[9]

The use of simplified models enables a man to overcome some of the limitations imposed upon his ability to handle complex situations. The components of any simplified model are approximations to the real choice situation. This means that information can affect all or any of the model's components (i.e. actions, outcomes, probabilities and utilities) and not just provide for the assessment and revision of the probabilities of outcomes as is the case within a perfectly

8.　Y. Ijiri, R.K. Jaedicke and K.E. Knight, The effects of accounting alternatives on management decisions, in R.K. Jaedicke, Y. Ijiri and O. Nielsen, *Research in Accounting Measurement*, American Accounting Association 1966, pp. 186–99.
9.　B. Lev, *op. cit.*, 1974, p. 100.

specified model. This wide role of information systems in relation to simplified decision models is, in summary:

  (i) in constructing the model, when the preliminary (*a priori*) set of relationships (hypotheses) comprising the model is indicated from experience;

 (ii) in testing the model, when sample information indicates the adequacy of the model's assumptions and implications (predictions) and suggests required modifications;

(iii) in using the model, when feedback control information will monitor the performance of the model and signal the required modifications in parameters and variables as the environmental conditions change;

(iv) in testing the rationality in the real situation of applying the solution derived from the simplified model, by comparing on an experimental basis the relative desirability of results based on the application of solutions derived from alternative simplified models in the real situation, and results which would have been achieved from the continued application of solutions derived from the simplified model in current use.

It has been argued that the purpose or multiple purposes of the user and the method of creation and development of the user's mental image are relevant to the value of information. The valuer of information in the real world is not in a position to *know* the type of decision which the information will influence, since he is remote from the user in space and time. Neither will the valuer know the way in which the decision taker will take his decision; he will not be certain of the decision model (or its component prediction processes) which the decision taker will employ in choosing his actions. The valuer must also make his own assumptions about the boundaries of the system which he considers relevant to his activities, and if he excludes some possible purposes for use of the information he is studying, his valuation will be understated. The human being evaluates information at a subconscious level when deciding upon facts of daily experience which are worthy of memory space, yet it is impossible to specify the process by which his decisions are taken.

An information system which supplements the human brain and nervous system will increasingly mingle functions concerned with the provision of information and functions concerned with taking decisions, but the overall objective of the information system remains an economic one. The ideal information system will contain descriptive and optimising models which are organised and inter-related to facilitate the accomplishment of the objectives of the system in which it is concerned. Interaction will continue between compilers and users of accounting information in an unending sequence of improvisation and compromise, as new contexts emerge. Attempts will continue to be made to tailor the provision of information to the programmed and unprogrammed needs of its users and to their ability to assimilate information, and information evaluation and re-evaluation will be recurrent features of contexts containing incompletely specified decision models.

5

Forecasting Models

MICHAEL THEOBALD

Lecturer in Accounting,
University of Manchester

Introduction

Decision making entails the selection of strategies from a set
of opportunities open to a particular decision maker. Each
strategy will lead to particular future consequences (or payoffs)
and in order to choose a strategy, some estimate of these
future consequences must be formed. It is the role of forecasting to provide information about the future consequences.
Hence, in a sense, forecasting is carried out to reduce the risk
in decision making.

In this chapter a number of forecasting techniques will be
described. A comprehensive description of all the forecasting
techniques available is not possible in a chapter of this length,
but most of the more popular techniques will be described.
Forecasting models may be classified into two groups — non-
causal and causal. The non-causal (or time series) models
develop forecasts on the basis of the past pattern of values of
the variable under consideration; causal models are based on
a theoretical relationship between the variable under consideration (the dependent variable) and a set of explanatory variables.
We will look at non-causal models first and then move on to
causal models. After that we will consider ways of evaluating
forecasts and comparing forecasting techniques.

A number of factors have to be taken into account in determining which particular forecasting model should be used. The type of data (i.e. whether trends, cycles or seasonal factors are present) from which the forecast is to be prepared is one of the prime determinants of choice of model. Another prime determinant is the amount of data available, since some need at least fifty observations of past results. Other factors to be considered are the costs of developing and operating the models, the benefits in terms of accuracy and the extent to which the model outputs can be understood and acted upon by the decision makers. One particular forecasting model will not normally be suitable for all the forecasting tasks of a firm; familiarity with a wide range of forecasting techniques is necessary in order that the optimal model for a specific forecasting task can be selected.

Components of Time Series

In order to gain some understanding of non-causal forecasting models, it is necessary to be aware of the basic components that are present in time series.

Let us denote the variable that we are studying as y_t, where the subscript t represents the time period in which we have observed y. The simplest time series will be the 'constant process' (time series are often described as 'stochastic processes') represented in the following equation (or model):

$$y_t = a + E_t \tag{1}$$

where a is the (unknown) constant of the process and E_t is a random disturbance term (sometimes referred to as 'noise'). The role of the E_t term is to represent random fluctuations of the y_t series about its constant value. For instance, annual ice cream sales might be described as a constant process, but due to random fluctuations in the weather actual sales in a particular year may be some way from the average level; E_t would represent the difference between actual sales (y_t) and average sales (a). Generally, we assume that E has an expected value of zero and a constant variance.

The values of some variables increase or decrease with the

passage of time, i.e. they have a 'trend'. Trends can be of a number of types and perhaps the simplest is the 'linear trend'. We use the same notation as before, with b as a second constant: then if y_t has a linear trend we can represent its behaviour as

$$y_t = a + bt + E_t \tag{2}$$

Analysis of linear trends is relatively easy, but many trends are best represented by more complex equations. Where a new (successful) product is introduced, the demand behaviour is typically described by an initial period of rapid growth followed by a gradual tapering off of demand. Demand behaviour of this type is often described by a logistic function. However, for ease of exposition and analysis we will continue to use the simple linear trend process throughout this chapter.

Cyclical factors may also be represented by terms in time series equations, but generally in the short run the cyclical effect becomes impounded in the trend term (known as the trend-cycle); consequently we will not consider cyclical factors separately here. However, seasonal factors are often important components of time series. Examples of time series exhibiting seasonalities are sales of Christmas cards, Easter eggs and raincoats; sales quantities vary systematically according to the time of year. The variables in a time series may be related in two distinct ways — additively and multiplicatively. If S_t is the seasonality in period t, the additive model may be represented algebraically as

$$y_t = a + bt + S_t + E_t \tag{3}$$

while the multiplicative model may be represented as

$$y_t = (a + bt)S_t E_t \tag{4}$$

Model (3) is the model often used in mathematical statistics, while model (4) is generally used in applied work. We shall use model (4) only.

Figure 5.1 depicts a constant process, curve (a), a linear trend process, curve (b) and a trend process with multiplicative seasonal variability, curve (c). One way to assess the components of a time series is to draw its graph. In the next sections we will consider other methods for preparing forecasts of time series incorporating the components described here.

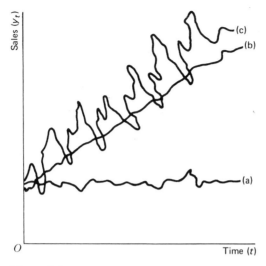

Figure 5.1

Classical Decomposition Analysis

This technique entails breaking the time series down into its constituent parts and then forecasting on the basis of the components found to be present in the data. The random and seasonal components are 'smoothed' out by taking moving averages of the series using a process described below. The smoothed series will contain only the trend component and hence may be used to estimate it. The ratio of the raw series to the smoothed series will then contain only the seasonal and random components and is termed the 'seasonal index'. The technique is best described with the help of an example. Suppose that we have the record of past sales given in table 5.1 and that we wish to forecast sales for the first quarter of 1979. A quick glance at the numbers indicates some quarterly seasonality. The influence of seasonal factors is confirmed when we plot sales against time in figure 5.2.

Table 5.1 Quarterly Sales Data

1976	1976	1976	1976	1977	1977	1977	1977	1978	1978	1978	1978
I	II	III	IV	I	II	III	IV	I	II	III	IV
100	104	101	109	103	109	103	114	108	110	106	119

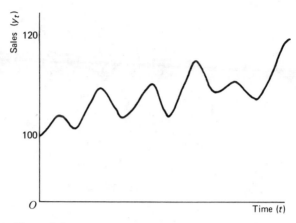

Figure 5.2

When one computes moving averages for a series which contains random components, provided the random components have an expected value of zero, the resulting smoothed series will be net of the random component. Similarly, if one takes a moving average over the period of seasonality of the series, the seasonality will be removed; that is, if we have one observation from each season in each moving average, then seasonal effects cancel each other out. Thus by calculating a four-period moving average for the data in table 5.1, we can generate a moving series consisting of a trend only. This data is contained in table 5.2.

The first number in the 'Four-period moving average' column is generated by taking the average of the first four observations: (¼) (100 + 104 + 101 + 109). The second number is obtained by dropping the 1976 I observation and substituting the 1977 I observation: (¼) (104 + 101 + 109 + 103). In this manner we can generate a series of moving averages. However, each moving average relates to a time between two quarters. The 'Centred moving average' column centres the moving average on one particular quarter by taking the average of the moving averages which straddle that particular quarter: the first number is generated by the expression ½ (103.5 + 104.25).

There are two important points to note about moving averages. First, the use of moving averages leads to a loss of

Table 5.2 Deriving a Trend

	Raw series	Four-period moving average	Centred moving average	Seasonal index
1976 I	100			
II	104			
III	101	103.5	103.9	0.97
IV	109	104.25	104.9	1.04
1977 I	103	105.5	105.8	0.97
II	109	106.0	106.6	1.02
III	103	107.25	107.8	0.96
IV	114	108.25	108.4	1.05
1978 I	107	108.5	108.9	0.98
II	110	109.25	109.9	1.00
III	106	110.5		
IV	119			

observations; the original raw sales series of twelve observations is reduced to eight. Second, as we would expect, the trend in the series becomes very much apparent after removal of the seasonal and random components.

The 'Seasonal index' column (which will also contain some random fluctuations) is determined by taking the ratio of the raw series to the centred smoothed series: the first entry is 101/103.9.

If we assume the trend to be linear we can 'fit' an equation to explain the smoothed series in the form:

$$y_t = a + bt \qquad\qquad (5)$$

by using ordinary least squares (this type of analysis is explained below). The estimates of a and b when we assign a value of $t = 1$ to the 3rd quarter of 1976 are $\hat{a} = 103$ and $\hat{b} = 0.84$.

If the 3rd quarter of 1976 corresponds to $t = 1$, then the 1st quarter of 1979 will correspond to $t = 11$. Thus our extrapolated trend forecast will be given by

$$\hat{y}_t = 103 + 0.84 \times 11 = 112.2$$

The seasonal index for the first quarter is 0.975 (i.e. the average of the two seasonal indices in table 5.2), so the forecast is $112.2 \times 0.975 = 109.4$.

In summary, there are four steps to a classical decomposition analysis:

  (i) the removal of seasonal and random factors by the use of moving averages;
 (ii) the determination of the trend from the smoothed series;
(iii) extrapolation of the trend line; and
(iv) adjustment back from moving averages by the use of seasonal indices.

A related and more elaborate technique is the 'Census II' method, which, despite some weaknesses, performs very well in practice.

Exponential Smoothing

A popular and simple alternative to the moving average technique is the exponential smoothing technique. The technique is perhaps best introduced by assuming a simple constant process (the technique is known as simple exponential smoothing).

If we denote the exponentially smoothed forecast at time $t-1$ as S_{t-1} (which will be the forecast of the variable at t), then the forecast error, e_t, will be given by

$$e_t = y_t - S_{t-1} \tag{6}$$

The next forecast S_t should incorporate the information present in the previous forecast error. The modified forecast may then be defined as

$$S_t = S_{t-1} + \alpha(y_t - S_{t-1}) \tag{7}$$

Equation (7) is the exponential smoothing formula, with α defined as the 'smoothing constant'. Thus, the exponential smoothing technique consists of adjusting prior smoothed statistics by the forecast error. The extent of adjustment is dependent upon the value of α, which can take values in the range zero to one. When $\alpha = 0$, there is no adjustment and the new statistic equals the old, while when $\alpha = 1$, there is full adjustment and the new statistic is equal to the most recent value of the variable to be forecast, y_t. The range of α

Table 5.3 Annual Sales Data

	Raw data	Simple exponential smoothing (S_t)		Double exponential smoothing (S_t')
		$\alpha = 0.3$	$\alpha = 0.5$	$\alpha = 0.3$
1976	414	414	414	379
1977	429	418.5	421.5	390.6
1978	442	426.5	434.8	401.4

reflects the conflicting objectives that are present in time series forecasting, namely the wish to smooth out random components versus the wish to adjust quickly to new information. Choice of a value for the smoothing constant is generally made by a comparison of forecast error statistics for differing values of α. For a constant process, α is usually assigned values in the range 0.01 to 0.3. Forecast numbers derived from this process may be considered to be weighted averages of past values (since it can be shown that the weights sum to unity), with the weights declining geometrically for older observations.

Application of model (7) to the sales data contained in table 5.1 would not be expected to be a very successful method of forecasting, since the data were not drawn from a constant process, or one which was changing only very slowly. It is possible to develop exponential forecasting models to handle both trend and seasonal components, but due to shortage of space we will consider here only the incorporation of a trend into the analysis.

The quarterly sales data contained in table 5.1 have been aggregated into annual data in table 5.3. The table illustrates the tendency of the simple exponential smoothing technique to predict values that are too low when the variable has a positive trend. This is confirmed in the simple exponential column using a smoothing constant of 0.3. Increasing the smoothing constant to 0.5 results in a forecast which more closely 'tracks' the actual series. In both cases S_{1976} has been assigned a value of 414, the first observation of sales. A number of alternative methods are available to obtain the first number in the series; and if it is desired to remove the effects of the initial value rapidly, a high smoothing constant can be used initially and then a more normal one once the starting value has been sufficiently 'washed out'. The smoothed value for 1977 is determined by

$$S_{1977} = S_{1976} + 0.3 \, (y_{1977} - S_{1976})$$
$$= 414 + 0.3 \, (429 - 414)$$
$$= 418.5$$

Double exponential smoothing entails smoothing the simple exponentially smoothed series; the resultant figures are shown in the fifth column of table 5.2. If this approach is applied to the trend process described in equation (2), the forecast is given by

$$F_{t+n} = a_t + b_t n \tag{8}$$

where

$$a_t = 2S_t - S_t{}'$$
$$b_t = \frac{\alpha}{1-\alpha} \, (S_t - S_t{}')$$

$S_t{}'$ represents the double exponentially smoothed series and n the number of periods ahead for which the forecast is required. This technique is generally referred to as 'Brown's one parameter linear exponential smoothing' method. It differs from the 'trend analysis' forecast of a linear trend in that the parameters of the process, a_t and b_t, change in response to patterns in the data. In trend analysis, a and b are constant over the whole of the data set. Again, it is necessary to determine an initial value for the double exponentially smoothed series; the best forecast is obtained from a starting value less than 414. There are formulae available for determining that initial value (see Chapter 3 of Montgomery & Johnson, included in the references at the end of this chapter). The fifth column of table 5.3 sets forth the double exponential smoothing series: the forecast for annual sales in 1979 is given by

$$(2 \times 426.5 - 401.4) + \frac{0.3}{0.7} \, (426.5 - 401.4)$$

$$= 462.0$$

With a short time series such as is analysed in this example, the starting values assigned to both series can be critical and lead to biases in the forecasts obtained. In practice, we generally have longer time series of observations, where small errors in the initial values are removed through time (systematically large errors could still lead to significant forecast biases, however).

A number of more sophisticated exponential smoothing techniques have been developed, whereby the smoothing constant can be monitored and modified when the process changes. These types of models are referred to as 'adaptive-control' methods and references describing these models as well as exponential smoothing models incorporating seasonal factors are provided at the end of this chapter.

Box—Jenkins Techniques

The Box—Jenkins class of forecasting models comprises a relatively powerful and general set of forecasting models. The models involve the use of complex techniques, a factor which is an obstacle to their wide-spread use.

It is in the presence of autocorrelations (the dependence of current values of the variable on past values of the variable) that Box—Jenkins techniques become particularly powerful. Many time series involve autocorrelations and such relationships are termed 'autoregressive', e.g. the value of a variable at time t, y_t, may be given by the following equation:

$$y_t = \Phi_1 y_{t-1} + E_t \tag{9}$$

where Φ_1 is a constant and E_t is a disturbance term. The equation (9) is termed an AR(1) process — AR for autoregressive and 1 for the maximum lag value of the variable. The general autoregressive process may be represented as AR(p) where p is the maximum lag on the forecast variable.

Another class of model is the moving average process, where the variable y_t is represented as dependent on so-called 'white noise' variables E_t, E_{t-1} ... An MA(2) process (moving average with two 'white noise' variables) is then given by

$$y_t = \mu + E_t + \Theta_1 E_{t-1} \tag{10}$$

where μ and Θ_1 are constants. The MA process reflects dependencies in the time series, since y_t and y_{t-1} are both functions of E_{t-1}.

The processes described in (9) and (10) may be combined to give an ARMA (1,2) process:

$$y_t = \mu_1 + y_{t-1} + E_t + \Theta_1 E_{t-1} \tag{11}$$

and we may define general processes in the form ARMA (p, q). The general type of ARMA (p, q) process can be used to model what are termed stationary time series. Definitions of stationarity can be subject to varying levels of precision; for present purposes, we define a stationary process as one in which the variable fluctuates randomly around a constant mean. If we have to deal with a non-stationary process, we may be able to use the technique appropriate to a stationary process by analysing differences in the values of variables; that is, if we have a simple linear trend, we analyse $y_t - y_{t-1}$ instead of y_t. The stages involved in a Box—Jenkins analysis will now briefly be described:

Stage 1 Identification

First the form of the model is determined: a choice is made between the general types of equation illustrated as equations (9), (10) and (11) and a decision is made as to how many variables are to be considered.

Stage 2 Parameter Estimation

The parameters (the Θ's and Φ's) have to be estimated. While AR processes can be estimated by ordinary least squares, MA and ARMA processes necessitate the use of non-linear least squares techniques which involve considerable estimating problems.

Stage 3 Diagnostic Checking

The adequacy of the specification has to be tested and, if necessary, improved.

Stage 4 Forecasting

The forecasts can then be generated.

Even in this short description of Box–Jenkins techniques, their complexity has been apparent. However, these techniques are powerful and of general applicability.

Causal Models: Building and Estimation

As the name implies, causal models specify a causal relationship between a dependent variable (the variable to be forecast) and a set of independent variables. The simplest form involves a linear relationship. The model

$$Y_t = a + bX_{1t} + cX_{2t} + E_t \tag{12}$$

is an example of a two-variable linear model where E_t is the disturbance term representing random fluctuations in period t, Y_t is the value of the dependent variable in period t and X_{1t}, X_{2t} are independent variables. Causal models may be developed in two stages:

(i) determination of variables to be included in the model; and
(ii) estimation of the parameters of the model (in model (12) a, b and c).

Generally the analyst will have some preconceptions of which variables should be included in the model, but it may be desirable to limit the variables that are actually included. Computer packages are available which 'dredge' the data and select the variables for inclusion in the model. The methods for estimating causal models will be outlined after we have considered a number of econometric terms.

The most common technique for estimating causal models is ordinary least squares (OLS) regression. This technique selects values for the parameters of the model in a manner that minimises the sum of the square deviations between the actual and estimated values of the dependent variable. Under certain conditions, OLS estimates are the best that can be made in the sense that they are unbiased, and of all linear estimates they have the minimum variance. The required conditions are that (a) the disturbance term has an expected value of zero; (b) the disturbance term has a constant variance; (c) the disturbances have zero serial correlations; and (d) the independent variables are independent of the disturbance term.

The coefficient of multiple determination, generally referred to as R^2, provides a measure of the goodness of fit of a relationship. It is the proportion of the variance of the dependent variable explained by the independent variables, i.e. the nearer to one that R^2 is, the better the fit. The R^2 statistic has the undesirable property, from the point of view of model building, that it will always increase when an additional independent variable is included, whether or not that variable is relevant. However, the R^2 statistic may be adjusted to eliminate this difficulty – it is then designated $\bar{R}^2$.

The statistical significance of the relationship described by a particular model can be assessed by use of the 'F–statistic'. Elementary statistics courses introduce the idea of hypothesis testing via the use of the 't–statistic'. However, these procedures are capable of testing only a hypothesis about a single variable. The F–statistic is the counterpart of the t–statistic; it is the basis of a test that *all* the coefficients of a model are statistically significant; it thus affords the means of testing a hypothesis about several variables. (In practice, the t–statistic of each of the parameters is often measured as well.)

It was noted that the $\bar{R}^2$ statistic does not always increase as a result of the inclusion of an additional explanatory variable. The condition for $\bar{R}^2$ to increase after inclusion of a variable is that the F–statistic of that variable should be greater than one. An F–statistic greater than one does not mean that that variable is statistically significant, so that a model building technique based on the criterion that $\bar{R}^2$ be maximised can lead to the inclusion of variables that are not statistically significant.

The final statistic to be considered is the standard error, a measure of the uncertainty of the estimates of the parameters of the model. A model building criterion calling for minimisation of standard errors is equivalent to calling for the maximisation of $\bar{R}^2$.

The statistics described above may now be used to outline, briefly, how one might build and estimate a causal model. When the number of variables to be considered is small, we can simply consider all combinations of the explanatory variables and select that model which minimises standard error (or maximises $\bar{R}^2$). However, this technique has the disadvantage that a large number of models have to be considered when the number of variables increases (the number of models to be compared when selecting from m variables is $2^m - 1$).

The most commonly used technique for model selection is a 'step-wise' regression, which is a brute-force mechanical technique. Variables are considered for inclusion on the basis of their F—values. A particular F—value may be selected by the model builder as a threshhold value for variable inclusion. There are a number of disadvantages in this procedure, but space does not permit their description here. The interested reader is referred to the references at the end of this chapter.

The importance of choosing the best model is emphasised by the fact that if relevant variables are omitted from the model, parameter estimates and perhaps also forecasts may be biased. Inclusion of irrelevant variables will not lead to biases, and this asymmetry has led to the so-called 'kitchen sink' philosophy — that is, when in doubt about a variable to be included, throw it in to the regression!

Causal Models: Forecasting

Once we have built and estimated our model, it can be used for generating forecasts. A causal model can be expected to generate adequate forecasts only if the forecast period has the same characteristics as the period over which the model was built. We may be interested in two types of forecast — *ex post* and *ex ante*. *Ex post* forecasts arise when we are comparing a forecast derived from a model with the known value of the forecast variable. This type of exercise is geared towards model validation. The type of forecast most managers are interested in is the *ex ante* forecast, a forecast of a future event.

Ex ante forecasts can be broken down into two types —

conditional and unconditional. Conditional forecasts occur when we do not know the values of the relevant explanatory variables (the independent variables). We then generate forecasts that are *conditional* upon values of the explanatory variables. Unconditional forecasts, on the other hand, arise when values of the explanatory variables are known. Values of the explanatory variables may be known when they are 'lagged' i.e. Y_t depends upon values of X in period $t-1$ etc.

It will be helpful at this stage to consider an example. Suppose that we are trying to forecast future sales of the supporters' club scarves of a particular football club, and that on *a priori* grounds we believe there to be only two possible explanatory variables — price and league position. Models have been estimated for combinations of the explanatory variables; they are given in table 5.4. On the basis of the maximum $\bar{R}^2$ (or minimum standard error) criterion described in the previous section, the optimal model is model 1. (The signs of all parameters are what we would expect and that may further support the choice of model).

If we know that the future price of the scarves will be £1, and if the team in question is Liverpool (so that the league position will be one), our forecast will be

$$\begin{aligned} \text{Sales} &= 98 - 0.34 - 1.94 \\ &= 95.72 \end{aligned}$$

Such a forecast cannot be made with certainty, however, since

  (i) the model parameters used are only estimates, and
 (ii) the outcome may be affected by random fluctuations.

We can recognise the uncertainty of our forecasts by calculating confidence (or prediction) intervals around our point

Table 5.4 Model Data

		R^2	F	Standard error
Model 1	Sales = 98 − 0.34 Price − 1.94 Position	0.991	388.6	1.10
Model 2	Sales = 104 − 1.44 Price	0.323	2.1	7.99
Model 3	Sales = 93.4 − 1.995 Position	0.988	566.4	1.29

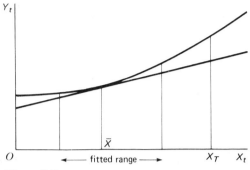

Figure 5.3

estimates. In generating forecasts, we can forecast either the mean of the dependent variable or the dependent variable itself. In both cases, the same point estimate will be obtained, but the confidence regions will differ (it is common practice to refer to the former as a confidence interval and the latter a prediction interval). For multivariate models the formulae become somewhat complex. The interested reader is referred to one of the standard econometric texts listed at the end of this chapter.

A number of points are worth noting about prediction intervals. First, prediction intervals will be smaller, the greater the number of observations used in development of the model. Also the interval will be smaller when the value of the explanatory variable is within the range of past experience. Related to this point are the dangers of extrapolation. For instance, suppose that we have used a simple linear model when a non-linear model would be preferable (see figure 5.3). If our forecasts are related to values of the explanatory variables experienced previously (i.e. we use interpolation), reasonable forecasts may be generated. Outside the range of previous experience, at X_T say, the generated forecasts become somewhat inaccurate.

Forecast Evaluation

We have considered above the main forecasting techniques open to management. We next review shortly some criteria for the evaluation of forecasts. We denote the forecast error in period t as

$$e_t = Y_t - \hat{Y}_t \tag{19}$$

where Y_t is the actual value in period t of the variable to be forecast and $\hat{Y}_t$ the corresponding forecast in that period. A desirable property of e_t would be that on average it should equal zero, i.e. $E(e_t) = 0$. If this condition holds, the forecast is said to be unbiased. An example of a biased forecast would be the use of the simple exponential smoothing model for a process which had a trend; use of that model would produce forecasts which were systematically too low.

We should also require the forecast errors to be small, on the average. Measures of the size of forecast error must avoid offsetting positive and negative errors; two common measures are the mean absolute deviation (*MAD*) given by

$$MAD = \frac{\Sigma_t |e_t|}{n} \tag{20}$$

and the mean square error (*MSE*) given by

$$MSE = \Sigma_t e_t^2 \tag{21}$$

Another commonly used statistic is Theil's *U*-statistic defined as

$$U = \sqrt{\frac{MSE}{\Sigma Y_t^2 / n}} \tag{22}$$

where n is the number of observations. For perfect forecasts, $U = 0$.

Comparison of Forecasting Models

Previous sections have described various forecasting methodologies without comparing them. This section identifies some of the relative advantages and disadvantages of the methodologies.

One strong advantage of causal models over simple time series models is that their functional form implies a more rigorous theoretical underpinning. However, some causal models have limited usefulness, because they show the variable to be forecast as depending on the *future* value of some other variable; that difficulty is avoided by time series models. Cost considerations also tend to favour the simple time series models over the causal models.

As mentioned earlier, Box–Jenkins techniques have advantages over the smoothing models. Box–Jenkins forecasts are generally more accurate (in terms of *MSE*'s) and the models have wider applicability and deal with some aspects which are ignored by the simpler smoothing models. However, Box–Jenkins analysis has the disadvantages of being relatively complex and of requiring large numbers of observations (generally greater than fifty).

Conclusions

The choice of a forecasting system should depend on the costs and benefits involved in the particular circumstances of its proposed use. No one system is preferable in all situations. Although much emphasis has been placed upon the generation of forecast point estimates, it must be stressed that the generation of multi-valued forecasts in the form of confidence (prediction) intervals is of considerable usefulness in showing the range of results that may follow a particular decision.

References

Two texts that cover broadly similar ground to the level of this chapter are:

D. Wood and R. Fildes, *Forecasting for Business: Methods and Applications*, Longmans 1976
and
M. Firth, *Forecasting Methods in Business and Management*, Edward Arnold 1977.
An excellent book in the area of smoothing is:

D. Montgomery and L. Johnson, *Forecasting and Time Series Analysis*, McGraw-Hill 1976.
This book also describes Box–Jenkins techniques as does:

R. Pindyck and D. Rubinfeld, *Econometric Models and Economic Forecasts*, McGraw-Hill 1976.

This text also discusses the econometrics necessary for an understanding of the causal forecasting models. Perhaps the best standard text at undergraduate level is:

J. Johnston, *Econometric Methods*, McGraw-Hill 1972.

An interesting comparison of time series techniques can be found in:

D. Reid, *Forecasting in action: a comparison of forecasting techniques in economic time series*, Joint Conference of OR Society's Group on Long Range Planning and Forecasting, OR Society, 1971.

6

Budgets for Decisions

JOHN ARNOLD

Professor of Accounting,
University of Manchester

Introduction

In this chapter we discuss the calculation of relevant costs
and revenues for decisions. Decisions are always concerned
with choices between alternative courses of action; if there
are no alternatives, there is no decision to be taken. The
fundamental importance of the existence of alternative courses
of action leads us to consider the role of alternative budgets,
i.e. budgets of the likely outcomes associated with each
available action. We explain ways in which the information
contained in a series of budgets may be summarised in a single
'profitability' statement and compare the results with those
obtained by the application of conventional historical cost
accounting.

The aim of this chapter is to introduce and discuss the basic
ideas of cost and revenue calculation. We do not, and could
not in the space available, consider all the problems involved
in determining costs and revenues for decisions. (Some of
those problems are discussed in other chapters.) The objective
here will be satisfied if the reader is left with a healthy
scepticism about the usefulness of conventional accounting
measurements of profitability. Nevertheless, we hope to
demonstrate that some methods of cost and revenue determination are based on sounder principles than are others.

Types of Decisions

Decisions fall into two basic categories: accept or reject decisions and ranking decisions. Accept or reject decisions arise when a firm is considering a particular opportunity, acceptance of which will not affect decisions on other projects that are expected to become available. In such a case, a decision may be taken about the worthwhileness of the opportunity under consideration, without having to compare it with other available projects — except that it remains necessary to consider alternative uses for the resources that would be needed if the opportunity was accepted.

Ranking decisions involve choosing between two or more competing opportunities, and generally result from either a shortage (scarcity) of resources or mutual exclusivity between opportunities. Scarce resources are said to exist when a firm has insufficient supplies of one or more of its resources (e.g. labour, materials, factory space etc.) to accept all available opportunities that appear to be profitable. In this situation, the firm must endeavour to apply its scarce resources in the most profitable way. How it might do so is considered in Chapter 7. Two or more opportunities are said to be mutually exclusive when acceptance of one of them precludes acceptance of the others, for reasons other than scarcity of resources. Mutual exclusivity normally arises when different means of achieving the same or similar ends are being considered, for example alternative production methods having the same output capacity.

Principles of Relevant Cost and Revenue Determination

A central problem facing firms, and a central concern of this chapter, is how to estimate the relevant costs and benefits associated with the various alternatives available to the firm. The principles involved will be explained with particular reference to costs, because these are generally more difficult to identify and evaluate than benefits. Similar principles should be applied to benefits, however.

The principles to be applied in determining costs and

benefits depend on the decision maker's objectives. Models for personal choice were considered in Chapter 3 and we shall not repeat the arguments developed there. For all decision models, the costs and benefits which are relevant are those which can be affected by the decision. Clearly, if a particular cost or benefit is independent of a decision, it should not be allowed to influence that decision. Recognition of this fact leads immediately to our first two principles of cost evaluation. The first is that only future costs are relevant. Decisions can be taken only about alternatives that affect the future. A firm cannot take decisions that will alter the past, and the inclusion of costs that have already been incurred may lead to an incorrect decision. Costs that have been incurred include costs that have already been paid and also costs that are the subject of legally binding contracts, even if payments due under the contract have yet to be made. This latter category is called committed costs. Although past costs are not of themselves relevant to decisions, they may be useful aids for predicting future costs (see Chapter 5).

The second relevant cost principle is that only those costs which will differ under some or all of the available alternatives are relevant; that is, only differential (or incremental) costs should be included in the analysis. For example, consider the case of an accountant deciding whether to travel to his office by train on five or six occasions during the coming week. Whether he travels five or six times, it is cheaper for him to purchase a weekly season ticket than to pay his fares daily. The cost of the season ticket is the same whether he travels five or six times and is not relevant to his choice between the two alternatives. It follows that any apportionment of the cost of the season ticket (say on an 'average cost per journey' basis) is also irrelevant for the decision. Suppose, however, that a third alternative were to be considered – the possibility of not travelling to the office at all in the coming week. In this situation there would be no need to purchase the season ticket, the cost of which should then be considered as differential and relevant to the decision.

We have argued so far that only future differential costs (and revenues) are relevant for decision purposes. There remains one outstanding problem: the choice of a unit of measurement for costs and revenues. Like the first two principles, this choice depends on the decision maker's objectives and on his decision model. It is generally accepted in the literature of accounting and economics (indeed it is probably a truism!) that the objective of each individual, and hence of the proprietors of a firm, is to maximise satisfaction (or consumption) over time. Broadly speaking, the goods and services of which consumption consists are available only in return for the payment of a cash price or its equivalent. Consequently we shall assume a decision objective which involves maximising future consumption potential, normally cash. Thus the third, and final, principle of relevant cost estimation is that only cash costs are to be included, suitably adjusted for differences in their timing if appropriate.[1]

Some decisions involve costs (or benefits) that are not easily expressed in cash terms. For example, suppose that a machine manufacturer has temporary spare capacity that could be used to produce guns at a cash cost far below the cash price at which they could be sold. If the manufacturer is a pacifist he may decide not to produce the guns, in spite of the high cash surplus they would generate, because there would be a further cost to him in doing so which is not reflected in the cash flows. Similar situations often arise in the public sector (central government, local authorities, nationalised industries etc.) where factors such as unemployment, pollution, energy conservation and national security often influence decisions. In situations like these, an attempt may be made to express such factors as cash flows. If this proves impracticable or inappropriate, the decision maker will have to make a value judgment as to whether net cash benefits are large enough to justify incurring 'non-cash' costs, or *vice versa*.

1.   Money, like many other things, has a price. Because of the existence of inflation, investment opportunities and borrowing costs, most people would rather have £1 immediately than the certain expectation of £1 at some time in the future. Thus, where the cash flows associated with a decision alternative are expected to arise at different points in time, adjustments are necessary to reflect their different timings. Such adjustments are usually effected by the use of interest rates. A detailed consideration of the procedures involved is outside the scope of this chapter.

The three basic principles discussed above may be summarised as follows: for making decisions, only expected future cash flows that will differ under some or all of the alternatives available should be considered. All changes to cash flows resulting from a decision should be taken into account and not just those easily identified with a particular project. So if a decision to be taken in one department of a firm would cause an increase in cash costs in another department, the increase should be taken into account in assessing the worthwhileness of the decision to be taken in the first department.

The Role of Alternative Budgets

Alternative budgets play an important part in the assessment of relevant costs and revenues. Where a number of opportunities have to be ranked, because they are mutually exclusive or because some resources are scarce, it may be necessary to prepare a series of budgets showing the worthwhileness of each opportunity. Even where only one opportunity is under consideration, two alternatives are implied: acceptance of the opportunity and rejection of it. In order to assess the desirability of the opportunity, future incremental cash flows associated with both acceptance and rejection must be considered. One way of doing this would be to prepare two (cash flow) budgets, one for acceptance and the other for rejection. In practice it is unusual, and would thus be unfamiliar and maybe confusing to the decision maker, to present two budgets as an aid to making a decision about a single opportunity. In consequence, the figures in the two budgets are normally combined in a single statement of 'profitability'. It is crucial to remember, however, that each figure in the statement represents the cash flow if the opportunity is accepted *compared with* the cash flow if it is rejected — the latter is always the implied alternative to acceptance.

In this section we concentrate on the determination of costs and revenues for inclusion in a single budget to evaluate an opportunity, acceptance of which will not impair a firm's ability to accept other opportunities. The extension of this procedure to ranking decisions is considered in Chapter 7. An important characteristic of the budget is that its 'bottom line' (i.e. the 'surplus' if the opportunity is accepted) should be easily interpreted. The most simple form of interpretation is presumably that if the surplus is positive the opportunity should be accepted, and if it is negative the opportunity should be rejected. In other words, the financial consequences of all alternative uses of resources required for acceptance are implicitly included in the budget and there is no need for further comparison of the budgeted surplus with anything other than a bench-mark of zero. A surplus indicates that acceptance of the opportunity would add more to cash resources than would alternative applications of the resources required for acceptance.

We consider now the general procedures to be followed in determining relevant costs. The procedures are illustrated in the numerical example in the next section. The relevant cost of using a particular resource on a project may be found by calculating the difference between cash flows expected if the resource is applied to the project and those if it is not. This is the differential cash flow approach to costing. In order to calculate the expected cash flow relating to a resource if the opportunity under consideration is rejected, it is necessary to establish the best alternative use to which the resource could be put in the event of rejection. Thus the procedure for calculating the relevant cost of using a resource is in two steps:

(a) estimate cash flows expected if the resource is put to its best alternative use;
(b) compare these cash flows with those expected if the resource is applied to the project under consideration.

If the cash outflow resulting from applying the resource is greater than the cash outflow resulting from the best alternative use, the difference is called a cost. If cash inflows are involved, rather than outflows, a cost arises if the cash inflow expected from the best alternative use is greater than the cash inflow expected from application to the project. A mixture of cash inflows and outflows may be handled using the same principles. Examples are given in the next section.

Illustration

Guilder Ltd manufactures a wide range of fashion products. The directors are considering whether to add a futher product, the Kyat, to the range. A market research survey, recently undertaken at a cost of £5,000, suggests that demand for the Kyat would last for only one year, during which 50,000 units could be sold at £18 per unit. Production and sale of Kyats would take place evenly throughout the year. The following information is available regarding the costs of manufacturing Kyats:

Raw Materials: Each Kyat would require three types of raw material, Krona, Krone and Krono. Quantities required, current stock levels and costs of each raw material are shown in table 6.1. Krona is used regularly by the company and stocks are replaced as they are used. The current stock of Krone is the result of over-buying for an earlier contract. The material is not used regularly by Guilder Ltd and any stock that was not used to manufacture Kyats would be sold. The company does not carry a stock of Kronos and the units required would be specially purchased.

Labour: Production of each Kyat would require a quarter of an hour of skilled labour and two hours of unskilled labour. Current wage rates are £3 per hour for skilled labour and £2 per hour for unskilled labour. In addition, one foreman would be required to devote all his working time for one year to supervision of the production of Kyats. He is currently

Table 6.1 Raw Material Information

Raw material	Amount required per Kyat (metres)	Current stock level (metres)	'Costs' per metre of raw material		
			Original cost (£'s)	Current replacement cost (£'s)	Current resale value (£'s)
Krona	1.0	100,000	2.10	2.50	1.80
Krone	2.0	60,000	3.30	2.80	1.10
Krono	0.5	0	—	5.50	5.00

Table 6.2 Details of Machinery

	Peso	Peseta
Original cost	£70,000	£50,000
Accumulated depreciation (straight line)	£30,000	£36,000
Written down value	£40,000	£14,000
Age	5 years	6 years
Expected remaining useful life	5 years	1 year
Expected resale value at end of useful life	£10,000	£8,000

paid an annual wage of £5,000. Guilder Ltd is currently finding
it very difficult to recruit new skilled labour. The skilled
workers needed to manufacture Kyats would be transferred
from another job on which they are earning a contribution
(surplus) of £1.50 per labour hour, comprising sales revenue
of £10.00 less skilled labour wages of £3.00 and other variable
costs of £5.50. It would not be possible to employ additional
skilled labour during the coming year. If Kyats are not manufactured, Guilder Ltd expects to have available 200,000
surplus unskilled labour hours during the coming year. Because
they intend to expand their activities in the future, and
because of the high cost of making staff redundant, the directors have decided not to dismiss any unskilled workers in the
foreseeable future. The foreman is due to retire immediately
on an annual pension, payable by the company, of £2,000.
He has agreed to stay on for a further year if necessary and to
waive his pension for one year in return for a year's wage.
His subsequent pension rights would not be affected.

Machinery: Two machines would be required to manufacture
Kyats, a Peso and a Peseta. Historical details of each machine
are given in table 6.2. Straight line depreciation has been
charged on each machine for each year of its life using the
formula: $D = (C - S)/L$, where D is the annual depreciation
charge, C is the original cost of the machine, S is the expected

Table 6.3 Values of Machines

		Start of year (£'s)	End of year (£'s)
Peso:	Replacement cost	80,000	65,000
	Resale value	60,000	47,000
	Discounted present value*	90,000	73,000
Peseta:	Replacement cost	13,000	9,000
	Resale value	11,000	8,000
	Discounted present value*	0	0

* Discounted present value of expected net receipts from continuing to operate machine in its present use.

resale value at the end of the machine's useful life, and L is the useful life in years, estimated when the machine was purchased. Table 6.3 contains details of various values of the two machines at the start and end of the year during which Kyats would be manufactured. Guilder Ltd owns a number of Peso machines, which are used regularly on various products. Each Peso is replaced as soon as it reaches the end of its useful life. Peseta machines are no longer used and the one which would be used for Kyats is the only one the company now has. If it was not used to produce Kyats, it would be sold immediately.

Overheads: In addition to machinery costs, Guilder Ltd incurs various other production overheads. Some, for example rent and rates, are fixed in total regardless of output levels and of the mix of products manufactured. Others, for example lighting and heating, have a fixed element and a variable element, the latter depending on the volume of activity. Fixed overheads (including costs which are fixed in total and the fixed elements of other costs, but excluding depreciation) are allocated by the company to products on the basis of total labour hours required. The allocation for the coming year is £3.50 per labour hour. Variable overhead costs for Kyat are estimated at £1.20 per unit produced.

We now consider the relevant cost to Guilder Ltd of using each resource required for the production of Kyats, applying the procedure outlined in the previous section; in each case we compare the cash flows associated with manufacture with those associated with non-manufacture. The difference between the two represents the incremental cost (or benefit) of each item.

Raw Materials: Cash flows are as follows[2] :

	Manufacture £'s	−	*Non-manufacture* £'s	=	*Difference* £'s
Krona:	−125,000		0		−125,000
Krone:					
sale of surplus	0		+66,000		
purchase of additional					−178,000
units	−112,000		0		
Krono:	−137,500		0		−137,500
					−440,500

50,000 metres of Krona would be required (50,000 Kyats each requiring 1 metre). As Krona is used regularly by the company, and stocks are replaced as used, the 50,000 metres required would be replaced at the current replacement cost of £2.50 per metre, a total cash outflow of £125,000. This cash outflow would not be incurred if Kyats were not produced. 100,000 metres of Krone would be required (50,000 Kyats each requiring 2 metres). If Kyats were manufactured, Guilder Ltd would use the 60,000 metres it has in stock, which have already been paid for, and would buy a further 40,000 metres at £2.80 per metre, a total cash ouflow of £112,000. If Kyats were not produced, the company would sell its current stock of Krones for £1.10 per metre, a total cash inflow of £66,000. 25,000 metres of Krono would be needed (50,000 Kyats each requiring 0.5 metre), and these would be specially purchased at £5.50 per metre, a total cash outflow of £137,500. There would be no cash flows associated with Krono if Kyats were not produced. To summarise, the relevant cost of raw materials is generally given by their

2.   A minus sign signifies a cash outflow and a plus sign a cash inflow.

current replacement cost, unless the materials are already owned and would not be replaced if used, in which case the relevant cost of using them is their current resale value or their value if applied to another product if this is greater than the current resale value.

Labour: Cash flows are as follows:

	Manufacture £'s	−	*Non-manufacture* £'s	=	*Difference* £'s
Skilled:					
wages	−37,500		−37,500		
contribution	0		+56,250		−56,250
Unskilled:					
wages	−200,000		−200,000		0
Foreman:					
wages	−5,000		0		
pension	0		−2,000		−3,000
					−59,250

Manufacture of Kyats would involve 12,500 skilled labour hours (50,000 Kyats each requiring a quarter of an hour) and 100,000 unskilled labour hours (50,000 Kyats each requiring 2 hours). Total wage payments for skilled labour (12,500 hours × £3 = £37,500) and unskilled labour (100,000 hours × £2 = £200,000) would be the same whether or not Kyats were produced. Thus they are not relevant costs. However, in the case of skilled labour, a contribution would be foregone elsewhere if Kyats were manufactured. The contribution *(before* charging skilled labour wages) is £4.50 per hour, a total of £56,250 (12,500 hours × £4.50) which would be received only if Kyats were not produced. The relevant cost of the foreman is the difference between the wages he would be paid and the pension cost that would be avoided. The above analysis of labour costs suggests the interesting possibility that, in many cases, wages paid are not appropriate measures of relevant cost, unless labour is employed specially for a particular contract. In the short run, at least, the relevant cost is generally given by the surplus that would be generated by workers in their best alternative use (assumed in our example to be £4.50 per hour for skilled labour and zero for unskilled labour). In the longer run, labour which has no worthwhile alternative use may be dismissed if the project under consideration is rejected. In this case, the relevant cost will equal the wages and other employment costs that could be avoided, less any redundancy payments that would have to be made.

Machinery: The likely effect of using a Peso machine is to bring closer the time at which it will have to be replaced. In order to estimate the relevant cost of using the Peso machine, we need strictly to estimate all future cash flows associated with Peso machines on the alternative assumptions that Kyats are and are not manufactured, and to discount them to present values to give measures of relevant cash flows. In practice, where a machine is used regularly, it may be sufficient to use the fall in its replacement cost (i.e. the cost of replacing it with an asset of identical age and condition) as an approximation to the relevant cost of using it.[3] Determination of the cash flows associated with the Peseta machine is straightforward; it will be sold either immediately (if Kyats are not manufactured) or after one year (if they are), at the prices given in table 6.3. On the assumption that fall in replacement cost is an adequate approximation to the relevant cost of using the peso machine, the cash flows associated with the machinery are:

	Manufacture £'s	−	Non-manufacture £'s	=	Difference £'s
Peso: replacement cost	−80,000		−65,000		−15,000
Peseta: resale value	+8,000		+11,000		−3,000
					−18,000

3.   A rigorous analysis of the cost of using fixed assets is beyond the scope of this chapter. Readers who wish to pursue this problem area further might refer to W.T. Baxter, *Depreciation*, Sweet and Maxwell 1970, or to B.V. Carsberg, On the linear programming approach to asset valuation, *Journal of Accounting Research*, Autumn 1969.

Overheads: Cash flows are as follows:

	Manufacture £'s	−	Non-manufacture £'s	=	Difference £'s
Variable overheads	−60,000		0		−60,000
Fixed overheads	−X		−X		0
					−60,000

Variable costs are £1.20 per Kyat produced, a total cash out-flow of £60,000 (50,000 × £1.20) incurred only if manufacture takes place. All other overhead costs are fixed; they are the same in total whether or not Kyats are produced. Whatever their level (we have assumed £X in total), it will be the same for manufacture and non-manufacture. This illustrates the important rule that, for decision purposes, only variable costs are relevant.

Sales Revenue: If we apply to revenues the differential cash flow analysis used for costs we find, not surprisingly, that relevant revenue equals unit sales price (£18) multiplied by the number of units expected to be sold (50,000):

	Manufacture £'s	−	Non-manufacture £'s	=	Difference £'s
Sales revenue:	+900,000		0		+900,000

For presentation to management, the results of the above analysis (i.e. the figures in the 'Difference' column) may be summarised in a profitability statement. A possible form of such a statement is given in table 6.4. Supplementary information should be provided concerning the basis of calculation of the figures in the statement, along the lines discussed previously in this section, dealing particularly with points of possible contention such as the cost of using the Peso machine.

The figures presented in table 6.4 may not represent the complete picture, however. As we noted earlier, the direct cash consequences of a decision may not be the only factors

Table 6.4 Relevant Costs and Revenues expected from the Manufacture
of Kyats

	£'s	£'s
Raw materials:		
Krona	125,000	
Krone	178,000	
Krono	137,500	440,500
Labour:		
Skilled	56,250	
Unskilled	0	
Foreman	3,000	59,250
Machinery:		
Peso	15,000	
Peseta	3,000	18,000
Variable overheads		60,000
		577,750
Sales revenue		900,000
Contribution (to fixed costs and profit)		322,250

of interest to the decision maker. In our example, production
of Kyats may have implications beyond those we have considered. For example, the new product may complement or
compete with existing products; it may entice new customers
to the company's whole range of products; it may change the
risk associated with the company's overall activities; and so
on. These, and other non-cash factors, should be quantified
and incorporated into the analysis as far as possible. At the
very least they should be mentioned in notes appended to
the decision budget, so that the decision maker can use his
own value judgement to balance them against the cash items
included in the budget.

We have made no attempt in our statement to adjust for
differences in timing between cash flows. In practice, where
cash flows arise at significantly different times (for example,
if all costs are payable at the start of a year and all revenues
receivable at the end), it will be necessary to apply an

interest adjustment to ensure that distortions created by the timing differences are removed.

One important conclusion to emerge from the analysis in this section is that in no case was the original, or historical, cost of a resource the appropriate measure of its relevant cost. This conclusion is unfortunate, because accounting records have conventionally been, and to a large extent still are, based on the measurement, recording and matching of the historical costs. We now turn to a more detailed consideration of this problem.

A Comparison with Conventional Historical Cost Accounting

The figures in table 6.4 differ from those we would have obtained by applying generally accepted (historical) cost accounting conventions to the problem of Guilder Ltd. In table 6.5 we show the sort of statement that might have been prepared using the conventional accounting approach. Broadly speaking, the conventional approach involves matching the original costs of the resources actually used on a project against its revenues. The statements in tables 6.4 and 6.5 illustrate several of the main differences between the conventional approach and the one recommended in this chapter.

The first difference concerns the treatment of historical costs (also called 'original', 'past' or 'sunk' costs). The application of conventional accounting practice involves charging resources to particular projects at their original cost as, for example, with the market research survey, raw material Krona and the first 60,000 metres of raw material Krone. In support of this procedure, it might be argued that if the value of a resource has fallen (or risen) since purchase, the loss (or profit) should be taken into account; but if the value has changed, the consequent loss (or profit) has already occurred regardless of any decision to be made now and should not be added to (or subtracted from) the costs of the opportunity under consideration. The crucial question is: which cash flows will be affected by the decision? The answer to this question depends

Table 6.5 Conventional Accounting 'Profitability' of Manufacturing Kyats

	£'s	£'s
Cost of market reasearch survey		5,000
Raw materials:		
Krona (50,000 metres at £2.10)	105,000	
Krone (60,000 metres at £3.30 +		
40,000 metres at £2.80)	310,000	
Krono (25,000 metres at £5.50)	137,500	552,500
Labour:		
Skilled (12,500 hours at £3.00)	37,500	
Unskilled (100,000 hours at £2.00)	200,000	
Foreman	5,000	242,500
Depreciation of machinery:		
Peso ([40,000 − 10,000] ÷ 5)	6,000	
Peseta ([14,000 − 8,000] ÷ 1)	6,000	12,000
Overheads:		
Fixed (112,500 × £3.50)	393,750	
Variable (50,000 × £1.20)	60,000	453,750
		1,265,750
Sales revenue		900,000
Loss from manufacturing Kyats		365,750

on the currently available alternative uses of the resource, and will be equal to its historical cost only by accident.

The second difference is the treatment of depreciation of assets. The straight line method of depreciation has already been mentioned. It is widely used in the reporting of financial information, and in common with other conventional methods of depreciation has the characteristic that the annual depreciation charge is based on an allocation of the original cost of the asset less its expected ultimate resale value. The treatment of depreciation is thus an extension of the conventional practice of matching or recovering past costs. For decision purposes we need to know the sacrifice involved in using the asset on the particular project under consideration. There is no obvious reason why this should correspond to the writing off of original cost that typifies the conventional accounting concept of depreciation.

A third area of difference concerns fixed costs. Costs that are fixed regardless of the decision under consideration (for example, unskilled labour wages and fixed overhead costs in the case of Guilder Ltd) are not relevant costs of that decision, for they cannot be affected by it. Nevertheless, in conventional accounting practice, fixed costs are often allocated to available opportunities.

The final main area of difference relates to the impact of a project on a firm's other activities (for example, the transfer of scarce skilled labour from another job and the deferral of the foreman's pension in the case of Guilder Ltd). Under conventional practice, only the amount paid for the resource is treated as a cost; cash flow changes elsewhere in the organisation are not usually considered, even though they are a direct consequence of the decision being taken.

The differences between conventional practice and differential cash flow analysis may lead to startling differences in 'profitability'. In our example a conventional 'loss' of £365,750 is in fact an incremental cash surplus of £322,250. In general, when prices are rising, the application of conventional historical cost accounting results in the understatement of the current relevant cost of using resources such as stock and fixed assets and a consequent overstatement of profitability. On the other hand, inclusion of allocated fixed costs overstates relevant costs and leads to an understatement of profitability. Such differences may lead to incorrect decision advice, as in the case of Guilder Ltd.

In fairness to conventional accounting practice, we should recognise that the information an accountant is expected to provide is often used for a number of purposes apart from internal decision making, including dividend determination, ascertainment of taxation liability and control by external users of accounts such as shareholders, creditors, lenders, government and customers over various aspects of a firm's activities. Just because conventionally prepared information is of limited use for internal decision making, it does not follow that it is not useful for at least some of the other purposes mentioned. Nevertheless, it is as well for the decision maker to be familar with accounting conventions, and their limitations, for the data provided by the accountant are often the main source of information available to him.

Summary

The main emphasis of this chapter was on the determination of relevant costs and revenues for decisions. We looked particularly at the role of alternative budgets in calculating incremental costs, recognising the fact that the cost of using a resource depends on the alternative uses to which it could be put. Such an interpretation of cost is consistent with the economist's concept of opportunity cost, which is normally defined in terms of the value of the best opportunity foregone by not applying a resource to an alternative use. Congruence between definitions of cost used by accountants and economists would have many benefits, particularly where accounting data were being used as input to economic models. Unfortunately, as we have seen, the relevant costing procedures described often bear only a slight resemblance to conventional accounting procedures.

7

Linear Programming and Production Planning

SUSAN DEV

Professor of Accounting,
London School of Economics and Political Science

Introduction

In this chapter we shall be concerned with linear programming. This is a mathematical technique that can sometimes help us select between alternative courses of action when, during the planning period, supplies of one or more resources are expected to be insufficient to enable the firm to accept all available opportunities that appear to be profitable.

Linear programming can be used to determine the optimal (i.e. best) solution to problems where the following conditions apply:

  (i) there is a specified objective
 (ii) there are feasible alternative courses of action
(iii) all or some of the resources are limited in quantity
(iv) the objective and the constraints (i.e. limitations) can be expressed as a series of linear equations or inequalities.

These conditions may apply to a variety of problems faced by the businessman, but we shall limit our attention to a simple short-term product selection problem, i.e. to a decision related to a single period which has no reactions on cash flows in later periods. We shall assume that the objective of the businessman is to maximise the profit of his firm (subject to the usual kinds of social, legal and policy constraints). Following the arguments put forward in Chapter 6, we shall focus our attention on the contribution that each unit of output makes towards fixed costs and profit, that contribution being the incremental net cash inflow generated from producing and selling a unit of output.

We assume that there are several different products, all with positive contributions per unit, that the businessman would be prepared to produce in the coming year. However, he is aware that he will be unable to meet demand for the entire product range because he does not expect there to be available sufficient quantities of one or more of the resources (e.g. machines, labour, material, storage space) required to provide inputs for several products. The problem is how to ration out, or allocate, the resources in producing the various products in such a way as to maximise total expected profit.

To comply with condition (iv), the linearity condition (which gives linear programming the first word of its name), the contribution per unit of each product to fixed costs and profit, and the utilisation of resources per unit, are assumed to be the same whatever quantity of that product is produced and sold within the output range being considered. Condition (iv) also implies that product units and resource units are infinitely divisible. Thus, an optimal plan that advises us to make 601.23 units of a product is acceptable for the purpose of this discussion, and we can view the 0.23 unit produced as the quantity of planned work-in-progress at the end of the year. We shall consider conditions (iii) and (iv) in some detail later.

Our aim in this chapter is not to delve into the mathematics of linear programming (which is more appropriate in a book on operational research techniques), but to give an understanding of the nature of the technique and to show how the solution to a product selection problem can be interpreted and used in a management accounting context.

A Product Selection Problem

We assume that Drak is formulating its production plan for the coming year and that the following estimates have been made in respect of the two products it is considering:

	(Input required)	Product A £	£	*(Input required)*	Product B £	£
Selling price per unit			11.10			7.00
Less avoidable costs: Material M @ £0.50 per kilo	(12 kilos)	6.00		(4 kilos)	2.00	
Skilled labour @ £1.50 per hour	(1 hour)	1.50		(2 hours)	3.00	
			7.50			5.00
Contribution per unit (to fixed costs and profit)			3.60			2.00

Inputs expected to be available during the year are as follows:

Material M 1,200,000 kilos
Skilled labour 400,000 hours
Fixed costs for the year are expected to be £280,000.

No stocks of material or finished goods will be held at the beginning or end of the year. The market for products A and B is perfectly competitive, so there are no constraints on the quantities that can be sold at the estimated selling prices.

For ease of exposition, we shall henceforth ignore the '000s.'

The Solution with No Resource Constraints

If there were no constraints, the firm would produce and sell as much of both products as it could, as each produces a positive contribution, so no choice between the two alternatives would be needed. We shall look at the matter of constraints later and simply observe for the present that, in reality, firms constantly meet constraints of some type or other.

The Solution with One Resource Constraint

We shall now assume that the firm faces one constraint only, that relating to material M (of which 1,200 kilos are expected to be available). What is its optimal production plan? Condition (iv) indicates that there are constant returns to scale, so the

Table 7.1 Product Selection with Material M Constraint Only

		Product A	Product B
(a)	Contribution per unit	£3.60	£2.00
(b)	Kilos of material M required per unit	12	4
(c)	Contribution per kilo of material M		
	(a) ÷ (b)	£0.30	£0.50
(d)	Ranking of (c)	2nd	1st
(e)	Maximum no. of units that can be produced with available material M:		
	1200 ÷ (b)	100	300
(f)	Contribution from maximum production		
	(a) × (e) *or* 1200 × (c)	£360	£600

company will maximise profit by expanding up to capacity the production of only one product, that which yields the higher contribution per unit of material M. Row (d) of table 7.1 shows that this is product B, and row (f) confirms that the largest contribution will be achieved by producing B only. (If there happened to be a limit on the quantity of B that the market was prepared to buy at £7.00, we would prefer to produce and sell that quantity and then allocate the remaining material M to the production of A.)

If, on the other hand, skilled labour was the only scarce resource, similar reasoning would lead us to conclude that A would be preferred, as indicated in table 7.2.

The Two-Resource Constraint Problem Formulated

The optimal solution is not as easy to find if *both* resources are in limited supply, because the rankings of contribution per unit of scarce resource differ. There are four solutions:

(a) produce A only,
(b) produce B only,
(c) produce some combination of A and B (and there is an infinite number of possible combinations!), or
(d) produce neither product.

The last alternative would be optimal only if neither product under consideration had a positive contribution per unit, so we can rule it out in the problem facing Drak.

Table 7.2 Product Selection with Skilled Labour Constraint Only

		Product A	Product B
(a)	Contribution per unit	£3.60	£2.00
(b)	Labour hours required per unit	1	2
(c)	Contribution per labour hour		
	(a) ÷ (b)	£3.60	£1.00
(d)	Ranking of (c)	1st	2nd
(e)	Maximum no. of units that can be produced with available labour hours: 400 ÷ (b)	400	200
(f)	Contribution from maximum production (a) × (e) or 400 × (c)	£1,440	£400

It is often helpful to write down problems in a standard way, particularly when they are complicated. Such a form also facilitates the handing over of a problem that has been formulated to the technical experts, or the computer specialists, for solution.

We formulate the problem algebraically in the standard form of a linear programming model, in which Q_a is the number of units of product A, Q_b is the number of units of product B, and C is the total contribution, as follows:

Maximise $C = 3.60Q_a + 2.00Q_b$ (i.e. maximise total contribution)

Subject to $12Q_a + 4Q_b \leqslant 1,200$ (material M constraint)

$Q_a + 2Q_b \leqslant 400$ (skilled labour constraint)

$Q_a \geqslant 0, Q_b \geqslant 0$ (non-negativity constraints)

Our aim is to find values of Q_a and Q_b (the quantities of each product to produce and sell) which will maximise the total contribution, bearing in mind the resource constraints facing the firm. The resource constraints are expressed as inequalities (of the form 'less than or equal to') because the best plan may not require the use of all resources to the limit imposed by the available supply. We have added non-negativity constraints (of the form 'greater than or equal to') to indicate that we do not wish to produce negative quantities of either product. This may seem unnecessary but, if a problem is solved using a computer, the program logic may otherwise advise us to produce negative quantities: if the solution indicates that it is more profitable to produce no units of a particular product than to produce a positive quantity, the program will assume that it is even more profitable to manufacture negative quantities. Clearly, we wish to avoid such a solution.

Fixed costs will be incurred anyway so, as they cannot affect the decision, we can omit them when formulating the model. Alternatively, we could deduct them in total from the objective function without altering the optimal solution, thus:

Maximise $C = 3.60Q_a + 2.00Q_b - 280$ (i.e. maximise total profit)

This formulation may be more helpful to the firm because, if the solution gives an unsatisfactory profit level, it may be an indication of possible long-run unprofitability, in which case the firm may be better off if it changes its line of business or goes into liquidation, unless the state is temporary. If the firm had overheads that varied linearly with output, it should be clear from the discussion in Chapter 6 that we would include them as a cost when calculating the contribution per unit of product to fixed costs and profit.

A Graphical Solution to the Product Selection Problem

There are a number of algebraic techniques available for the solution of linear programming problems, of which the simplex method is the best known.[1] In fact, all but the simplest problems are normally solved using a standard computer program. We shall solve Drak's two-product problem using a simple graphical method, because this will illustrate a number of the principles involved in algebraic methods of solution and more complicated cases. The interpretation of the results is the same regardless of the method of solution used.

1. For an explanation of the simplex method see W.J. Baumol, *Economic Theory and Operations Analysis*, Prentice-Hall 1977, pp. 84–99.

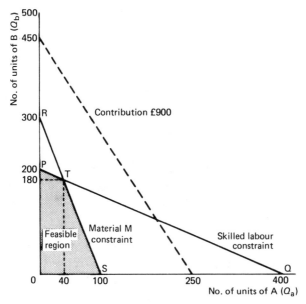

Figure 7.1 *Graphical Representation of Drak's Problem*

As there are only two products being considered, we are able to graph the problem on a two-dimensional diagram (figure 7.1) and solve it in the following three steps:

(1) *Label the axes:* one (the *x* axis) for the number of units of output of A and the other (the *y* axis) for the number of units of B.

(2) *Plot the two constraints using straight lines.* We need to calculate at least two points for each constraint to enable us to do this. It is simplest to calculate for each constraint the output level if all the scarce resource were devoted to (i) producing A only, and (ii) producing B only, plot the resultant outputs on the two axes, and draw a straight line between them. We can take the quantities from row (e) of tables 7.1 and 7.2 for material M and skilled labour, respectively.

The line RS in figure 7.1 connects all the combinations of outputs of A and B that are feasible with the available material M, and with none to spare. Similarly, PQ connects all the combined outputs of A and B that are just possible with the skilled labour hours available. The diagram then shows that the output combinations within the triangle PRT (and on PR and RT) are not possible, because they require more skilled labour than is available.

Similarly, the output combinations within the triangle STQ (and on SQ and TQ) are not feasible, for they require more material M than is available. The only outputs that are feasible are shown by the area bounded by OPTS. This area, shaded in the diagram, is known as the *feasible region*. We should note that, if a resource was required for only one product — say for product A — and there was sufficient to produce 200 units of it, we would depict the constraint as a vertical line on the graph cutting the *x* axis at 200.

So far we have not considered money values. The resource constraints represent physical quantities of the inputs required in production. They are represented by straight lines, owing to condition (iv) that relates to constant returns to scale. The slopes of the lines represent the *relative* quantities of each resource required for the two products. The figures of inputs required per unit may have been obtained from the firm's standard costing system.

(3) *Plot a contribution (or iso-profit) line on the graph.* This will indicate the *relative* contributions earned by the two products. The line is drawn by connecting all combinations of outputs of A and B that earn a particular amount of contribution. For example, we can plot a line representing a contribution of £900 on the graph (see the broken line in figure 7.1), its position being calculated as follows:

Contribution of £900 earned on 250 units of A (900 ÷ £3.60) plus 0 units of B.

Contribution of £900 earned on 450 units of B (900 ÷ £2.00) plus 0 units of A.

None of the various combinations of output levels of A and B on the broken line is, in fact, possible, because the line is outside the feasible region, whose shape and size are determined by the technological requirements of production

		Re-allocation of:		*Effect on*
		Material M (kilos)	*Skilled labour (hours)*	*contribution (£)*
(i)	Resources released by reducing output of B by one unit	− 4	− 2	− 2.00
	Use resources released to produce $\frac{1}{3}$ unit of A	+ 4	+ $\frac{1}{3}$	+ 1.20
	Reduction in contribution			− 0.80
or				
(ii)	Resources released by reducing output of A by one unit	− 12	− 1	− 3.60
	Use resources released to produce ½ unit of B	+ 2	+ 1	+ 1.00
	Reduction in contribution			− 2.60

and by the availability of resources. The optimal quantities of A and B that can be produced are given by the point T, where another contribution line (which will be parallel to the one plotted because contribution per unit of output is the same for A and B whatever the levels of output) is tangential to the feasible region. It should be apparent that none of the infinite number of other output combinations within the feasible region OPTS will be as profitable as that at point T because, as the contribution line is moved nearer to 0 (the origin), the profit it represents becomes less.

Reading from the graph, we find that the optimal output levels given by the coordinates of T are 40 units of A plus 180 units of B. This gives a total contribution for the year of £504 and a net profit of £224, calculated as follows:

	£
A 40 × £3.60	144
B 180 × £2.00	360
Total contribution	504
Less fixed costs	280
Net profit	£ 224

We can check that the output combination of 40 units of A and 180 of B is the most profitable by calculating the effect on contribution if the output of one product is reduced marginally and the freed resources are used to produce more of the other product. This is shown in the box on p. 129.

We can see that neither rearrangement of the resources at the margin adds to the firm's contribution, so the most profitable mix of products must have been found.

There is a theorem of linear programming which shows that the optimal solution will be given by one of the corners of the feasible region, the corners in the above problem being at O, P, T and S. Thus, instead of plotting a contribution line on the graph, we can compute the contribution given by each of the four corners and, by inspection, locate the optimum, *viz*:

Corner	Output	Contribution
		£
O	0 units of A and 0 units of B	0
P	0 units of A and 200 units of B	400
T	40 units of A and 180 units of B	504 (optimum)
S	100 units of A and 0 units of B	360

Our solution shows that the limited amounts available of both material M and skilled labour prevent Drak from producing as much as it would like of the two products. If more material M could be purchased at £0.50 per kilo, the material constraint line would move out to the right, parallel to RS, so enlarging the feasible region and enabling a larger total profit to be earned. Alternatively, it would be profitable if more skilled labour at £1.50 per hour could be hired and this would push the labour constraint up and to the right, parallel to PQ. In this problem, both skilled labour and material M may be called *binding constraints,* or effective constraints.

When formulating a problem prior to solving it, we cannot usually be sure which constraints will be binding. For example, in addition to the skilled labour and material M constraints, assume that Drak pays a fixed annual rent (included in the fixed costs figure of £280) for sufficient factory space to produce an annual maximum of either 250 units of A or 450 units of B, or any linear combination in between. If this were the case, we should plot the factory space constraint on the graph in figure 7.1 in the position where the broken contribution line now is. We can see that this lies outside the feasible region, indicating that production would not be constrained by the availability of factory space. If products A and B are the only alternatives we are considering, the firm would not therefore enhance its profits by renting additional factory space, and factory space may be termed a *slack constraint* or a non-binding constraint. This is a contradiction in terms; but it should be clear that the expression is used to indicate that, although a limited amount is expected to be available, the solution shows that this is more than enough for the firm's requirements in the planning period, given the existence of the other constraints.

A Test of Understanding

To test understanding of the discussion so far, the reader should check that he agrees with the following statements (a ruler may be found helpful to alter the positions of the lines on the graph in figure 7.1 as appropriate):

(i) If more material M can be acquired at £0.50 per kilo, the output of A should be increased and that of B decreased, and the slope of the labour constraint line indicates that the ratio of the change will be 2:1. If more than a total of 4800 kilos can be acquired, material M becomes a slack constraint. Skilled labour is then the only binding constraint and the optimal production plan (given by corner Q) is to produce 400 units of A only. The solution is then as given in table 7.2.

(ii) As an alternative to (i) above, if more skilled labour can be hired at a variable cost of £1.50 per hour, the slope of the material M constraint line indicates that the output of B should be increased and that of A decreased in the ratio of 3:1. If more than a total for the year of 600 hours can be obtained, skilled labour becomes a slack constraint. Production will then be constrained by the availability of material M only and the optimal production plan (given by corner R) is to produce 300 units of B only, the solution being as given in table 7.1.

As a further test of understanding of the diagram (and, again, a ruler may be helpful) assume now that, instead of (i) and (ii), the relative profitability of the two products changes (e.g. due to a change in the selling price of one product), so the slope of the contribution lines changes.

(iii) If the contribution of B remains at £2.00 per unit and that of A increases, the parallel contribution lines will become steeper because it will take a smaller output of A to earn a particular total contribution. If they become steeper than the material M constraint line,[2] with a contribution per unit of A in excess of £6.00, the optimal corner of the feasible region is S. Here, only the material M constraint is binding and the limited supply of it should be used to produce 100 units of A and none of B.

(iv) As an alternative to (iii), assume now that the contribution of B per unit again stays at £2.00, but that of A falls so the slope of the contribution lines will become shallower than that of the one shown in the graph. If they become shallower than the skilled labour constraint line, with the unit contribution of A being less than £1.00, the optimal corner will be P. Skilled labour will then be the only binding constraint and 200 units of B should be produced and none of A.

2.   If the contribution line has the same slope as one of the binding constraints, there is an infinite number of optimal product mixes.

The Calculation and Interpretation of Dual Values (or Shadow Prices)

We shall now show how Drak's production plan and the size of its profit will alter if it is able to obtain, at the expected market price, a little more of one or other of the resources which impose binding constraints on the firm.

If there is only one binding constraint, the answer is easy to find. Assuming for the time being that only material M is limited in supply, so that product B alone is produced, row (c) of table 7.1 shows that each kilo contributes £0.50 towards fixed costs and profit. This is the average contribution per kilo and, because of condition (iv) which implies a constant contribution per unit for all quantities within the range being considered, it is also the contribution per unit at the margin. Thus, an additional kilo will be used to produce ¼ unit of B, which will add £0.50 to the firm's total contribution. Conversely, if the firm is deprived of a kilo, its production of B will fall by ¼ unit, so the contribution will be £0.50 less. Using linear programming terminology to describe the value at the margin, the *dual value* or *shadow price* of material M is £0.50 per kilo.

Using similar reasoning, and assuming that skilled labour is the only binding constraint so that product A alone will be produced, we can see from row (c) of table 7.2 that its dual value is £3.60 per hour. Thus, if an extra hour is available, it will be used to produce another complete unit of A. Resources that do not impose binding constraints (i.e. slack constraints) have dual values of zero because a marginal increase, or decrease, in the quantity available will not affect the firm's optimal plan nor the size of its total profit.

The calculation of linear programming dual values, and the effect on the production plan of a marginal change in the availability of a resource that constrains production, is not so straightforward if we have more than one binding constraint, because a change in the amount of one constrained resource leads to a re-shuffle of uses of the others. We can, however, demonstrate the basic procedure using the diagrammatic representation of Drak's simple two-product, two-constraint problem.

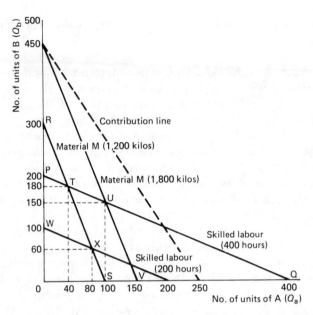

Figure 7.2 *The Effects of Marginal Changes in Resources available to Drak*

In figure 7.2 the material M constraint has now been relaxed for illustration purposes to 1,800 kilos and, assuming that the skilled labour constraint is unchanged, it can be seen that U is the optimal corner of the new feasible region OPUV. So, reading from the figure, 100 units of A and 150 units of B will be produced. We can calculate the effect of the marginal change in the availability of material M as follows:

	Material M available (kilos)	Production plan A (units)	B (units)	Dual value (£)
(a) Initial constraint	1,200	40	180	
(b) New constraint	1,800	100	150	
(c) Change, (b) − (a)	+ 600	+ 60	− 30	
(d) Production change for 1 kilo extra of material M, (c) ÷ 600		+ 0.10	−0.05	
(e) Profit change for (d) £3.60 × 0.10 £2.00 × −0.05		+ £0.36	−£0.10	£0.26

Row (d) confirms that the product substitution will take place in the ratio of 2:1, as mentioned in the first part of the previous section (where the quantity of material M was increased until it ceased to be a binding constraint). This is because skilled labour must be redistributed from B to A in order to enable the increment of material M to be used by A. Thus, the way in which a production plan will change in response to a change in the quantity available of a particular resource will be affected by the relative utilisation of *other* scarce resources.

If, instead, available skilled labour was reduced to 200 hours (material M remaining at its original availability of 1,200 kilos), corner X of the new feasible region OWXS in figure 7.2 shows that 80 units of A and 60 units of B should be produced. As mentioned in the second part of the previous section, the substitution from A to B will be in the ratio of 3:1. The relevant calculations to confirm this are as follows:

		Skilled labour available (hours)	Production plan A (units)	B (units)	Dual value (£)
(a)	Initial constraint	400	40	180	
(b)	New constraint	200	80	60	
(c)	Change, (b) − (a)	− 200	+ 40	− 120	
(d)	Production change for 1 hour less of skilled labour (c) ÷ 200		+ 0.20	− 0.60	
(e)	Profit change for (d) £3.60 × + 0.20 £2.00 × −0.60		+ £0.72	− £1.20	£0.48

The effects of changing the availability of material M or skilled labour, described above, demonstrate that the dual value of a resource may be defined as the increase (decrease) possible in the value of the objective function if the available supply of the resource is increased (decreased) by one unit.

It should be noted that, as in the single material M constraint problem considered at the beginning of this section, condition (iv) means that linear programming dual values

place an average, as well as a marginal, valuation on all resources which constrain production. The dual values are
calculated in such a way that the entire planned contribution
is divided between the products to be produced. Thus, we
could say that Drak 'owes' its entire contribution to the two
scarce resources and, if the dual values are charged as costs to
products A and B, both will have a contribution of zero, *viz:*

		Product A			Product B		
	(Input required)	£	£	*(Input required)*	£	£
Contribution per unit (as before)			3.60			2.00
Less dual values:						
Material M @ £0.26 per kilo	(12 kilos)	3.12		(4 kilos)	1.04	
Skilled labour @ £0.48 per hour	(1 hour)	0.48	3.60	(2 hours)	0.96	2.00
Surplus			—			—

In this type of calculation any products considered and
rejected, as not forming part of the optimal set, would show
a deficit when costed in this way. This can be illustrated by
the single skilled labour constraint problem in table 7.2,
where product B was rejected:

		Product A		Product B
	(Input required)	£	*(Input required)*	£
Contribution per unit (as before)		3.60		2.00
Less dual value:				
Skilled labour @ £3.60 per hour	(1 hour)	3.60	(2 hours)	7.20
Surplus (deficit)		—		(5.20)

These calculations will be referred to later when we consider
how dual values can be applied to management accounting
problems.

The Solution Summarised

The information we have calculated relating to Drak's optimal plan for the coming year may be summarised as follows:

(a) The quantities of each product to produce and sell:
40 units of A and 180 units of B.

(b) The contribution, and net profit (contribution minus fixed costs), that will be earned for the year if all estimates turn out to be correct:
contribution £504, net profit £224.

(c) The resources which are expected to constrain the firm's ability to earn a greater profit (i.e. the binding constraints):
material M and skilled labour.

(d) The total amount of each resource in (c) that the firm can profitably use without altering the range of products in the optimal solution given in (a) above, assuming that the supply of either one or the other resource can be increased:

   (i) material M 4,800 kilos (i.e. an extra 3,600 kilos) and
   (ii) skilled labour 600 hours (i.e. 200 hours extra).

(e) The change in production plan if additional units of one or other of the constrained resources can be acquired, up to the limit in (d) above:

   (i) for an additional kilo of material M, A goes up by 0.10 unit and B goes down by 0.05 unit;
   (ii) for an additional hour of skilled labour, A goes down by 0.20 unit and B goes up by 0.60 unit.

(f) The extra profit that will be earned if one, or the other, of the binding constraints can be relaxed by a unit:

   (i) £0.26 per kilo for material M, and
   (ii) £0.48 per hour for skilled labour.

(g) Holding the contribution of B constant at £2.00 per unit, the limits within which the contribution of product A can lie (e.g. due to a change in its selling price) without affecting the quantities of A and B to be produced:

(i) between £1.00 and £6.00 per unit.

Similar calculations to those given earlier would show that if, instead, A's contribution is held constant at £3.60 per unit, B's contribution can vary as follows without affecting the optimal plan:

(ii) between £1.20 and £7.20 per unit.

Sensitivity Analysis

From the figures in (d) and (e) we can get an indication of the sensitivity of the optimal production plan, and from (f) and (g) of the sensitivity of the optimal profit stated in (b), to possible errors in the estimates used in the model. Thus, if at the planning stage we are not certain of the value of one of the variables (e.g. selling price of a product, cost of a resource, availability of a resource), we know the limits within which the value can lie without altering our product range, and we also know the effect that another value of the variable in question (within the limits indicated in (d) or (g), as appropriate) will have on our production plan and on the total contribution.

Sensitivity analysis, of which this application is an example, is a useful practical tool when making decisions under uncertainty. When a linear programming problem is solved using a computer program, the computer program will normally provide for sensitivity data, of the type indicated above (but maybe covering more aspects of the problem), to be printed out at the same time as the optimal solution.

Some examples of the types of question that our sensitivity data can help to answer, say before Drak's optimal plan is put into operation, are given in table 7.3. We should note that a change in the value of any variable outside the sensitivity limits (e.g. the equivalents of (d) and (g)) requires the problem to be re-formulated and a fresh solution found. We can, in fact, determine the answer to question 6 posed in table 7.3[3]

3. Product B will no longer form part of the optimal solution if its contribution falls below £1.20. Corner S of the feasible region shown in figure 7.1 then becomes the optimal corner, so 100 units of A will be produced and sold earning a total contribution of £360 for the year.

Table 7.3 The Sensitivity of Drak's Optimal Plan

What if . . . ?	Comment*	Effect on production plan A (units)	B (units)	Effect on profit (£)
1. The accountant were to work harder	From (c), the accountant's time is not given as a binding constraint.	None	None	None
2. 1000 extra kilos of material M are acquired at £0.50 per kilo	Within the sensitivity range in (d)(i). From (e)(i) 1000 × 0.10 − (1000 × 0.05) From (f)(i) 1000 × 0.26	+100	−50	+260
3. 50 hours less of skilled labour is available	From (e)(ii) 50 × 0.20 − (50 × 0.60) From (f)(ii) − (50 × 0.48)	+10	−30	−24
4. Up to 300 extra hours of skilled labour can be employed at £1.50 per hour	Exceeds limit in (d)(ii), so restrict to 200 hours. From (e)(ii) − (200 × 0.20) 200 × 0.60 From (f)(ii) 200 × 0.48	−40	+120	+96
5. A's selling price rises by £2, giving contribution per unit of £5.60	Within range in g (i). From (a) 40 × 2	None	None	+80
6. B's selling price falls by £1.10, giving contribution per unit of £0.90	Outside range in g (ii). Problem needs re-formulating, as product range will change.	—	—	—

* The reader should refer to the section entitled 'The Solution Summarised' for the references given in this column.

without difficulty, but few real-life linear programming problems are as simple as Drak's. We should also note that our calculations relate to changes in the value of one variable at a time and that the questions posed in table 7.3 are independent of each other; care needs to be taken in interpreting the impact on the firm if the value of more than one variable changes, especially if we are near the sensitivity limits — in which case a complete re-formulation may be necessary.

The Notion of Effective Constraints

We shall now look further at the information given in points (d) and (f) of the preceding section as far as material M is concerned. Drak has estimated that 1,200 kilos of the material will be available during the coming year at a cost of £0.50 per kilo and we have shown that it could profitably use a further 3,600 kilos on the understanding that only 400 hours of skilled labour can be acquired. Having drawn this conclusion to management's attention, a special effort by Drak's buyers to acquire more at the market price would be justified. If this proves unsuccessful, it might be suggested that the firm should be willing to pay a premium of up to £0.26 per kilo above the expected market price to induce a seller to supply further quantities, assuming there are no adequate substitutes for the material. If the premium were, for example, £0.15 per kilo (i.e. a purchase price of £0.65), Drak would make a profit of £0.11 from using each additional kilo up to a maximum of 3,600 kilos.

However, the existence of a dual value implies that, according to Drak's expectations, there will be excess demand in the market for material M at a price of £0.50 per kilo. If firms like Drak indicate a willingness to pay a premium for extra quantities, this may cause a rise in the market price for the material, so that Drak has to pay more for its originally planned purchases as well. In this case its expected contribution may not be achieved.

Alternatively, Drak's estimate of the constraint may be wrong. An excess demand for material M at £0.50 per kilo may bring forth more supplies on to the market (e.g. by overtime working or by imports) and it may encourage the supply and use of substitutes.

In reality, both the market price and quantity on offer may increase towards a situation where demand is equated with supply at a higher price. However, there will usually be a time lag before the adjustment is complete, the delay varying according to the technological conditions of supply of the material, the degree of imperfection in the market pricing mechanism for it, and other market conditions.

Once a firm has adopted a plan and has decided on the range of products to produce and sell during the coming year, and in roughly what quantities, it may be difficult in practice to alter the plan later. The necessary grade and quantity of labour may have been recruited, contracts placed for materials, machines set up, catalogues printed and orders taken from customers. If at the planning stage it appears likely that there will be binding short-term constraints due to market imperfections, it may be worthwhile checking estimates especially carefully and considering whether the prices and/or quantities of the inputs concerned are likely to change during the year and, if so, how and when.

We assumed that a single price for material M would hold throughout the year, but we could break the problem down into a number of shorter periods (e.g. each of a month) in order to allow for different prices, and quantities on offer, if we expected these to apply at different times during the year. The solution to such a problem would yield a different plan and, needless to say, the more careful and accurate are the estimates, the more helpful should the solution be to the firm in scheduling its production and in managing its working capital for the coming year.

Effective constraints are not necessarily caused only by market imperfections. They may also arise as a result of a firm's operating policy (e.g. the desire by management to keep the firm a manageable size). Thus, Drak may have correctly estimated the market rate for skilled labour for the year to be £1.50 per hour and, for some reason, management may not wish to increase the size of its labour force, even though suitable additional labour is readily available at the same rate. If this is the case, the dual value gives a measure of the cost, in terms of profit sacrificed, of management's policy to restrict the skilled labour force to a size that will offer a total of only 400 labour hours during the coming year.

Other Applications of Dual Values

We have shown that, if dual values are charged to products in respect of the scarce resources they employ, each product that forms part of the optimal plan will show a surplus of zero.[4] This result gives dual value data potential usefulness in managerial decision making as the following examples indicate.

(i) *Screening a new product*

Say Drak has introduced the plan that we calculated to be optimal and, some time during the year, management is considering whether to add to its range a new product, C, which uses material M and the same skilled labour as is required for A and B. We can calculate the expected contribution from C (using the expected market values of the resources needed) and charge against this the dual values of the scarce material M and the skilled labour, obtained from our original linear programme. If C then shows a deficit, its introduction is not expected to increase the profit of the firm as a whole, so we need spend no more time in investigating its viability. On the other hand, a surplus indicates that it is worth introducing and the time spent on further investigation is justified. The linear programme will need to be re-formulated to include C. Its solution will tell us the quantities of A, B and C that are now most profitable to produce.[5] (A surplus of zero for C indicates that a revised plan that includes it is equally as profitable as the one based on A and B alone.)

4. If there are binding demand constraints, the dual values of these must also be charged. This is considered in S. Dev, Linear programming dual prices in management accounting and their interpretation, *Accounting and Business Research*, Winter 1978.

5. According to a theorem of linear programming, the number of products in the optimal plan will not exceed the number of binding constraints. Thus, the optimal solution will indicate that C should be produced together with A or B, or neither (but not both) of them.

(ii) *Minimum price setting*

Following on from (i) above, if we are asked instead to calculate the minimum price at which it is profitable to sell the new product C, we can add to the estimated avoidable costs of producing C the dual values (given by the original linear programme) of the scarce resources it requires. The total we obtain is the price at which Drak would, on short-term profit grounds, be indifferent to introducing C: at this selling price, the expected profit of the firm from the optimal plan which includes C will be the same as that based on A and B only.

(iii) *Decentralised decision making*

In a divisionalised organisation, where each division has a certain amount of autonomy in making adjustments to planning decisions during the year as the need arises, we can use a similar approach. We can instruct the divisions to use avoidable costs in all their estimates and, so far as resources that are limited to the firm as a whole are concerned, to charge in addition the dual values previously obtained by head office from a linear programming model of the whole organisation. The divisions should be instructed to plan to at least break even on all activities on the basis of these costings.

This procedure requires that the firm's optimal plan, on which the dual prices are based, incorporates plans for each division for the year. So it can be argued that there are, in fact, no decisions left for the divisions to make during the year. However, it is unlikely in practice that events will turn out exactly as planned and, although the overall linear programme for the firm should, in principle, be re-formulated and re-solved when significant changes take place anywhere in the firm, dual values based on an earlier formulation may be sufficiently accurate to give a reasonable idea of the extra value to be attributed to scarce resources when divisions are faced with the need to make marginal adjustments.[6]

6. For more on the application of linear programming in decentralised organisations, see Chapter 5 of G. Salkin and J. Kornbluth, *Linear Programming in Financial Planning*, Prentice-Hall 1973.

The Linearity Condition Reviewed

We now review condition (iv), noted at the beginning of the chapter, and consider how its assumptions may affect the applicability of linear programming methods to the production planning decision, as we have described it. To avoid giving the impression that linear programming is appropriate only where very simple assumptions are made, we shall briefly refer to ways of dealing with more complex situations which can be handled by a standard computer program. It is not the purpose of this chapter to consider these in detail and suitable reading is specified in the footnotes.

First, the objective function of our linear programme assumes a constant contribution per unit of output (or per fraction of unit of output) regardless of the level of activity. This implies:

(i) There is a constant unit selling price, as in a perfectly competitive market situation, for all units sold within the range determined by the demand constraints (if any) built into the model.

(ii) The avoidable cost per unit of each resource is the same, whatever the level of acquisition and use. Thus it is assumed that there will, for example, be no bulk discounts if the optimal solution shows that the firm will require large quantities of a particular material.

(iii) Fixed and avoidable costs can be separated, so that any costs not treated as avoidable are fixed for all levels of output from zero to the maximum imposed by the constraints. Thus, there are assumed to be no 'step costs' as may occur in practice, for example, when an additional supervisor has to be employed at a fixed weekly wage to help cope with an increased level of activity.

Second, as far as the physical usage of resources is concerned, the condition assumes that there will be no savings in the usage of inputs when producing large output levels, or large batches, as opposed to smaller ones. In practice, savings may be made with long production runs because there is less starting and stopping of machines. Also, labour may be more efficient when working on large production runs (though, at some stage, diminishing returns may occur as boredom and fatigue set in).

One can get round the implicit assumption that product units and resource units are perfectly divisible by the use of the method known as integer programming, which can also handle step costs. Here, where fractional units are inappropriate, suitable constraints are added to the linear programming formulation to permit only the acquisition of whole numbers of a resource (e.g. one machine, a man's labour for a year) or the production of a complete product (e.g. an aeroplane or a bridge). Integer programming methods give dual values to the integer constraints as well as to the more usual constraints. However, the interpretation of the new set of dual values differs to some extent. Also, there are different methods of solving linear programming problems with integer constraints and these can result in different sets of dual prices, according to the method used.[7]

Another implicit assumption of linear programming, apparent from our diagrammatic representation of Drak's problem, is that the demand functions for the various products under consideration are independent of each other. Thus, in Drak's problem we took no account of the possibility that the two products, A and B, might be substitutes for each other or, alternatively, complements. An analogous problem may arise where there is interdependence between the input factors required to manufacture two or more products. In both cases, if the dependence can be expressed algebraically, suitable constraints can be added when formulating the linear programming model prior to solution using a standard computer program.

Where the data for a particular business problem involve non-linear relationships, a modified version of linear programming may yield solutions that are sufficiently accurate for many purposes. For example, if the expected selling price of a product is not independent of the volume sold, the total revenue function may be approximated by a number of linear

7. The nature of integer programming is explained in B. Carsberg, *Introduction to Mathematical Programming for Accountants*, Allen and Unwin 1969, pp. 92—9.

segments of different slopes. Each segment may be represented by a linear equation and an algebraic expression obtained for the total revenue function for use in the linear programming model. In cases where such approximations are inappropriate, we may need to employ techniques of non-linear programming. These are more complicated and more difficult and slower to solve than correspondingly sized linear problems.[8]

The basic linear programming model that we have described is an optimisation model and the objective we assumed for Drak was profit maximisation though, for other business problems (e.g. product blending, choice of production process, transport routing, manpower planning), the objective might be expressed as cost minimisation. In practice, however, management may wish to attain a number of goals concurrently, so the objective will be to find the most satisfactory plan in terms of a set of goals rather than the best possible value for a single objective with specified constraints.[9] An example is goal programming, which is a special type of linear programming for dealing with such problems.[10] The decision-maker must either rank or weight the quantitatively expressed goals in terms of his subjective opinion of their relative importance and an objective function is set up which incorporates the ranking or weighting. Due to the way the problem is formulated, the dual values associated with the solution to a goal programming problem do not indicate the value of scarce resources at the margin. Therefore, their interpretation differs from the dual values of the single objective optimising model dealt with in this chapter.

8. Readers who wish to pursue the use of mathematical programming where there are non-linear relationships might refer to B. Carsberg, *Economics of Business Decisions*, Penguin 1975, pp. 187—202, or W.J. Baumol, *op. cit.*, Chapter 7.
9. The so-called 'satisficing' objective of management calls for this approach. See R.M. Cyert and J.G. March, *A Behavioural Theory of the Firm*, Prentice-Hall 1963.
10. Goal programming is dealt with in Chapter 7 of Salkin and Kornbluth, *op. cit.*

Summary

We have indicated the basic idea underlying the mathematical technique of linear programming and have shown how it may help in the selection of an optimal production plan. The interpretation of the solutions given by this technique can be important in the work of the management accountant. In order to show how dual values and other sensitivity data are derived and can be explained, we focused our attention on a very simple one-period problem. We referred at the end to some complications that can arise in practical model-building which may require the use of more complex linear programming formulations or, alternatively, the use of other programming techniques, some of which require more sophisticated mathematics.

Linear programming is a very powerful computational tool for dealing with a wide range of situations that involve the examination of many combinations of alternatives. Practical linear programming models can be very large. Most models have at least a few hundred constraints and variables, and these can be solved in a matter of minutes on most computers.

8

The Accountant's Contribution to the Selling Price Decisions

JOHN SIZER

Professor of Financial Management,
Loughborough University of Technology

Introduction

The determination of selling prices is an important decision in most companies and one to which the accountant normally makes a significant contribution.

Pricing is a difficult and complex subject. In many companies, decisions on selling prices interact with decisions on which products are to be sold, to which customers, in which markets, by which sales promotion methods, and through which channels of distribution. A full discussion of the accountant's contribution to selling price decisions is not possible in this chapter, but some aspects of the accountant's role in the pricing of consumer products are considered, methods of arriving at costed selling prices are illustrated and the impact of inflation is examined.[1]

1. The aspects of selling price decisions and the examples in this
    chapter, and other aspects of pricing, are examined in more detail
    in J. Sizer, Accountants, product managers, and selling price
    decisions in multi-consumer product firms, *Journal of Business
    Finance*, Vol. 4, No. 1, Spring 1972; and in J. Sizer, *An Insight
    into Management Accounting*, 2nd edn, Penguin 1979, Chapters
    11 and 12.

Selling price is only one of a number of variables on which decisions have to be made as part of a firm's marketing plan. The importance of each variable may change from stage to stage of the life cycle of a particular product. Product and marketing managers require from accountants financial information which they can use when determining the best set of decisions on marketing variables for each stage of the life cycle of a product.

Long-Range Planning and New Product Decisions

We start by considering how the concept of a product life cycle, and the management of the variables in the marketing mix over the life cycle, relate to a company's profit planning and control procedures. Planning and control should be a continuous process of analysing past performance, setting objectives, developing a plan, implementing the plan and measuring results. The analysis of past performance and the establishment of broad objectives leads to the formulation of a strategy to achieve the objectives. A company should have a marketing plan which sets out the company's marketing policy and strategy; that plan is likely to include a programme for the marketing of new products.

The acceptance of the new product plan by the board of directors, as part of the corporate long-range plan, would not normally imply approval of the introduction of the individual new products envisaged in the plan. Eventually each proposed new product will be included in the annual marketing plan and also in the capital expenditure budget, probably in a form that differs from the original proposal in the long-range plan. At this stage the proposal can be submitted for detailed approval by the board of directors, and the merits of the new proposal can be appraised in the light of the current situation.

A typical product life cycle is illustrated in figure 8.1. The management is first concerned with deciding whether the investment to be made in periods 2–6 will produce a satisfactory return compared with the company's cost of capital and the return on alternative investments.

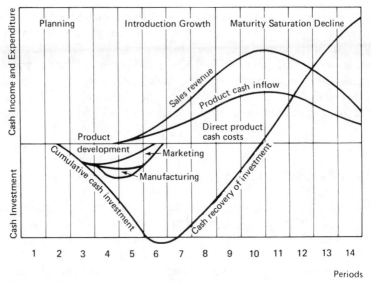

Figure 8.1 *Investment Life Cycle of Hypothetical New Product*

Price Reviews

After introduction of a new product has been approved and
the investment made, the next important decisions arise in
period 5. The product manager is then concerned with
managing the variables in the marketing mix (selling price,
sales promotion, distribution channels and so on); decisions
on those variables can be changed over short intervals, which
frequently correspond with budget periods. Until recent
years, there has been a general reluctance to review selling
prices more than once or possibly twice a year. Changes in
selling prices can be expensive and complicated. The changes
frequently were made as part of the annual preparation of
the budget. Between price reviews, product managers can
manipulate the non-price variables in the marketing mix in
response to competitors' actions and other market forces.
The high rate of inflation in recent years has increased the
importance of frequent reviews of selling prices. The continuous pressure on profit margins has forced many companies
to review prices more frequently and in many cases almost
continually.

A company requires a system which signals the need for selling price reviews. How many firms have such systems? Frequently, information is collected independently by the management accountants and the marketing staff. An integrated system might collect and present some or all of the following information:[2]

1. Sales (in units and value)
   (a) previous year comparisons,
   (b) different markets/channels comparisons,
   (c) budget *versus* actual comparisons,
   (d) forecast *versus* budget comparisons,
   (e) forecast *versus* actual comparisons,
   (f) latest forecast *versus* previous forecast comparisons.
2. Competitors' prices and conditions of sale.
3. Enquiries from potential customers about a product.
4. Company's sales at 'below list' prices
   (a) measured as a % of total sales,
   (b) revenue as % of sales at full list price.
5. Types of customers getting the most and largest price reductions.
6. Market shares in individual markets.
7. Current and forecast product costs
   (a) production, marketing, etc.,
   (b) fixed—variable.
8. Product unit and total contributions in different markets.
9. Price competition from
   (a) customers,
   (b) salesmen.
10. Stocks of finished goods at different points in distribution chain.
11. Customers' attitudes to firm's prices, packaging, etc.
12. Number of lost customers (brand switching).
13. Inquiries and subsequent purchases.

What cost information should accountants provide to product managers when selling price reviews are being made? The author's own research and other recent research studies

2. Adapted from A.R. Oxenfeldt, A decision making structure for price decisions, *Journal of Marketing*, Vol. 37, No. 1, January 1973, p. 50.

indicate that the accountant's advice to management is invariably based upon full cost at normal capacity in the first stage of price fixing. To understand the various methods (and their limitations) of arriving at a 'costed' or target selling price, let us consider the following case study.

James Wilson & Son (B)[3]

Mr Hawkeye, the management accountant of James Wilson & Son of Milchester, calculated three possible costed selling prices for a garment. Wilson's was an old-established company producing knitted underwear, leisurewear and children's outerwear. They had premises in Bridge Street and South Street, Milchester, and recently had opened a new factory in North Ashfleet, ten miles south of Milchester. Underwear and leisurewear were produced at Bridge Street, and knitwear at South Street and North Ashfleet. The company had an annual turnover of £1,300,000 and some 500 employees.

The three methods Mr Hawkeye employed to calculate costed selling prices for a garment are illustrated in table 8.1. The weight of yarn per dozen garments was determined from production samples and a fixed percentage was added for waste. Yarn cost was obtained by multiplying the yarn weight by the standard cost per pound of yarn (standard cost is the normal cost under acceptable levels of efficiency). For needles, cost was estimated on the basis of past experience, and trimmings were charged at standard cost. Labour-time standards and piece rates were established by the work-study engineer, and the allowances were multiplied by the standard wage rates. If times or piece rates had increased in a department since the standards were established, separate allowance was made for the increase. Overheads were included by multiplying the total labour cost by the overhead recovery rate for the factory in which the garment was to be produced (i.e. by assuming that overheads were incurred in proportion to labour costs). The sums of the two columns in the table represent

3. This case is taken from J. Sizer, *Case Studies in Management Accounting*, Penguin 1976, and first appeared in *The Hosiery Trade Journal*, February 1972.

total cost and variable cost. For example, the total cost of the boys' jersey was £16.08 and variable cost £12.66.

The three costed selling prices were determined by the following additions to total or variable cost:

(i) Total cost plus 8.5% gave a costed selling price of £17.45 for the boys' jersey.
(ii) Variable cost plus 43% gave a costed selling price of £18.10 for the boys' jersey.
(iii) Variable cost plus three times making-up labour gave a costed selling price of £17.50 for the boys' jersey.

The mark-ups of 8.5% and 43% were calculated by Mr Hawkeye in the following manner.

Knitwear Division Budget 1970

Budgeted Sales	£510,000
Estimated capital employed, with fixed assets valued on an assumed current-cost basis	£270,000
Required return on capital employed	15%
Required profit	£40,000
Fixed overheads	£112,000

$$\text{Mark-up on total cost} = \frac{\text{required profit}}{\text{total cost}} \times 100$$

$$= \frac{£40,000}{£(510,000 - 40,000)} \times 100$$

$$= 8.5\%$$

$$\text{Mark-up on variable cost} = \frac{\text{required total contribution}}{\text{total variable cost}} \times 100$$

$$= \frac{£152,000}{£358,000} \times 100$$

$$= 43\%$$

Table 8.1 Illustration of Calculation of Costed Selling Prices

		Boy's jersey size 26 in.	
Yarn usage per dozen		*(lb)*	
Weight		8.88	
Waste		0.56	
		9.44	
		£	£
Cost per dozen			
Yarn cost		7.08	
Draw thread and swatches		0.02	
			7.10
Needles			0.06
Buttons		0.13	
Sewing/Tabs/ Tapes		0.26	
Plastic		0.90	
			1.29
Bags/Boxes			0.15
Knitting labour		0.66	
Making-up labour		1.62	
		2.28	
Holiday pay/Increase(24%)		0.55	
			2.83
Carriage/Packing			0.18
		11.61	11.61
Overheads	(121%)	3.42	
		15.03	
Commission discount (7%)		1.05	1.05
Total cost/Variable cost		16.08	12.66
+ 8.5%/43%		1.37	5.44
Costed selling price per dozen		£17.45	£18.10
Variable cost + 3 × *making-up* labour		£17.50	

SELLING PRICE DECISIONS 155

	Baby's cardigan size 18 in.			Maxi-cardigan size 36 in.	
	(lb)			*(lb)*	
	2.26			16.44	
	0.16			1.03	
	2.38			17.47	
	£	£		£	£
	1.93			14.15	
	0.02			0.02	
		1.95			14.17
		0.06			0.06
	0.03			0.50	
	0.25			0.30	
	—			—	
		0.28			0.80
		0.13			0.30
	0.46			2.80	
	0.89			2.29	
	1.35			5.09	
(24%)	0.25		(11%)	0.56	
		1.60			5.65
		0.16			0.18
	4.18	4.18		21.16	21.16
(121%)	2.03		(135%)	7.63	
	6.21			28.79	
	0.43	0.43		2.02	2.02
	6.64	4.61		30.81	23.18
	0.56	1.99		2.64	9.97
	£7.20	£6.60		£33.45	£33.15
	£7.30			£30.50	

The factor that frequently limited Wilson's capacity to manufacture additional garments was making-up labour. The
making-up capacity involved a labour cost of £50,000.
To achieve the budgeted contribution of £152,000, the company had to obtain a little over £3 of contribution for every
£1 spent on making-up labour. Therefore, the third pricing
rule was to take variable cost plus three times making-up
labour.

Mr Hawkeye used his costed selling prices in the following
manner:

'I recommend to Mr Simpson, the sales manager, the
highest costed selling price produced by the three
methods. Everyone's criterion is then met. Mr Simpson
cannot always negotiate the highest selling price and
sometimes has to come down below the lowest costed
selling price, but I am very unhappy with any selling
price below total cost. For example, as you are no doubt
aware, maxi-cardigans are very fashionable at the present
time, and last month we introduced them to our knitwear range. For the maxi-cardigan in table 8.1, I recommended a selling price of £33.45 per dozen to Mr
Simpson, and, in the event, he has sold twelve dozen at
£40 per dozen. Business is hard to come by at the moment
and our North Ashfleet factory, which produces the maxi-
cardigans, is working on short time. I could not recommend the price of £30.05 based on making-up labour;
the total cost per dozen is £30.81 and we would not
recover our overheads.

Each quarter I produce an analysis of sales which
distinguishes between:

   (i)   sales below total cost;
  (ii)   sales between total cost and lowest desirable selling
         price;
 (iii)   sales between desirable selling price on labour and
         desirable selling price on variable cost;
  (iv)   sales above highest desirable selling price.'

Analysis of James Wilson & Son (B)

This is an interesting case study in that Mr Hawkeye appears to use a 'belt and braces' approach to pricing. He employs the full cost plus, the rate of return on capital employed variant, and marginal cost methods to determine recommended 'costed' selling prices for garments.

Mr Hawkeye calculates separate overhead rates for each of Wilson's factories, even though two of the factories appear to be capable of producing the same knitwear. The result is that in table 8.1 an overhead rate of 121% is applied to the boys' jersey and the babies' cardigan, and a rate of 135% to the maxi-cardigan. Furthermore, a single overhead rate is applied for each factory. Mr Hawkeye appears not to recognise that there are two distinct parts to a knitwear factory — the capital intensive knitting operation and the labour intensive making-up operation. It will be noted that in table 8.1 the ratio of knitting labour to making-up labour varies significantly between the three garments. There should, perhaps, be separate overhead rates for each operation, e.g. one rate for the knitting operation and another rate for the making-up operation. It can be seen that a number of equally qualified and competent accountants may produce different costed selling prices depending upon the methods they employ.

Mr Hawkeye sees the costed selling price he recommends as the starting point from which Mr Simpson, the sales manager, arrives at the final selling price. He does not object to Mr Simpson's negotiating a higher price, but is 'very unhappy with any selling price below total cost'. Mr Hawkeye's system fails to take formal account of price—demand relationships. Mr Hawkeye would have been unhappy to recommend the maxi-cardigans at a selling price of less than £33.45 and appears to be happy that Mr Simpson has sold 12 dozen at £40 per dozen. He appears not to have taken into consideration that, for example, at a lower price of £30 per dozen Mr Simpson might have sold not twelve dozen but fifty dozen when business is 'hard to come by'. Twelve dozen at £40 per dozen gives a total contribution of £201.84 (i.e. 12

X (£40 − £23.18)), where fifty dozen at £30 per dozen would give a total contribution of £341.00 (i.e. 50 × (£30 − £23.18)).

The strength of Mr Hawkeye's system is that it is directed towards achieving clearly defined objectives, namely £40,000 profit and 15% return on capital employed; and it also takes account of making-up labour, the factor that frequently limits Wilson's capacity. When the company achieves or exceeds budgeted sales, provided Simpson achieves the 'costed' selling prices, the profit and return on capital employed objectives should be achieved. Furthermore, Hawkeye directs management's attention to the relationship between his recommended pricing decisions and actual prices, highlighting those prices which appear to fall short in their contribution to the profit and return on capital employed objectives; no doubt this leads management to consider price−demand relationships.

The weakness of the system is that it does not provide Simpson with guidance on how to take account of price−demand relationships when arriving at the final selling price, particularly when the company is working below capacity. Such guidance could be given by using the contribution graphs as illustrated in figure 8.2. Variable cost is assumed to be constant over the relevant output range. Each curve shows different ways of earning a fixed contribution. For example, a total contribution of £1,200 can be generated by any of the following combinations: 1,200 dozen at £1.00, 2,000 dozen at £0.60; 2,400 dozen at £0.50; 4,000 dozen at £0.30, etc. The graphs can be segmented to show the high and low contribution areas, and high and low volume areas. The most profitable products are shown in the top right hand segment − styles 11, 2 and 8. They have high unit contributions and high volume, and therefore generate a high total contribution. Products in the bottom left hand corner − styles 1, 6 and 10 − are those which management may wish to re-design, or exclude from its range altogether. Alternatively, Hawkeye might develop a ready reckoner for Mr Simpson so that he can quickly compare alternative prices against estimated sales volumes in terms of total contribution. Of course, Hawkeye and Simpson may have developed a good working

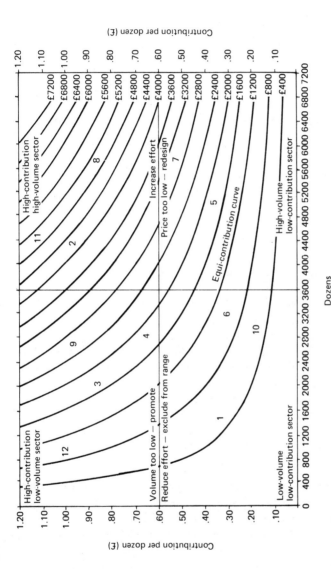

Figure 8.2 *James Wilson & Son: Contribution Picture for Men's Knitted Briefs in the British Market*

relationship which encourages Simpson to request the information he needs and allows Hawkeye to provide informal advice on price–volume relationships.

It has been argued elsewhere[4] that the accountant should not simply provide the product manager in a multi-consumer product firm with 'full unit cost estimates for evaluating alternative selling prices'. Critics of full-cost pricing, including the rate of return pricing variant, have identified a number of shortcomings in systems of full-cost or 'cost plus' pricing:

1. They tend not to take account of demand directly and assume that prices should depend simply on costs.
2. They fail adequately to allow for competition.
3. They do not distinguish between incremental costs and fixed costs.
4. They overplay the precision of allocated fixed costs, and possibly capital employed, in a multi-product business.
5. The allocation of common fixed costs to product groups is a crude measure of the opportunity cost of directing managerial effort at particular products, because opportunity costs should be measured in terms of profit foregone and not cost incurred.
6. They are based on a long-run pricing concept, and it is doubtful whether it is useful to think in terms of the long run given the rapidly changing external environment in which companies operate.
7. Selling price is one of a number of variables in the marketing mix and, if selling price decisions are based on full-cost data, there is danger that decisions about variations in the non-price variables are incorrectly evaluated.

While 'cost plus' pricing does not take account of demand directly, a decision maker may do so indirectly by varying the required mark-up on total cost. However, such a procedure may be a poor substitute for price–demand information. For example, a manufacturer of fully fashioned knitted outerwear calculated the total cost and selling price of a garment as illustrated in table 8.2. The managing director

4.   J. Sizer, 1972; see footnote 1.

Table 8.2 Cost Sheet

Style No. 7317
Type: Long line halter polo with belt

Yarn: matt tricel bonde

Department	Overhead (%)	Direct Labour (£)	Overheads (£)	Yarn (£)	Trim and packaging (£)	Dye and print (£)	Total (£)
Flat-knit ribs	304	0.04	0.12	—	—	—	0.16
Run on steam iron, etc.	110	0.26	0.28	—	—	—	0.54
FF knit	128	0.62	0.79	4.13	—	—	5.54
Pre-dye make-up	145	0.29	0.42	—	0.11	—	0.82
Flat-knit trim	304	0.09	0.26	1.54	—	—	1.89
Dye/scour	—	—	—	—	—	2.13	2.13
Print	—	—	—	—	—	—	—
Post-dye make-up	121	1.04	1.21	—	0.07	—	2.32
Press and counter	287	0.19	0.53	—	0.20	—	0.92
		£2.53	£3.61	£5.67	£0.38	£2.13	£14.32

Cost summary

	£
Factory cost brought down	14.32
Seconds allowance	0.34
Pack and dispatch	0.44
Sub-total	14.70
Profits 12½%	1.83
Total per dozen	£16.53
Cost per garment	£ 1.38

maintained that he wished to obtain a 12½% mark-up on total cost, and that he did not like to see any of his products falling below this mark-up. On investigation it was found that frequently the selling price of a style was not fixed at total cost plus 12½%, but increased to a slightly higher level. The final selling price appeared to be based on the managing director's subjective judgement. He explained that he adopted an increased price where he believed that there had been some extra input of skill in make-up or design, and the market could bear the extra price. However, his variation of the mark-up percentage was based on 'extra input' and not on any systematic assessment of price—demand relationships.[5]

Baxter and Oxenfeldt have neatly summarised the major criticism of 'cost plus' pricing:[6]

> ... inability to estimate demand accurately and in time scarcely excuses the substitution of cost information for demand information. Crude estimates of demand may serve instead of careful estimates of demand, but cost gives remarkably little insight into demand.

Nevertheless, 'full cost' appears to be used by many firms as a starting point in selling price decisions, while managerial judgement determines the size of the 'plus'.

Relevant Costs for Pricing Decisions

If 'full' unit cost data are not relevant for selling price decisions in multi-product firms, what information should the accountant provide for the product manager? The accountant should recognise that decision making is essentially a process of choosing between competing alternatives, each with its own combination of receipts and costs; and that relevant information for decisions comprises estimates of future incremental costs and revenues and opportunity costs, rather than full costs which include past or sunk costs.

5. See 'Kettle Knitwear Ltd' in J. Sizer, *Case Studies in Management Accounting*, Penguin 1976.
6. W.T. Baxter and A.R. Oxenfeldt, Costing and pricing: the cost accountant versus the economist, in D. Solomons (ed.), *Studies in Cost Analysis*, Sweet & Maxwell 1968.

The accountant must provide relevant cost and revenue data and also ensure that the product manager understands why the data are relevant. Experience of conducting seminars with marketing executives, including product managers, indicates that many have a limited understanding of relevant cost concepts. When considering a selling price decision or a decision concerning the non-price variables in the marketing mix, the product manager should have sufficient understanding of the relevant cost and revenue concepts to be in a position to discuss his financial information needs with the management accountant. He must have sufficient understanding to ask the management accountant the right questions, and to evaluate the significance of the answers. Provided assumptions are clearly stated, product profit—volume charts can be effectively employed to explore the relevant cost and revenue concepts and provide such an understanding.

Let us consider an example. We assume that a manufacturer seeks to fix its prices so as to maximise total contribution to fixed costs and profit. Unless the manufacturer's products are in competition with each other, this objective is achieved by considering each product in isolation and fixing its price in each market at a level which is calculated to maximise the total contribution in that market.

The Bang Bang Manufacturing Company is reviewing the selling price of product X, a consumer durable, and after carrying out extensive market research has estimated the following annual demands for the product at varying prices:

Price		Estimated Annual Demand
£17		8,000
£17.5		7,800
£18	(existing price)	7,600
£18.5		7,200
£19		6,600
£19.5		5,700
£20		4,200

It is anticipated that at least 8,000 units can be manufactured and marketed with existing capacity. The forecast average

Table 8.3 Review of Selling Price of Product X

Selling price (£)	17.0	17.5	18.0	18.5	19.0	19.5	20.0
Marginal cost (£)	12.0	12.0	12.0	12.0	12.0	12.0	12.0
Contribution (£)	5.0	5.5	6.0	6.5	7.0	7.5	8.0
Estimated demand (units)	8,000	7,800	7,600	7,200	6,600	5,700	4,200
Total contribution (£)	40,000	42,900	45,600	46,800	46,200	42,750	33,600
Separable fixed costs (£)	25,000	25,000	25,000	25,000	25,000	25,000	25,000
Direct product profit (£)	15,000	17,900	20,600	21,800	21,200	17,750	8,600
Product break-even							
Sales (units)	5,000	4,545	4,167	3,846	3,572	3,333	3,125
Percentage of demand	62.5	58.3	54.8	53.4	54.1	58.5	74.4

variable cost per unit over the relevant output range is constant at £12 per unit, i.e. marginal cost equals average variable
cost. The separable fixed costs (the fixed costs associated with
the product, such as the product manager's salary, as opposed
to the common fixed costs, such as the managing director's
salary) are £25,000. The calculation of the price which will
make the greatest contribution towards fixed costs and profit
is shown in table 8.3. It will be noted that the greatest profit
would result from raising the selling price of product X from
£18.0 to £18.50. With a 'cost plus' pricing procedure, this
price would be arrived at only by accident.

The information in table 8.3 is presented in the form of a
profit—volume chart in figure 8.3. *CC* is the contribution
curve for product X. It shows the relationship between sales
in units, direct product profit and total contribution: it also
shows break-even sales volume for each price. For example, a
selling price of £18.50 would result in sales of 7,200 units of
product X, a total contribution of £46,800, a direct product
profit of £21,800, and a product break-even at 3,846 units.
In establishing the contribution curve and determining the
price which promises the highest contribution, the relationship between price and volume has been taken into consideration and cost is based upon a concept of cost (future marginal
cost) that is relevant to the pricing decision at hand.

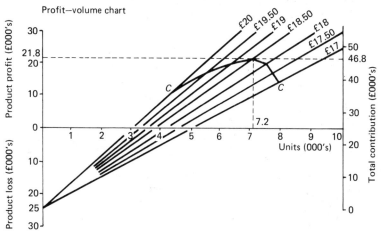

Figure 8.3   *Product Profit—Volume Chart for Product X*

The profit--volume chart can be related to marketing strategy at different stages of the product life cycle. The introductory stage can be contrasted with the maturity stage. At the introductory stage, the product manager may shade upwards or downwards the price found from the normal analysis, to create a more favourable demand in future years. Limited productive capacity may rule out low prices. The initial price may be set at P_6 (see figure 8.4) with a view to progressively reducing price, if and when (a) the price elasticity of demand increases, or (b) additional capacity becomes available. If the new product introduction is successful, demand will increase and both the position and the shape of the contribution curve will change.

If there is no production capacity constraint, a price such as P_3 or P_4 may be preferred at the introductory stage. Such a price would yield early high volume accompanied by slow competitive imitation, but lower unit product profit. Again, if demand grows, the position and shape of the contribution curves will change, but the company would rely on the low initial price to maintain market share in a growing market without resort to successive price reductions (or increases less than the rate of inflation).

At the maturity stage, the firm will be less concerned with the future effects of current selling prices. Prices probably will have fallen during the growth stage (at least in comparison with general price levels) as a result of economies of scale and

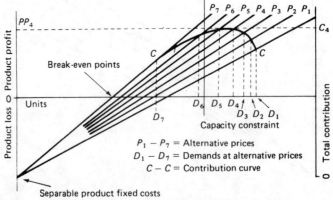

Figure 8.4 *Product Profit--Volume Chart for Product X*

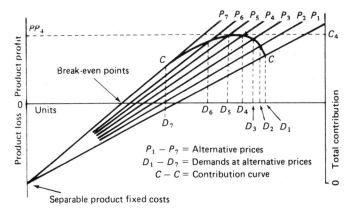

Figure 8.5 *Product Profit–Volume Chart for Product X*

competitive pressures. Prices may decline further in the maturity stage, but eventually stabilise. The profit–volume chart in figure 8.5 shows that P_4 is the selling price promising the highest direct product profit. At this stage of the product life cycle, the firm probably would be wise to maximise short-run direct product profit. The management may, for what are described usually as 'long-run policy reasons', decide upon some price other than P_4. If they do, they will be consciously deviating from the short-run optimal price, and should consider the short-run cost of such a policy.

Accuracy of the Demand Forecast

The author often conducts seminars on marginal pricing for marketing executives. In these seminars he points out that the analysis of pricing is dependent upon the estimation of a demand curve. Invariably the participants agree that they cannot provide precise estimates. However, after some discussion the following conclusions are frequently reached:

1. Profit–volume charts can be used to answer questions about the sensitivity of results to variations in policy. For example, a manger may wish to know if the price of product X is increased to £18.50, how far demand can

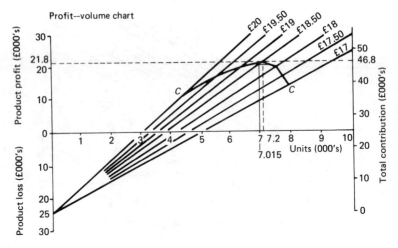

Figure 8.6   *Product Profit—Volume Chart*

fall before the new total contribution falls below the current contribution. As illustrated in figure 8.6, the answer to this question can be read directly from the product profit—volume chart.

2. The contribution curve *CC* can be shown as a band; for each price there will be a range of possible units demanded, product profits and total contributions. Marketing has long been viewed as requiring mainly judgement, intuition and experience, but marketing researchers are increasingly combining scientific techniques with judgement and intuition. Some firms offer specialised consultancy services to assist with the estimation of demand. For example, they may produce graphs which contain estimates of the optimal price for a product and which predict what the fall in sales would be if the product was priced higher or lower. While market researchers cannot predict accurately the shape of the demand curve, they should be able to attach subjective probabilities to a range of possible outcomes for each possible price. The accuracy of demand curve estimates can normally be improved, but the worthwhileness of such refinements may be limited because

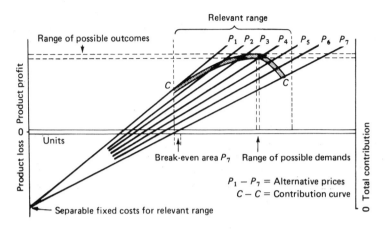

Figure 8.7 *Product Profit–Volume Chart under Uncertainty*

the cost of refining the estimates may outweigh the benefit derived.

3. There are many assumptions underlying the product profit–volume chart, and the analysis may have limited relevance outside a particular range of output levels. Figure 8.7 illustrates a product profit–volume chart which takes account of the uncertainty surrounding the pricing decision.

4. Normally, at the growth and maturity stages of the product life cycle, the product manager should be concerned with choosing between a limited number of alternative prices on the crown of the contribution curve. The lower and higher prices on the tails of the contribution curve are not normally relevant, except when capacity is limited or when a 'skimming policy' or a 'penetration policy' is considered at the introductory stage. There is some evidence that low prices can deter consumers, just as much as high prices.

5. The subjective probabilities attached to demand curve estimates by market researchers can be incorporated into diagrams, and graphs or tabulations can be presented which array the probable price–contribution outcomes according to a rational combination of possibilities

involved. Risk profiles can be developed for each
alternative price indicating the likelihood of achieving
various total contributions. The author has proposed a
simple risk analysis procedure which uses a discrete
probability density function.[7] A more sophisticated
approach has been recommended by Flower.[8]

It may well be argued that while the results of analyses that
employ subjective probabilities look impressive, they are
based on purely subjective judgements. It is true that no one
has yet developed a completely reliable method to measure
precisely the demand for any brand or product at various
prices. However, the product manager must estimate the
effects of a proposed price change. He will rarely find precisely
comparable circumstances in either his own or his firm's
experiences. However, as Baxter and Oxenfeldt[9] have emphasised, crude estimates of demand may serve instead of
careful estimates of demand, but cost gives remarkably little
insight into demand. Subjective estimates of the range of
likely outcomes based on the aggregate experience of executives are better than single-valued estimates based on the
same experience. As management becomes more accustomed
to the estimation of subjective probabilities for demand and
cost forecasts, its ability to make such estimates improves.
The result is a formalisation of a normal part of decision
making: weighing the odds.

Individual Pricing Decisions in Inflation

A full discussion of individual pricing decisions in inflation is
beyond the scope of this chapter.[10] However, some of the

7.   J. Sizer, A risk analysis approach to marginal cost pricing,
     Accounting and Business Research, No. 1, Winter 1970.
8.   J.F. Flower, A risk analysis approach to marginal cost pricing: a
     comment, *Accounting and Business Research*, Autumn 1971.
9.   W.T. Baxter and A.R. Oxenfeldt 1968; see footnote 6.
10. J. Sizer, Pricing policy in inflation: a management accountant's
     perspective, *Accounting and Business Research*, Spring, 1976,
     reprinted in J. Sizer (ed.), *Readings in Management Accounting*,
     Penguin 1980.

policy implications for individual pricing decisions under a high rate of inflation can be highlighted.

The high rate of inflation in recent years has increased the importance of the timing of pricing decisions. The continuous pressure on profit margins has forced companies to review prices frequently, and in many cases almost continuously. The introduction of state control of pricing in the Price Code of 1973 provided companies with a means of justifying price increases, and also resulted in a more systematic review of pricing decisions in the context of a company's pricing and marketing policy. An essential first stage in the pricing decision is a comprehensive monitoring system, such as that described earlier in this chapter, to signal the need for a price review. This type of monitoring system is forward looking and is likely to identify some of the shifts in demand that are occurring in the market place and trends in costs and product profitability. In this respect, it is important for the management accountant to recognise that the marketing manager requires a system for reporting current and forecast segment profitability, that is the profitability of different products in different markets. Segment reporting has become important because the high rate of inflation, and the Chancellor's successive Budget measures, affect products and markets in different ways. When making price and other marketing decisions, managers require financial information on the implications of these shifting patterns of consumer demand on product and market profitability, which implies the need for *segment reporting*.

The monitoring system, including segment reports and contribution pictures, may signal the need to review prices. Product profit–volume charts may be used for this purpose. Let us consider the impact on a product profit–volume chart of (a) a high rate of inflation and rising real disposable incomes, and (b) a high rate of inflation and falling real disposable incomes.

High Rate of Inflation and Rising Real Disposable Incomes

With a high rate of inflation and rising real disposable incomes, period costs, variable product costs and break-even volume

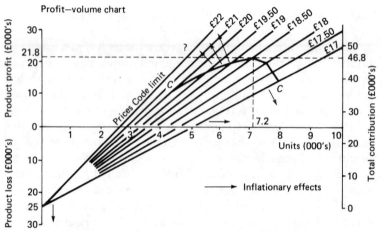

Figure 8.8 *Effect of Inflation with Rising Real Disposable Incomes*

for existing prices are increasing continuously, but it is likely that changes in demand will allow the higher costs to be passed on in higher prices. The contribution curve is likely to move upwards and to the left. The company is likely to generate a higher total contribution and higher direct product profit in money terms at the optimal price, assuming that the company is not prohibited (by government regulation) from charging this price. The 1973 Price Code placed an upper limit on the price that could be charged. The optimal price may have been below this limit, but many companies appeared to assume in 1973 and 1974, during a period of rapid inflation and buoyant demand, that the appropriate price was that allowed by the Price Commission. These effects of inflation are illustrated in figure 8.8. While increases in costs and break-even volume for a given price can be forecast with a reasonable degree of accuracy, the move in the contribution curve cannot. An effective monitoring system should assist in this direction.

High Rate of Inflation during a Period of Falling Real Disposable Incomes

Consider now the situation in a period of high inflation and falling real disposable incomes. Period and variable costs again

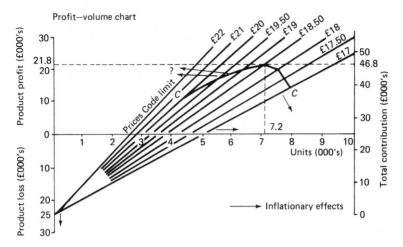

Figure 8.9 *Effect of Inflation with Falling Real Disposable Incomes*

rise continuously, but as real disposable incomes fall, it may be impossible to increase selling prices to compensate for the increase in costs. The contribution curve may move *downwards* and to the left. The shape of the contribution curve may also change as consumers switch to cheaper products, to substitutes, or stop purchasing the product. Many companies in the period 1975–7 found themselves in the position illustrated in figure 8.9, facing rising costs, falling demand, and disappearing total contribution. The optimal price was no longer that allowed by the Price Code, or a higher price, but some lower price difficult to determine.

Thus, during this period, many companies' selling prices were below those allowed by the Price Commission; as real disposable incomes fell, it became increasingly difficult for companies to pass on higher costs in the form of higher prices and at the same time maintain their sales volume. For example, the fall in consumer expenditure in the United Kingdom during the second quarter of 1977 was greater than had been anticipated. Only expenditures on basic necessities, such as housing, fuel and light, food, drink and tobacco, escaped a downturn. Spending on clothing fell by 4% in real terms compared with the first quarter, consumer durables by 3¾%, and motor vehicles by 7%. One result of the continuing

erosion of real disposable incomes and of the associated fall
in consumer expenditure was that only about half of the
respondents to a CBI August 1977 economic survey expected
to increase domestic prices over the next four months (the
lowest figure recorded since companies first were asked two
and a half years previously about price intentions each month),
despite the continuing cost inflation. This situation forced
many companies to take a long hard look at both variable
product costs and period costs.

A similar analysis can be undertaken for producers of
industrial products. An important difference is that the
customers in these markets are professional buyers. In a
recession, companies that market industrial products can
quickly find themselves in a buyers' market. The effect on
producers of industrial products of a high rate of inflation in
a period of recession is similar to the effect on producers of
consumer goods. Period costs are rising, contribution margins
are eroded by increasing variable costs, and demand is falling
at the same time. It is difficult to raise prices in a buyers'
market, and if losses are to be avoided it is necessary to reduce
period costs.

Impact of the 1977 Price Code

A new Price Code applied from 1 August 1977 and a new
Price Commission (disbanded in 1979) took office on that
date. Under the new legislation the Government retained the
powers to maintain control over the net profit margins of
manufacturing and service firms and the gross and net profits
of distributors for one more year. The detailed control over
price increases by reference to allowable costs was superseded
by a new investigatory system.

Larger manufacturing and service companies were still
required to give advance notice of proposed price increases.
The Price Commission selected proposals for investigation
and the Secretary of State could order inquiries into prices
and pricing practices of industries or other large economic
sectors. The Price Commission made detailed recommendations
to the Secretary of State for Prices and Consumer Protection,

with reasons, as to whether price increases should be allowed and whether pricing practices were reasonable.

In selecting price increases and pricing practices for investigation, the Price Commission and Secretary of State had to take account of criteria such as cost levels, efficient use of resources, the adequacy of rates of return on capital employed, the maintenance of quality and satisfaction of changing consumer demands, the encouragement of competition, protection of the consumer against abuse of market power, and maintenance and expansion of the British share of world markets. The criteria were intentionally broad and the Commission had the difficult job of balancing the need to allow industry to generate adequate profits and the political need to control price rises. There were a number of specific safeguards to protect firms during and after an investigation:

(i) the Commission had discretion to allow one or more interim price increases during an investigation;

(ii) protection was given against compulsory reductions in price levels prevailing at the start of an investigation and in interim price increases; and

(iii) the Secretary of State's powers were limited so that he could not act more severely than the Price Commission recommended.

Regulations under Clause 9 of the Price Commission Act 1977 laid down minimum rates of profit which must not be eroded through the operation of the Act. They provided for a return on capital after interest and before tax approaching 12½% per annum. These safeguard clauses severely limited the Price Commission's powers to restrict prices and in February 1979 the minimum profit level safeguards were repealed. However, the Price Commission (Amendment) Act 1979 required the Commission to permit interim price increases to cover increased imported raw material costs.

The investigatory powers under the Act applied especially where it appeared that market forces were exercising insufficient price restraint. Some forty investigations a year were undertaken. For the great majority of enterprises, pricing decisions were not subject to external rules. Nevertheless, in making those decisions, larger enterprises had to take account of the possibility of triggering off a Price Commission investigation.

What was the effect of the 1977 Price Code on the previous analysis? Under the Code there was no detailed control over price increases by reference to allowable costs, and therefore the Price Code limit that appears in figures 8.8 and 8.9 could no longer be calculated. Enterprises had to determine their selling prices in the light of their view of how future costs and demand conditions would affect the position and shape of the contribution curve. If, and when, real disposable incomes started to rise, the position of the curve would move upwards and to the left. The difficulty surrounding computation of the contribution curve has been referred to earlier. The monitoring system advocated would signal the need, and provide essential information, for price reviews.

Summary

Selling price decisions are complex. The accountant should provide financial information relevant to the decision at hand. In many multi-product, multi-market companies, selling price has to be seen as one of a number of variables in the marketing mix. Cost-based prices are a reference point in determining selling prices. The principal methods of determining cost-based prices are full-cost and marginal-cost pricing. The major criticism of full-cost pricing is that it fails to take direct account of demand and assumes that prices are a function of costs. On the other hand, the principal problem associated with marginal or relevant cost pricing is that of forecasting price–demand relationships. Full-cost pricing appears to be used by most firms as a starting point in 'primary' pricing decisions; managerial judgement determines adjustments to obtain the actual price. A high rate of inflation increases the importance of the timing of reviews of pricing decisions. Price controls restrict the ability of companies to increase prices in expanding markets, but are less important in a recession. An essential first stage in individual pricing decisions is a comprehensive monitoring system which signals the need for a price review. With a high rate of inflation, costs are increasing continuously; management then has the difficult task of deciding to what extent higher costs can be passed on in higher prices. Some attempt then needs to be made to determine the position of contribution curves on product profit—volume charts.

9

Stock Control Models

L R AMEY

Professor of Accounting,
McGill University

and

D A EGGINTON

Senior Lecturer in Accounting,
University of Bristol

Introduction[1]

Stocks play an important part in the decision making of firms. Most firms hold stocks of goods for sale to customers and most manufacturing firms keep stocks of components and raw materials for production purposes. Consequently, firms commonly have large investments in stocks — which involve them in *carrying costs* of financing, warehousing, insurance and so on. However, employees who have everyday control of stocks in their jobs as storekeepers and salespeople may tend to be less sensitive to the costs of holding large stocks than to the burdens of frequent re-ordering or to the complaints and lost sales that occur when stocks run out. All these aspects involve costs of different kinds, and firms therefore need to establish guidelines that seek to minimise overall costs. Such guidelines are the function of stock control.

Stock control requires a decision framework and an administrative structure to implement the decisions. We are concerned here only with the decision framework, which is

1. This chapter is largely based on relevant sections from L.R. Amey and D.A. Egginton, *Management Accounting: A conceptual approach*, Longman 1973, Chapter 19.

provided by stock control models. There is a substantial literature on stock control,[2] dealing with a wide variety of problems encountered by firms, and nowadays models for stock control are frequently applied via computer systems. We shall be providing a glimpse of some relatively simple models, after first considering the motives for stockholding and the important management acccounting issue of relevant costs.

A firm's reasons for stockholding are the basic determinants of stock policy. The three fundamental reasons for stock-holding are the same as the three motives originally advanced by Keynes for the holding of cash[3]: the transactions motive, the precautionary motive and the speculative motive. Any or all of these motives may be relevant to a particular class of goods.

The holding of goods for *transactions* purposes alone can be distinguished where demand for goods is assumed to be known with certainty and the goods can be replenished either immediately or with a certain waiting period. It is worthwhile to hold some stock in these circumstances, because although there are costs of carrying goods there are also costs of re-ordering and it is evident that some balancing of costs must take place: any household carries stocks of easily replenish-able goods on a similar principle, rather than buying 'hand-to-mouth'.

The *precautionary* motive arises because demand for goods and/or the waiting period for replenishment are not known with certainty. Customer demand may fluctuate, and depleted

---

2. The interested reader is referred to the following range of texts: J. Buchan and E. Koenigsberg, *Scientific Inventory Management*, Prentice-Hall 1963, for a succinct introductory chapter on fundamentals and studies of applications of a wide range of models; A.J.H. Morrell (ed.), *Problems of Stocks and Storage*, ICI Monograph No. 4, Oliver and Boyd 1967, for a compact treatment of the more typical problems arising in manufacturing industry; G. Hadley and T.M. Whitin, *Analysis of Inventory Systems*, Prentice-Hall 1963, for a wide spectrum of models.

3. J.M. Keynes, *The General Theory of Employment, Interest and Money*, Macmillan 1949, Chapter 15. Similarities and differences for holdings of cash and goods are examined by Keynes on pp. 226–7.

stocks will result in lost sales unless customers are prepared to 'place an order' that can be satisfied later. On the replenishment side, suppliers are not always reliable in their delivery periods; they may face such problems as industrial disputes or variations in the demand for their products. Consequently stocks are held as buffers against uncertainty. In determining the level of these *safety stocks*, the carrying costs of stocks have to be balanced against the costs of being out of stock.

Finally, the *speculative* motive relates to expected price changes. A firm may increase stocks in expectation of a price rise, or decrease them below the 'usual' operating levels in expectation of a price fall. The anticipated gains from a price rise must be balanced against carrying costs, or the anticipated savings from buying after a price fall must be balanced against the net cost of being out of stock in the interim period. The crucial element in speculative holding is the expectation of a price change, which will be formed by officers (such as buyers) within the firm. That is a forecasting problem, to which stock control models can offer no contribution. The major control issue for speculative stockholding is administrative: there is a clear need to ensure that limits to a firm's financial risks in speculative stockholding are established and observed. In the present context of stock control models, however, the speculative holding of goods need not be examined further.

In the following sections the general issue of relevant costs is examined, before turning to deterministic stock control models that deal with the transactions requirements of stockholding. These 'transactions' sections cover the basic economic order quantity (EOQ) model and basic economic lot size. The precautionary motive is recognised in a succeeding section which illustrates a probabilistic approach to safety stocks.

Relevant Costs for Stock Control

The relevant costs for a stockholding decision, as for any decision, are those which are variable with the actions under consideration (see Chapter 6, for example). These costs need not, and in very many cases will not, coincide with the costs designated as variable in the routine accounting records.

Three possible approaches can be used for the less amenable costs: adjustment of available accounting data for the purpose in hand, separate investigation/estimation of cost elements, or the use of a stock model to 'backtrack' from an assumed decision to discover if the implied costs seem plausible.

The major categories of costs associated with stocks are procurement costs, carrying costs and stockout costs, each of which will be considered in turn.

Procurement Costs

Procurement costs are incurred in acquiring a batch of goods. Two distinct elements can be distinguished. The first is the cost of the goods themselves, either the price paid or the cost of manufacture. It is convenient to treat these acquisition costs as constant per unit, although quantity discounts would make this assumption invalid and necessitate separate investigation.[4] Acquisition cost per unit would not in itself be relevant to the stockholding decision, because it would be incurred even if no stocks were held; *but* it will be seen that acquisition cost is relevant as a measure of funds tied up in stocks for the calculation of carrying costs.

The second category concerns costs caused by the act of acquiring a batch of units. Goods purchased by the firm incur an *order cost*, the costs of clerical time spent in ordering, processing the invoice and payment, arranging for delivery, etc. Goods manufactured by the firm may incur a similar *set-up cost:* the cost of setting up equipment for a production run, administrative arrangements for production scheduling, etc. The major elements of both order and set-up costs are independent of the *quantity* of units in a batch and can be deemed fixed in relation to quantity; where procurement elements are variable with quantity (e.g. costs of unloading), it is usually convenient to include them in the cost of goods.

A major difficulty in estimating order cost, and to a lesser extent set-up costs, is that they are likely to include significant cost elements common to different functions, particularly

4. Quantity discounts are covered in all three books mentioned in footnote 2.

in the administrative area. However, employee time is commonly a substantial element of both order costs and set-up costs, and costings at the appropriate wage rates can therefore often provide estimates.

Carrying Cost

Carrying cost of stock includes several component elements:

(i)   *Interest* on the 'value' of goods carried in stock. This is an opportunity cost; if stockholding were lower, the funds released could be employed elsewhere or borrowing could be reduced. The appropriate interest charge would depend on the relevant opportunities for the released funds.

The 'value' of goods carried in stocks will be the acquisition costs which would be avoided if stocks were reduced, or the acquisition costs which would be incurred if stocks were increased. Stock decisions relate to goods which the firm intends to replace; consequently the appropriate measure of value should be replacement cost for the decision period. This value will be termed cost of stocks.

(ii)   *Storage costs* include such out-of-pocket costs as the running expenses of warehousing (light, heat, wages, rent), *provided* these expenses are variable with the stock decision under consideration. When warehousing is owned by the firm, the depreciation cost as such is irrelevant; the usual considerations of opportunity cost and capacity constraints apply. If there is spare capacity (owned or committed for renting in the period), the opportunity cost is zero: if there are alternative uses, the value of the best alternative is the opportunity cost of storage. In capacity constrained situations the stockholding decision should be made in the context of the constraints,[5] although approximate opportunity costs may be employed in the simpler models. Clearly, outlay costs are relevant for warehouse acquisition decisions which incorporate stock considerations.

5.   For examples see Hadley and Whitin 1963 (footnote 2), pp. 54–61 and 304–7.

(iii) *Deterioration costs* include such elements as breakages, evaporation and pilferage; *insurance* against losses is also relevant. These costs have an approximately linear relationship to the time held in stock.

Obsolescence is a further cost associated with carrying stocks. A charge for obsolescence may be included on a similar basis to deterioration costs, but this implies that obsolescence is continuous over time, whereas its uncertain incidence really makes it inappropriate for incorporation in this simple (deterministic) manner.

Stockout Cost

Stockout cost is the opportunity loss which occurs when the firm is unable to meet a demand for a good; it may include loss of profit margins on sales or the additional costs of filling backorders, and also the cost of lost goodwill affecting future sales. By nature, the stockout cost is particularly difficult to estimate.

Only the above three major groups of costs will be recognised in the following subsections, but the list is not exhaustive. We have ignored costs of the information system, and also cost interrelationships in dynamic systems, which need to be considered jointly with regard to potential cost savings (e.g. amalgamation of orders to a single supplier).

The Basic EOQ Model

The economic order quantity (EOQ) model has provided the basis for many applications and extensions since its development early this century. The model adopts a fixed order quantity for goods purchased by the firm, and this quantity is reordered at a regular replacement interval. The objective is the selection of the order quantity which minimises costs of stock policy; implicitly, examination of the overall profitability of dealing in these goods takes place outside the model.

The assumptions of the model are stated below.

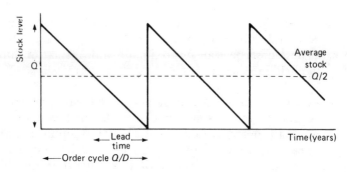

Figure 9.1   *Stock for Basic EOQ Model*

1. Demand is certain, constant and continuous over time (e.g. sales are not made at discrete intervals).
2. *Lead time* (the time between placing an order and receiving it) is certain and constant.
3. All prices and costs are certain and constant.
4. Demand cannot be postponed, which means that backordering is not permitted (i.e. customers' orders cannot be held awaiting the replenishment of stock).
5. There is an infinite time horizon, unless the optimal replacement interval coincidentally divides into the (finite) time horizon an integral number of times. This is because average costs being minimised include an order cost occurring at replacement *intervals*.

The first two assumptions exclude the precautionary motive for holding stocks; the third excludes the speculative motive.

Under these assumptions it will be evident that it is feasible to re-order when stock is just sufficient to satisfy demand during lead time. Thus the pattern of stock levels will take the form shown in figure 9.1.

The time between orders (which is equal to the time between deliveries with a constant lead time) is termed the *order cycle*. Since stock declines uniformly over the order cycle, the average stock must be half the order quantity. The following notation will be adopted, assuming a demand period of one year:

Q = order quantity in units
D = annual demand in units
C = unit cost of good
I = carrying cost of stock as a percentage of unit cost C per year
A = cost of placing an order

From figure 9.1 it can be seen that the average number of units in stock is given by $Q/2$. Each unit involves a money cost C for funds tied up in stocks, and the percentage carrying cost of stock value is I, so that IC = carrying cost *per unit* per year. (IC can be expressed as an absolute money amount without necessarily employing I as a percentage of unit cost — thus components of carrying cost which are not variable with the money value C, such as handling costs during storage, can be incorporated directly into IC.)

The carrying costs of average stock are therefore given by:

annual carrying costs $= ICQ/2$ (1)

The number of orders in a year is given by D/Q. Since each order incurs a cost A:

annual order costs $= AD/Q$ (2)

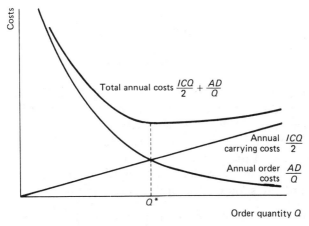

Figure 9.2 *Annual Costs of Stock Policy*

Thus, where V = total annual costs of stock policy:

$$V = ICQ/2 + AD/Q \qquad (3)$$

Figure 9.2 illustrates the way in which the cost elements in expressions (1) and (2) combine to give the total costs of expression (3). Annual carrying costs increase with the size of Q, while annual order costs decline with the order quantity. The objective of minimising total annual costs can be achieved by determining the optimal order quantity Q^* that balances annual carrying costs against annual order costs.

The formula for the optimal order quantity Q^* is derived by calculus. Treating Q as a continuous variable, the total annual cost of stock policy from expression (3) can be minimised by differentiating with respect to Q:

$$\frac{dV}{dQ} = \frac{IC}{2} - \frac{AD}{Q^2},$$

and setting the derivative equal to zero, giving:

$$Q^2 = \frac{2AD}{IC}$$

and

$$Q^* = \sqrt{\frac{2AD}{IC}} \qquad (4)$$

where Q^* is the optimal (i.e. economic) order quantity.[6]

The expression in (4) is the core of the EOQ model; orders of Q^* units minimise the sum of order costs and carrying costs.

The EOQ formula shows that when stock is being held for transaction purposes, the optimal order quantity (and average stock $Q^*/2$) will vary with economies of scale for items with a high level of demand. The formula also reflects the flatness of the total cost curve around Q^* in figure 9.2. A small shift from Q^* makes relatively little difference to total cost, and the square root formula correspondingly moderates

6.   This gives an absolute minimum because $dV/dQ = 0$ and d^2V/dQ^2 > 0.

the impact on order quantity of any error or variations in the estimated data.

The minimum cost of stock policy, V_{min}, can be derived by substituting for Q in (3):

$$V_{min} = \frac{IC}{2}\sqrt{\frac{2AD}{IC}} + AD\sqrt{\frac{IC}{2AD}}$$

$$= \sqrt{2ADIC} \tag{5}$$

Applications of EOQ

The application of the basic EOQ model is easily demonstrated. Assume that a firm has an annual demand D of 100,000 units for one of its products. The unit cost C of the good is £16 and the carrying cost I is estimated at 15% per year. Finally, the cost of placing an order A is assumed to be £12 per order. The optimal order quantity can be calculated:

$$Q^* = \sqrt{\frac{2AD}{IC}} = \sqrt{\frac{2 \times 12 \times 100,000}{0.15 \times 16}} = 1,000 \text{ units}$$

Thus the firm's annual costs of stock policy would be minimised by ordering in quantities of 1,000 units (at intervals of about 3½ days over the year).

With the order quantity of 1,000 units, the carrying costs and order costs can be shown to be equally balanced, to give minimum total costs for the year:

$$\text{annual carrying costs} = \frac{ICQ}{2} = \frac{0.15 \times £16 \times 1,000}{2} = £1,200$$

$$\text{annual order costs} = \frac{AD}{Q} = \frac{£12 \times 100,000}{1,000} = £1,200$$

$$\text{minimum total costs} = \sqrt{2ADIC}$$
$$= \sqrt{(2 \times £15 \times 100,000 \times 0.15 \times £16)} = \underline{\underline{£2,400}}$$

The EOQ model can be adapted to an economic lot size (ELS) model for batches of goods manufactured within the firm. The decisions to be made concern the size of batches of different goods to be manufactured on multi-purpose equipment. The major difference from EOQ is that the order cost is replaced by a set-up cost for each batch manufactured, as explained earlier under relevant costs for stock control. All that is needed to change the basic EOQ formula into the basic ELS formula is to define A as the set-up cost per batch, instead of the order cost. In fact, historically the ELS model was first developed for production decisions within firms, and later adapted into the EOQ model.

An amendment to the basic model is desirable when demand for a good takes up a significant proportion of productive capacity. Those goods that are despatched to satisfy demand as soon as they come off the production line do not incur stock carrying costs — thus they permit an upward adjustment of economic lot size. The firm is relieved of carrying costs in proportion to the size of annual demand relative to the production rate, so that the carrying cost element can be reduced in that proportion for the square root formula, as follows:

$$\text{economic lot size} \quad Q_L^* = \sqrt{\frac{2AD}{IC\,(1 - D/R)}}$$

where R is the maximum annual production rate.

The application of this formula can be illustrated by slightly adapting the earlier figure example. As before, $D = 100,000$ units, $C = £16$ and $I = 0.15$. This time, A is still £12, but represents set-up cost per batch manufactured. The only new element is R, which will be assumed to be 400,000 units per year. Thus:

$$\text{economic lot size} = \sqrt{\frac{2AD}{IC\,(1 - D/R)}}$$

$$= \sqrt{\frac{2 \times 12 \times 100,000}{0.15 \times 16\,(1 - 100,000/400,000)}}$$

$$= 1,155 \text{ units}$$

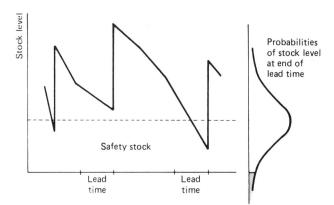

Figure 9.3   *Variable Sales with Constant Lead Times*

The adjustment for demand relative to the production rate is the only difference from the earlier calculation which produced an answer of 1,000 units. Thus the adjustment has pushed up optimal quantity by 155 units, a relatively small amendment for a product that takes up a quarter of productive capacity.

Safety Stocks

The precautionary motive for stockholding is relevant when demand and/or *lead time* (the waiting period between ordering and delivery) cannot be treated as certain. In addition to the holdings for transactions purposes, it is necessary to employ safety stocks to absorb variations in the calls on stock.

The effect of a safety stock is illustrated in figure 9.3, where demand is no longer certain but lead times remain constant.

Order quantity calculated on (mean) expected demand can be calculated in the deterministic manner already considered. The safety stock constitutes a separate component of stock, which *on average* will be carried all year round.[7] On the

7. In fact the independent calculation of order quantity and safety stock implied here is not strictly valid, but sufficiently close for the present purpose. See Hadley and Whitin 1963 (footnote 2), Chapter 4.

right-hand side of figure 9.3 there is an upended probability
density function for stocks remaining on hand at the end of
lead time, illustrated here quite arbitrarily as a normal distribution. EOQ based on mean expected demand would leave
sufficient stock to meet demand during lead time on 50% of
occasions — because demand during lead time would be less
than the mean for half the time. The remaining 50% of
variations in demand would either be met by safety stocks,
or would result in stockouts.

If the stock policy is optimally determined, the safety
allowance will be that for which the probability of stockouts
balances the expected costs of depletion against carrying cost
for the marginal unit stocked. The technique will not be
examined here. The alternative approach is to select a specific
risk of stockout by arbitrary policy decision. In either case,
an assumption about the probability distribution of demand
is required. Past data on demand can be examined to justify
the adoption of a particular distribution; often it is convenient
to assume that whole classes of stock items share some
characteristic distribution.

For an illustration of an arbitrarily determined probability
of stockouts, consider a firm which requires that there shall be
only one chance in 100 of being understocked on a particular
item. Sales occur in a random manner and the Poisson
distribution is assumed to be appropriate. A convenient
characteristic of the Poisson distribution is that standard
deviation is given by the square root of the mean; thus only
average demand during lead time need be known in order to
determine the distribution. The direct normal distribution may
then be used as an approximation to the Poisson distribution
for small probabilities.

If I_0 = number of units on hand at the beginning of the
period which will reduce the probability of running out of
stock during the next period to $1/100$, and d = average demand
during lead time, then

$$I_0 = d + 2.326\sigma = d + 2.326\sqrt{d}$$

2.326σ either side of the mean of the normal distribution
(the 2% probability level) includes all but 1% of cases on either
side of the mean. We are concerned with only one tail of the

distribution; stock needs to be sufficient to meet all but the 1% probability of stockouts shown as the shaded area in figure 9.3.

The firm's safety stock is given by:

$$I_0 - d = 2.326\sqrt{d}$$

If lead time is one week and average weekly demand is 24 units, a safety allowance which would on average give a stockout only one week in 100 can be calculated:

$$I_0 = 24 + 2.326\sqrt{24} = 35.4, \text{ say 36 units,}$$

and safety allowance = 12 units.

When the probability of stockouts is selected by policy decision, it is still possible to calculate an implied cost of stockout to permit managerial assessment of the plausibility of stockout costs.[8]

The above discussion considered briefly only that type of amendment to the deterministic approach which accommodates demand variations. Variations in lead time could be treated in a similar manner, but to deal with variations in both demand *and* lead time would require a different approach. Simulation can be used to tackle this type of problem.[9] Moreover, the discussion has been concerned exclusively with static models; significantly different treatment is required to accommodate dynamic changes in the determinants (demand, lead times, prices) of stock policy.[10]

Conclusion

This chapter has explained the fundamentals of stock control models. The models adopted within firms may be more complex in their formulation and they certainly require a good administrative framework for implementation, but the same essential ideas have universal application to stock policy.

The central square root formula is highly adaptable to

8.   For example see Morrell 1967 (footnote 2), pp. 27–34.
9.   See Buchan and Koenigsberg 1963 (footnote 2).
10. For treatment of dynamic changes, see Hadley and Whitin 1963 (footnote 2), Chapter 7.

different circumstances of transactions demand, and can be modified to cope with problems like economic lot size and financial constraints on stockholding. Further models are developed to determine the safety stocks to meet stochastic demand, where the characteristics of the model depend upon the nature of the probability distribution that can be assumed for demand. In all models the correct specification of relevant costs is important, although the decisions obtained from the models fortunately tend to be relatively insensitive to minor variations in the estimated data.

10

Standard Costing for Planning and Control

MICHAEL BROMWICH

Professor of Finance and Accounting,
University of Reading

Introduction[1]

It has been said that an understanding by the accountant of what *variances* mean is the first step to their practical and useful application. But perhaps not enough thought has been given to the production of meaningful variances. The major part of this chapter, therefore, considers from the perspective of the economist and managers within the firm the usefulness for planning and control of the traditional methods of standard costing. Many of the findings and suggested improvements to standard costing apply equally to budgetary control as currently practised. The last section of the chapter recognises that though long-term objectives are often urged upon management, both budgetary control and standard costing systems

1. The major part of this chapter draws extensively on my article, Standard costing for planning and control, *The Accountant*, April–May 1969, pp. 547–9, 584–7 and 632–4. The last section is similarly based on Measurement of divisional performance in the long run, in H.C. Edey and B.S. Yamey (eds), *Debits, Credits, Finance and Profits*, Sweet and Maxwell 1974, pp. 15–20. The kind permission of the publishers of these two articles to reprint parts of them is gratefully acknowledged.

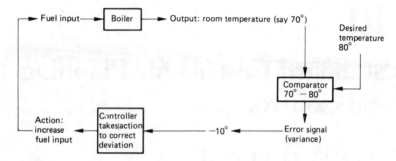

Figure 10.1 *Central Heating Thermostat*

have a short-term orientation. The final section, therefore, considers the additional problems that flow from using such short-term control devices to aid in achieving long-run objectives.

Standard Costing and Feedback Systems

The model for planning and control used in standard costing compares actual and expected results, significant deviations hopefully giving rise to action either by the responsible manager or his superiors.

This type of model belongs to a general class called feedback systems. The latter include such diverse systems as central heating temperature regulators, missile guidance systems, and all the automatic control systems of the human body, e.g. those which stabilise body temperature. A study of the ideas of feedback theory may therefore be useful to the accountant. For example, the theory about the effects of lags in feedback on system output may apply directly to delays in producing accounting reports.

Probably the best known feedback model is the central heating system, where differences between actual and desired warmth are used as signals for automatically changing boiler activity. In figure 10.1 the controller using error signals received from the comparator (which compares actual and desired temperature) automatically alters fuel input. Thus by use of feedback the output of the system, the actual temperature, causes changes in the input to the system. Here negative feedback, where the action required is inversely related to the error signal, is used as it is in the standard costing model.

Merely altering the names of the boxes gives us a representation of the accountant's standard costing system. If output of the information system is actual material prices, then the error signal becomes a price variance and the controller represents the responsible manager.

Feedback Models and the Accountant

The feedback approach to standard costing and budgetary control brings out very clearly the link between planning and control. In the central heating system, past performance is monitored and, on the assumption that any past error will continue unless action is taken, a planning decision about fuel input is made. Similarly, standard cost variances can only be used to guide future actions, as any past mistake is a sunk (i.e. lost) cost. Thus, if the manager who was £10,000 overrun last month is sacked, it is not because of his past error, but because it was assumed that he will continue to perform inefficiently in the future. Unfavourable control variances (which I prefer to call appraisal variances owing to the emotive connotation of control) are planning variances which serve to highlight the need for improved performance or planning in the future.

One area of feedback theory rich in potential applications to accountancy involves the use of error signals other than simple actual—standard differences. For example, the *rate of change* of variation between actual and standard is often used in feedback theory. In accounting, this would indicate the trend in a manager's performance over time. A variance showing the *rate of change* of a *rate of change* variance is conceivable. This might indicate whether the rate of improvement in a manager's performance was increasing or decreasing. Such dynamic variances (of which more later) could be produced easily, and perhaps continuously, by computer. Many of the received principles of standard costing can be derived from feedback models. For instance, the manager is supposed to take action on error signals (variances) reported to him; thus it is pointless to communicate to him those beyond his control. But to avoid the dangers of sub-optimisation (local profit at the expense of loss elsewhere in the firm), all the significant effects of his actions throughout the firm should, ideally, be monitored and reported.

The Limitations of the Accountant's Feedback Model

Although looking at a standard costing system as a feedback model clarifies thought, many difficulties stand in the way of the direct application of the ideas. Most of these problems, and indeed most of the general limitations of the accountant's model, stem from the fact that, unlike physical feedback systems, we are dealing with human beings whose behaviour is but poorly understood.

In the central heating system the response to error signals is both automatic and well understood, whereas people have to be motivated to respond to accounting variances. Further, even assuming the causes of off-standard condition are known, management often has little idea of the action necessary to eliminate variances.

In contrast to the central heating system, where for every significant variation a precise remedial action exists, management has only a small set of blunt instruments, such as the threat of non-promotion, and motivational devices like bonuses, to use in obtaining desired results. Little is known about the effects of these tools.

The accountant's model consists of not one system, but rather layers of feedback systems, one for each level of management. Each layer combines the lower ones and gives less detailed information. The reports are prepared, often well after the event, by accountants who are, as it were, outside the system and who may have different views of what is relevant to those comprising the system. Thus top management, who may be distant from actual operations, must plan and control with only a few imprecise tools to aid them.

For these reasons, plus the time constraint on top management, effective planning and control must depend heavily on action by the responsible subordinate manager generated by self-appraisal based on past variances. Therefore motivating subordinates to act correctly on the basis of accounting information is a very important management function, and one in which at present the accountant (*qua* accountant) does not usually participate.

Causes of Variances

Now we come to the most important difference between simple feedback systems and those of the accountant. In the central heating system, the cause of an error signal is normally of little importance. In the accountant's system, the cause may be of paramount importance, as very different responses may be required to correct variances resulting from different factors. Indeed, some variances cannot be eliminated, but must be taken into account when re-planning — for example, a price variance following a currency devaluation (after all, even a central heating system might have to be re-planned if there were a drastic change in climate). Thus our ability to distinguish between different causes of variation requiring different management action is fundamental to the whole success of standard costing and budgetary control.

The following are some of the major causes of off-standard conditions:

1. Inefficiency in operation, e.g. failure to obtain a reasonable standard in the prevailing circumstances, through inability in one form or another, or through lack of motivation.
2. Incorrect original plans and standards, or originally correct plans and standards that have been invalidated by environmental changes. Here, the reporting of variances may result in the revision of plans: and the process of variance analysis for planning can be described as being educational. In this situation the one thing we do not want is to encourage adherence to the original plans.

3. Poor communication of standards and budgetary goals.
4. Random fluctuations around standards and goals which are likely to be average targets (this is especially true of budgetary goals).
5. If in budgeting (and in decision making) the interdependence of departments has not been taken into account, then action taken by one department may cause variances elsewhere in the firm (the suboptimisation problem).

I believe that variance analysis designed with such causes and the particular circumstances of the business explicitly in mind may be more useful to management than the ritual calculation of all-purpose textbook variances. A different kind of variance might then be used for each cause. For example, as Stedry has said, it is not obvious that variances designed to control planning can also usefully serve as a motivational device.

For some of these, such as cause 3 above, we lack the theoretical background for this approach (though a possible approach might be regularly to compare subordinates' concepts of goals and standards with the beliefs of top management). For others, the basic theory has been developed (e.g. cause 4) or is being developed (e.g. the use of transfer prices to solve the sub-optimisation problem of cause 5).

Variances for Planning and Appraisal

The remainder of this chapter reviews the usefulness of the conventional variances for planning and appraisal in relation to causes 1 and 2, and tries to show how information can be obtained that is more meaningful than that derived from the usual variance computations. I shall call those variances which highlight cause 1 (inefficiency and poor motivation) *appraisal* variances. At present it is not possible to suggest an analytical approach for splitting the appraisal variance between these two causes and a detailed investigation of specific actual variances seems to be the only solution. Recent work has, however, contributed substantially to our understanding of the motivational effects of accounting methods of planning and control.[2] By isolating off-standard results due to these causes, we hope to learn about a manager's past performance. That is, given the environment he faced and the decision variables at his command (those items over which he has authority), how near did he come to optimum performance?

Both for self-appraisal by the manager, the importance of which has already been underlined, and for top management review of subordinates, only controllable variances are of interest. Thus, where the environment has shifted, performance should be compared with a standard reflecting these changed conditions — showing how well the manager has grasped new opportunities, or to what degree he overcame an unfavourable environment. The difficulty lies in defining optimum performance, but I hope to show that some useful approximations to this exist. Of course, any attempt to define optimum performance for changing circumstances introduces a greater element of subjectivity into variance analysis than is usual, but I believe that any difficulties associated with this are likely to be offset by the provision of more meaningful information to management.

Variances which monitor cause 2 I shall call *control of planning* variances; these being used to evaluate plans and standards as distinct from executive performance. When used in conjunction with the variance between original plans and the current appraisal standard (which reflects the prevailing environment), a comparison between unadjusted original plans and actual results may be a useful check on forecasting ability. Further, and more importantly, a persistently unfavourable trend in this variance may suggest the revision of original plans; a persistently favourable variance may hint at new opportunities for the firm.

Direct Cost Variances

Material Price Variances

The usual price variance ((actual material price − standard material price) × actual material usage for actual production)

2. See list of references at end of this chapter for details of some of this work.

may be of little use for appraising the performance of the purchasing officer, as price changes may be due to market-wide forces beyond his control, especially in inflationary conditions. The recent pattern of oil prices gives an instance of seemingly uncontrollable price changes. In such cases a more meaningful variance, for both self-appraisal and top management review, may be a comparison of the actual price paid with the best available estimate of the general market price reigning at the time of purchase. A favourable variance then indicates the buyer's ability to 'beat the market', either by bulk buying or by special arrangements.

A major weapon of the 'market beating' buyer is speculative purchasing, though his ability to engage in this depends on the market in which he buys, the finances of the firm, and his management's attitude. Various approximate measures of speculative success can be suggested. Where the buyer is ordering quantities larger than would normally seem economically necessary (e.g. above those called for in the production schedule), he may justify this by saying that prices will be higher in the later period in which he would normally be expected to buy these items. By computing the variance between the prices which actually obtain in the later period and his earlier estimates of these, we can measure his forecasting success. The profitability of his speculative activities can be gauged by deducting from these actual later prices the lower prices he paid plus the holding costs he incurred.

The above illustrates the general point that variances for appraisal purposes should ideally show how well managers did in the prevailing circumstances and should abstract from uncontrollable environmental changes.

As a check on forecasts and standards, the usual price variance may, however, be useful for planning purposes, particularly if used in conjunction with the appraisal variances suggested above. Further, if an appropriate external forecast of prices were available, an assessment of relative forecasting ability could be obtained by comparing the mistakes of this index with the firm's own errors. Such an external index may be useful as an approximate measure, even if it covers a much wider range of goods than the firm uses.

Another use for the price variance is as an indicator in

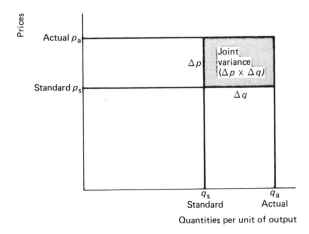

Figure 10.2 *The Joint Variance*

assessing whether the trend in prices necessitates a change in existing plans (e.g. to raise final output prices or to change production methods). Here a rate of change variance, namely a comparison showing the trend in the price variance over time, may be more helpful than the standard computation.

Thus it is suggested that the usual price variance could be usefully split into a 'control of planning' and an 'appraisal' variance. The control of planning variance shows how the market price differed from that previously assumed; and the appraisal variance, by being net of uncontrollable market changes, measures the purchasing agent's ability in the conditions that actually prevailed. The formula for the control of planning variance is $(p_c - p_s)mX$ and that for appraisal variance $(p_a - p_c)mX$, where the symbols p_c, p_s and p_a are, respectively, the general market price at the time of purchase (based on external indicators), the original standard price, and the actual price paid for the commodity in mind. The standard material usage for actual output is represented by mX, where m is the standard usage per unit of final output and X is the actual number of units produced.

Material usage is evaluated in this case at standard usage per unit in order to avoid complications that arise when actual usage is used. Using actual quantities and actual prices in ordinary variance calculation gives rise to what has been called the 'joint variance', which is the product of the price variance and the quantity variance.

This variance is illustrated in figure 10.2, where actual price p_a per unit is above standard p_s, giving a variance of Δp. Actual quantity usage q_a per unit is similarly above standard q_s, indicated by the variance Δq. The joint variance is illustrated in this case by the shaded area (equal to $\Delta p \times \Delta q$).

Fairly apportioning this variance to the responsible manager is impossible. The manager responsible for quantities may argue that the only reason the joint variance arose was because the purchasing officer paid over standard for his purchases. The latter manager can argue with equal conviction that the joint variance flows from the use of extra quantities over standard. If these additional quantities had not been used, the purchasing officer would not have had to buy additional units at above the standard price.

To avoid these insoluble arguments, it is probably wise to report joint variances separately and not attempt to apportion them to responsible managers. For practical purposes, traditional variance calculations normally include joint variances within either the quantity or price variance. With material, it is usually included in the price variance by using actual usage in the calculations of the conventional price variance.

Even the above modified variances only reflect part of the buyer's responsibility. By bulk purchasing he may show a favourable price variance, but at the expense of inventory holding cost. Thus, some attempt should be made to lay down inventory standards so that such effects can be detected. Similarly, provided that the information obtained is worth its cost, standards could be set for other of his responsibilities. For example, a transport cost variance would highlight the cost of rush orders and could be charged to the responsible department. One could argue that, in general, accountants have been too slow in extending their activities in this way.

Material Usage Variance

This variance is less likely than the price variance to be affected by uncontrollable changes in the environment; even so, such cases are easily conceived. For example, poorer quality labour than expected may be used, owing to conditions in the labour market. Here, for appraisal, actual material usage should be compared with an adjusted standard. However, if the use of inferior labour is due to, say, poor performance in the personnel department, then the responsible manager should, in principle, incur a variance equal to the difference between the revised and the original standard.

In such a situation, where the use of lower grade labour is due to general economic conditions and therefore uncontrollable, the modified usage variance suggested above should be used for appraisal; but the conventional variance should be used in conjunction with it for the control of planning. A conventional usage variance that becomes increasingly unfavourable over time may indicate a need for more capital-intensive methods. This suggests the reporting of a rate-of-change variance.

The Accountant's Mix Variance

Substitutions between materials may also be profitable. If such decisions are technically possible, then whoever is responsible for them should have an indicator that tells him when they are profitable. The usual material usage variance gives no hints about this to the production manager, as usage is evaluated at standard prices to avoid contaminating the variance with items beyond the manager's control. This may be reasonable, if somewhere else in the accounting system signals are given that substitution decisions could be profitable. But in general, material usage is priced at standard throughout the system and, therefore, operational management is not informed when it is profitable to change material proportions.

One would expect the mix variance to highlight the possibility of substituting cheaper materials for more expensive ones. But this it cannot do, as it is priced at standard cost. The variance generally serves the far less important role of an appraisal variance, denoting the cost of changes in mix on the basis of given constant relative prices. Further, owing to the assumptions it implies about feasible material substitutions, it does not even do this well.

Ideally, for planning there should be 'on the shelf' material usage plans for different relative prices — that is, usage recipes giving mixes for various relative material prices. Depending on prices, some materials will be in one recipe but not in others; or larger quantities of any specific material will be in some recipes than in others. These recipes can be used to calculate a control of planning variance called a substitution variance. For each material, actual usage is compared with the 'off the shelf' optimal usage for the relative prices that actually reigned in the period and the difference valued at the actual price for the period of that material. These components are then summed over all materials to give the total substitution variance. For each material the following comparison is made: $(m - m^*) \, p_a^* X$. The new symbols m^* and p_a^* are respectively the optimal usage for each material and its current price, and m is the actual usage of material per unit of final output. Summing these comparisons gives the total substitution variance. An unfavourable overall variance would suggest that the use of different material proportions should be considered. This may seem a costly exercise, but with computers and the use of mathematical programming it is practicable.

Apart from serving as a control of planning variance, the overall substitution variance is useful for appraising the executive responsible for decisions of this type. This is a case where the same variance can be used for both planning and appraisal. But if this revised mix variance is to be useful for appraisal, the reasons for any substitutions must be known. For example, there may have been a departure from the optimal mix, not owing to inefficiency in production, but as a result of a failure in the buying department.

Here, for appraisal, the optimal usage m^* should represent the best operating management could do in the light of the purchasing department's failure. A separate comparison based on the difference between this optimum (which is available to the production department) and the optimum which should have been attained but for the inefficiency of the purchasing department, indicates the cost of the latter. This cost will be useful in appraising the purchasing department's performance and may point up the need for re-planning.

Mix and yield calculations in their usual form give no clear guidance to the correctness of the original technical specifications and therefore worthwhile revisions may not be made. The only remedy seems to be routine engineering studies of existing technical specifications.

For the above reasons it seems doubtful if the computation of the *conventional* mix and yield variances is worthwhile.

Labour Rate and Efficiency Variance

My criticisms of the conventional material price variance apply with full force to the labour rate (price) variance, ((actual wage per hour − standard wage) × number of hours worked to produce the actual output). Indeed, the personnel department may be even more at the mercy of the market than the buying department. The conventional rate variance may be useful for the control of planning, but is less likely to make a good appraisal variance.

The conventional formula for labour efficiency variance is: actual labour hours *less* standard hours for actual production *times* the standard labour cost per hour. It is generally regarded as an appraisal variance, off-standard conditions reflecting on the production manager. This is reasonable if the standard used reflects the environmental conditions that prevailed during the period; but if, for example, owing to conditions in the labour market, labour of less than standard skill had to be used, then the standard used for appraisal purposes should be adjusted to reflect this fact.

A rate-of-change variance may be useful for appraisal purposes, as the responses of both top management and the responsible manager depend on whether or not any unfavourable variance is expected to persist. Watching the trend in labour, and other appraisal variances, may be helpful in validating standards; a persistent trend should be a signal for a thorough study of targets.

In computing labour efficiency variances (and, indeed, all variances), attention should be paid to all those that are mutually dependent. For example, by allowing higher than standard material waste, greater labour efficiency may be obtained. Here, labour efficiency and material usage variances cannot be looked at in isolation.

The efficiency (appraisal) variance based on current attainable standards, and the uncontrollable efficiency variance (which represents labour inefficiency due to environmental conditions, and is therefore a useful control of planning variance), together explain deviations from forecast capacity due to labour inefficiency. Thus they may suggest that management should employ more capital intensive methods, consider price increases or investigate switching to a product which needs less skilled labour. The two variances together are thus relevant for the control of planning.

Cost of Labour Inefficiency

The conventional efficiency variance, even when adjusted to take account of attainable standards, may understate the cost of excess labour usage. This cost variance is taken to be the wage payments for which standard performance was not obtained, whereas the true cost is the opportunity cost of production lost due to inefficiency (that is, approximately the lost total contribution to profits and overheads after meeting variable costs).

A simple example may help to explain this. Let us assume that 100 labour hours produced only 90 units of final output where the standard was 100. The conventional efficiency variance would price the ten extra hours at the standard rate per hour (say, £1.50), giving an unfavourable variance of £15. However, if the factory will always be running at full capacity in the conceivable future, the real loss associated with these ten hours includes the loss of ten units of output evaluated at their standard contribution to overheads and profit. These units will now never be sold.

Under the above assumptions, the true cost of labour inefficiency is the conventional variance *plus* any lost contribution. On the other hand, the conventional variance accurately reflects the cost of inefficiency if idle capacity is expected in the future and if unsatisfied demand in any period is carried forward to the next. (But if overtime has to be worked in the next period to make up lost units, the cost of this should be included in the variance as a cost of excess usage.)

The approach suggested above, which entails a forecast of the future effects of past inefficiency, is more subjective than the usual calculations. However, it shows more clearly the effect of sub-standard performance, and illustrates the need to consider its future effects.

Sales Variances

Sales Volume Variance

Here, the need to compute separate appraisal and planning variances may be imperative. Management by exception using the conventional sales volume variance may be of little help in appraisal. If changes in market conditions since the standard was set have been ignored, a variance computed in the normal way may disguise inefficiency. This is illustrated in figure 10.3.

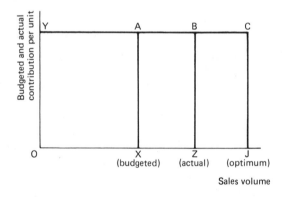

Figure 10.3 *Sales Volume Variances*

OY is the budgeted and the actual contribution per unit (it is assumed that budgeted prices and costs are actually realised). Budgeted and actual sales are, respectively, OX and OZ.

The conventional volume variance may be calculated as the difference between actual and standard sales priced at the standard contribution (in our case a favourable variance represented by the rectangle AXZB). This merely tells us that the sales manager has sold more than expected (OZ − OX), whereas the important question is: how well has he exploited his opportunities in the period? Whether or not he has met a possibly obsolete target is irrelevant. We may be able to ascertain that, in the prevailing circumstances, he should have sold more than the budgeted amount (say OJ in the diagram). This can be done in the motor vehicle industry, where sales figures for firms within the industry are published monthly. In this way, we can see that the manager has in fact performed rather badly, even though the accountant's conventional variance suggests otherwise.

If these calculations suggest that the optimum sales for the period is shown by, say, OJ in the diagram, the variance BZJC is really an opportunity cost variance which indicates the cost to the firm of neglected opportunities. Conversely, if the market demand had fallen for reasons outside the manager's control, he should be assessed against a more realistic lower standard.

To compute such a variance in any precise way would require more knowledge about demand conditions than firms normally possess, but some useful approximations may be possible. One approach is to compare the actual market share in the last period with both desired and earlier ones. In our diagram, OJ could represent the firm's average past market share applied to total industry sales for the period under review. This, of course, assumes that all unusual factors such as strikes and the introduction of new models have been abstracted. A favourable difference between the actual and the average past market share may give an indication of the sales manager's ability to beat the market. In a favourable environment, however, the average market share may be of less use as a standard than in an unfavourable one, as its attainment may merely reflect previously neglected opportunities.

Other information may be helpful in this situation. For example, the number of orders and inquiries received by the firm could be monitored, a large build-up perhaps leading to a revision of standards. A careful watch should be kept on changes in total industry sales and on the fortunes of similar industries, as the firm's performance should, at least, exhibit a similar pattern. I believe that appraisal variances of this type will, provided their subjectivity is recognised, give better results than the conventional variances.

Original plans should be compared with the appraisal standard to give a control of planning variance. This comparison may give clues about forecasting ability (the conventional variance will also be useful here), shifts in the environment, and whether plans need revising, especially if a rate-of-change variance is used and read in the light of past trends.

Plant expansion decisions may follow from a persistently favourable difference between actual sales and the sales manager's estimate of what he could have sold in the absence of any capacity constraint.

Pricing the Sales Volume Variance

For appraisal we need some measure of the profits foregone in not achieving the appraisal standard. Often the standard profit margin per unit is used to evaluate lost sales. This may be confusing, however, if the margin includes allocated overheads that are the result of past planning decisions, for such allocations by their nature are arbitrary and so, therefore, are profit margins calculated using such figures.

Contribution to overheads and profits per unit of final output may be a useful approximate measure of the opportunity cost of a lost unit of sales. It, however, assumes that any sales lost are lost forever. This is unlikely where the firm is not working to capacity (provided that any unsatisfied demand will not be transferred by customers to other goods). If lost volume can be made up later, the only cost to the firm is the 'time' cost of receiving cash flows later. This illustrates, yet again, the interdependence of variances through time. Thus, pricing the sales volume variance using the contribution may overstate the cost to the firm of incorrect planning. But this point may be less important in appraising performance, for if the sales manager has persistently sold less than the standard volume it seems reasonable to assume this inefficiency will continue and hence that lost sales will not be made up in later periods unless top management intervenes.

Sales Price Variances

In some industries the market dictates the firm's selling price and the sales price variance is then useful only in checking on planning, as it is beyond anyone's control.

Even where firms do have pricing discretion, prices in real terms may be stable for long periods, owing to either the administrative difficulties of alteration or to the market structure in which the firm operates. In either case, a careful watch should be kept on the prices of other firms, as this may give hints on the need for price revisions of one's own.

In situations where the reporting of price variances is considered useful they may, nevertheless, be confusing if looked at in isolation from the sales volume variance. Where the economic environment has not altered during the period, an unfavourable price variance will tend to be associated with a favourable volume variance and *vice versa*. A lower price and increased sale quantities may result from a shift along the demand curve. Thus it can be argued that little is gained by splitting the overall sales variance. This is shown in figure 10.4. OA and OB are respectively actual and budgeted prices, and OV and OW are budgeted and actual sales volume. OC is

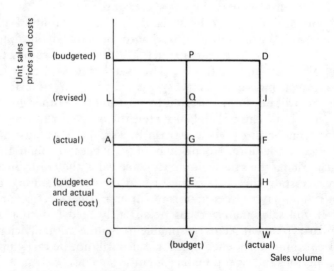

Figure 10.4 *Sales Variances*

the budgeted and actual direct cost. The usual sales volume variance, priced using the contribution, is shown by PDHE ((actual *minus* standard volume) *times* the standard contribution) and the (unfavourable) price variance is shown by the rectangle BDFA ((actual *minus* standard price) *times* actual volume).

However, it is unrealistic to expect to sell more than the budgeted volume without some associated reduction in price. The two variances (price and volume) should be computed using an adjusted price. The minimum adjustment is to use, instead of the standard price, the price that we would expect to obtain for the *actual* volume of sales. In our case this is assumed to be OL. This adjusted price ought also to be used in calculating the standard contribution. Thus, our new price variance becomes ALJF — still unfavourable, but less than with the conventional computation. The volume variance is QJHE — again favourable. The conventional variances are overstated, as the irrelevant rectangle LBDJ is included. For control of planning, we should also compare the contribution that ought to have been obtained from the actual sales (the rectangle CLJH) with that expected if the original price and sales had been adhered to (CBPE).

Where there has been a change in the external economic environment the above procedure is of little use, as both price and volume variances may be favourable for reasons beyond the control of management. The analysis now becomes even more subjective. What is ideally needed for appraisal is a comparison between actual results and an estimate of the best attainable performance in the conditions which faced the firm in the period under review. For control of planning, the comparison needed is between the previous planned sales volume and the appraisal standard. A comparison between planned prices and an estimate of the prices at which the appraisal sales volume could have been sold in the actual conditions in the market should also be helpful. Thus, in analysing sales variances, it is important to try to recognise shifts in the economic environment, e.g. by using market share and inventory variances as clues.

Fixed Overhead Variances

Overhead Variances for Appraisal

Most treatments of overhead variances involve the computation of overhead under-recovery or over-recovery and its
division between capacity and efficiency variances. Is the
feedback of such information useful for appraisal? The
answer must, on the whole, be no. In the first place, it is
redundant information. Under-recovery results from either
not selling the budgeted quantity, or inefficiency in not producing the budgeted quantity within the standard time
allowed. Both causes will be reported either as sales or direct
cost variances and the responsible executives should be
aware of the situation without a report of overhead variances.

Secondly and more importantly, fixed overheads are the
consequence of past decisions to invest in plant, the difficulties
of dismissing labour, etc. and are by definition fixed for any
volume of production within a given range. To treat them as
variable with production (which is what overhead recovery
rates do) is at the best confusing, especially as the various
methods of computing overhead rates give different answers,
all arbitrary.

Normally, for appraisal purposes an overhead efficiency
variance is calculated based on a comparison of standard and
actual output for a given amount of input. Let us assume that
fixed overheads are recovered on the basis of £0.50 per labour
hour per effective unit of final output and that only 5,000
units were produced using labour that ought to have produced
7,000 units. The efficiency variance is (7,000 *minus* 5,000)
times the standard recovery rate of £0.50 per efficient labour
hours — that is £1,000 (unfavourable). This merely tells me
that a figure of under-recovery shown in the firm's formal
book-keeping can supposedly be explained by inefficiency in
the use of labour.

What is the real loss? It is the labour efficiency variance
discussed earlier, namely the cost of the opportunities lost
due to the inefficient use of labour. If the 2,000 units are
lost forever, the cost is the value of the lost contributions,
plus the wages paid to inefficient labour. At the other ex-

treme, if the units could not be sold anyway, it is merely the labour cost. Even this assumes that labour costs are really variable with output.

Similarly, the under-recovery resulting from the sales force's inability to sell the budgeted amount is quite irrelevant for appraisal purposes. Again, the cost of such failures is measured by the opportunities lost. The aim of appraisal variances ought to be to show the cost of deviations from the best short-run utilisation of capacity attainable under prevailing conditions. Overhead recovery has no close relationship with this.

Cost of Idle Capacity

A measure of the cost of idle capacity is required for two purposes: to check on forecasts used in the past to justify investments, and to highlight the opportunity cost of unused facilities (e.g. for planning).

Monitoring the validity of forecasts is best done by a straight comparison of planned and actual cash flows and sales volumes. A comparison between the sales volumes used to justify a project and those achievable if the firm had worked efficiently (the appraisal standard) is also helpful. Persistent large adverse variances may suggest to management that a project is no longer profitable and that alternative uses of funds should be considered and investigated. Favourable variances may help management in its search for new opportunities.

To evaluate the opportunity cost of idle capacity, we must distinguish between a variety of measures of capacity. For example, technical capacity may be irrelevant, as in order to obtain economies of scale it may be worthwhile to invest in a plant with greater capacity than is expected to be used. In this way the expected level of production may be manufactured at a lower cost than in a plant of exactly the required capacity, but with higher operating costs. For planning purposes, an expected idle capacity variance should be computed prior to the period under review, so that management is informed of expected idle capacity early enough to be able to investigate alternative uses. This expected variance should be compared with the actual variance. Both variances should be evaluated at their opportunity cost — the profits foregone due to idle capacity — for example, the return from renting out the idle capacity or using it to produce some other product. If no alternative use is feasible, then idle capacity has no cost. Thus, the evaluation of idle capacity is subjective and cannot be measured by the under-recovery of overheads, as this in no sense measures foregone profits.

I have argued here that overhead efficiency variances can be both misleading and redundant, and that overhead capacity variances do not measure the cost of idle capacity. Of the conventional overhead variances, only the expenditure variance is left. For appraisal, the standard used here needs to be net of uncontrollable influences. This implies that when the variance is computed an estimate should be made of the expenditure level justified by actual conditions, so that it can be split into controllable and uncontrollable elements. This is the concept of the flexible budget. It seems likely, however, that there are many situations in which a pre-set flexible budget will not satisfactorily reflect the attainable standard, because of the large number of conditions that may change. Specific assessment of the standard that could reasonably have been attained may be needed for each period at the time when its results are received.

Control in the Long Run

The first part of this chapter has concentrated on the advantages and weaknesses of standard costing (and budgetary control) as a tool for planning and control over relatively short periods of time, say a month, a quarter or a year. This final section considers the additional problems and challenges for standard costing which arise with the nearly universal view that the firm's objective should be sought over a longer period of time than is normally covered by standard costing reports. There has been a major revolution in the practice of corporate financial management and capital budgeting in the last 20 or 30 years. Many firms now use investment appraisal techniques that allow, in a systematic way, for the timing of the cash flows expected from proposed investment projects. Unfortunately, no similar transformation has yet occurred in standard costing and budgetary control methods used by firms to monitor, evaluate and control the progress of such projects.

This short-term orientation of traditional control and appraisal methods makes it difficult to relate the performance of a business in any period to the capital resources it used during that period. Such models have no direct connection with the concepts underlying discounted-cash-flow methods of investment appraisal.

The use of the usual standard costing and budgetary control systems may cause non-optimal behaviour in various ways. These systems may indeed sometimes highlight what seem to be irresponsible or mistaken forecasts made in the past. Such signals may, however, become apparent only late in a project's life. By then, with the advantage of hindsight, the responsible manager may be able to produce plausible reasons for these variances. It is hard to assess such arguments unless there is a system to monitor lifetime forecasts over a project's complete span and, as the project proceeds, highlight alterations in productions and plans. I would argue that such a system would allow a partial appraisal of forecasting ability to be made well before the completion of a project, and would go some way towards inhibiting the production of irresponsible forecasts. It should also give early warnings that plans may need to be revised.

Non-optimal behaviour may also arise where top management relies primarily on traditional measures of short-term performance to monitor the operational efficiency of its subordinates. In this situation, managers responsible either for making investment decisions or for suggesting worthwhile projects may opt for those giving good short-run performance, rather than those which would most help to achieve the enterprise's long-term financial objective. Worthwhile projects may, when traditional accounting measures are applied in their early years, produce apparently poor short-term results over several periods.

For similar reasons, the emphasis of traditional accounting methods on short-run performance may mean that indications of a need to take new decisions and revise plans may be lost.

However, an evaluation system has been suggested recently which attempts to gauge more precisely how satisfactorily a manager has used his or her capital assets. This has been labelled the 'residual income method'. It involves deducting from the profit for a period an interest charge based on the value of the manager's or department's capital assets, and comparing the residue with a budgeted residual profit figure computed in the same way. The major advantage of this system is that it forces subordinate management to consider the cost of existing and proposed investments in decision making, for any decision that affects their investment base also alters their residual income.[3]

A Suggested Improvement

This method represents a step towards an evaluation system based on the same theoretical foundation as discounted cash-flow models. Indeed, Solomons claims that 'the long-run counterpart of this objective (using the excess of net earnings over the cost of capital as a measure of managerial success) is the maximisation of the discounted present value of the enterprise'. A combination of this method of control and the appraisal concepts of standard costing does offer some promise of a control technique which is consistent with the usual assumed long-run objective of firms.

The central idea on which this suggested performance evaluation system is based is the making, at the end of a period, of a revised forecast of likely future performance, based on those changes in expected cash flows, and hence in present values, that result from alterations to either the forecast environment or the level of managerial performance assumed at the beginning of the period. This revised estimate is to be made on the assumption that no managerial act has yet been planned to counteract or to exploit any of these altered expectations. For ease of presentation, it will be assumed that decisions are made only at the end of each current period.

3.   For a more detailed description and discussion of residual income, see chapter 12.

These changes in expectations may be partitioned into at least three categories. The first encompasses revised forecasts concerning the behaviour of those uncontrollable factors in the environment to which management can respond only by altering future activity in a given way. The only response that a profit-maximising management can make to such changes is to alter its future plans to reflect their effects. An extreme example of this type of environmental change would be a new law, the provision of which could be avoided only by quitting the enterprise's existing area of activity.

The second category incorporates those environmental changes that can be modified or exploited by managerial action, even though their occurrence is beyond the influence of management. Many instances of the second type of expectational change could be cited. It is, for example, unlikely that a firm can influence the trend of world steel prices, but it may escape many of the consequences of such price changes by stockholding in the short-run and by using substitute materials in the long-run.

The third type of expectational change built into the suggested forecast is that generated by expected alterations in factors within managerial control. This category may be split into at least two sub-divisions. One element of the sub-division would indicate the expected change if no action were planned to correct past inefficiencies in execution of the plan; a second would indicate, on a similar basis, the effects of incorrect original forecasts concerning factors within management's control.

Uses of the Model

I realise that none of the above forecasts can be made with precision. However, it is likely that at least some of the advantages claimed for the proposed system are relatively insensitive to a considerable degree of inaccuracy. These ideas are merely an extension of the concepts shown earlier to underlie standard costing and budgetary control procedures. The distinction between controllable and uncontrollable variances has been made in order to give management a picture of what the future will be like if the situation met in the current period is allowed to continue. The monitoring scheme based on the forecasts suggested in this section attempts to fulfil this role over a longer time period, in a way that is consistent with the investment appraisal models likely to be in use to appraise the projects currently being monitored.

The variance between the original and currently estimated present values, combined with the variance between the actual and planned cash flow covering the period between the two estimates, in so far as these variances could be assigned to uncontrollable factors, would give an idea of the uncertainty surrounding a division's activities, particularly when calculated over successive periods, so that a time series of variances could be made available.

Further analysis of such variances, into those which the management could meet only by a change of plan and those that could be offset by appropriate action within the given plan, would give a further indication of the nature of the uncertainties facing the division.

In so far as such variances were controllable and could be analysed into those due to errors in earlier planning and to those due to errors in execution of the plan, they would provide a direct indication of the need for management action to improve efficiency. The overall comparison of the actual cash flow of the period and the newly estimated end-period present value, with those forecast and planned at the beginning of the period, would give direct information for control related to the whole future lifetime performance of the division; and, subject to the range of error created by the need to re-estimate future performance, would thus reduce the risk of management favouring projects on the basis only of an expected good short-term performance.

Various other control procedures suggest themselves. A manager's forecasting ability might be tested by comparing the success of his predictions against those of other people. In some instances it might be possible to utilise published forecasts of particular parameters used in the manager's own forecasts. It might even be possible to compare the extent that longer-term published forecasts changed over time relative to the estimates made by the divisional manager charged with similar forecasts.

The above procedure could not be expected to give a precise picture of the estimating ability of a manager; but combined with a requirement by top management that all major changes in forecasts be fully justified and analysed with the same rigour as is normally recommended for initial proposals, it could provide an effective instrument for discouraging careless planning. Moreover, with the suggested system, the trend over time in a manager's forecasting variances would be monitored, and unrealistic forecasts could be highlighted relatively early in a project's life.

Some Problems

Two limitations of the above scheme as a control method may be noted. The first arises because, if there is much interdependence between parts of the firm, it may be impossible to arrive at the discounted present value of the enterprise as a whole by aggregating the present values obtained by individual departments. This problem arises, however, with all monitoring systems.

Second, the comparisons suggested implicitly assume that the departmental manager has no alternative but to use existing assets in approximately the way that is planned at present. Thus, the suggested system, in common with existing evaluation methods, does not report possible performance if assets were used in a way different from that planned or actually undertaken. Neither it, nor more conventional standard costing systems, is, therefore, a substitute for the continuing exploration of alternatives.

References

On feedback systems:

W.R. Ashby, *An Introduction to Cybernetics*, J. Wiley 1956.

On statistical significance of variances:

R. Kaplin, The significance and investigation of cost variances: survey and extensions, *Journal of Accounting Research*, Autumn 1975.

On transfer prices:

J. Hirshleifer, On the economics of transfer pricing, in M. Alexis and
     C.Z. Wilson (eds), *Organisational Decision-Making*, Prentice-Hall
     1967.

On behavioural effects of standard costing:

W.T. Bruns Jr. and D.T. de Coster (eds), *Accounting and its Behavioural
     Implications*, McGraw-Hill 1971.
A.C. Stedry, Budgetary control: a behavioural approach, in Alexis and
     Wilson, *op. cit.*

On the residual income method:

D. Solomons, *Divisional Performance: Measurement and Control*,
     Irwin 1965, Chapters 3, 4 and 5.

Other useful references on standard costing:

J. Demski, Variance analysis using a constrained linear model, in D.
     Solomons, see below.
C.T. Horngren, The analysis of capacity utilisation, *The Accounting
     Review*, April 1967.
D. Solomons (ed.), *Studies in Cost Analysis*, Sweet and Maxwell 1968.

11

The Organisational and Behavioural Aspects of Budgeting and Control

ANTHONY G HOPWOOD

Professor of Accounting and Financial Reporting,
London Graduate School of Business Studies

Introduction

In accounting texts, budgeting and other related procedures of financial control are portrayed as technical phenomena. Emphasis is placed on the rules and calculative procedures by which budgets are formulated and thereafter used to provide means for evaluating the adequacy of actual performance. Consideration is given to the identification of key budgetary constraints, to the alternative mechanisms for assembling and analysing the mass of expectations for the budgetary period, and to the technical possibilities for analysing the variances between budgeted and actual performance. Although such statements of the technical apparatus of budgeting and financial control invariably commence with appeals to the underlying organisational processes and roles which they serve, the detailed discussion of the technical means for their attainment invariably results in a distancing of the technical from the organisational — a distancing which once achieved is often difficult to reverse.

Unfortunately such an emphasis on the technical rather than the organisational has resulted in an appreciation of budgeting which is detached from the organisational setting in which it operates and the ways in which it is implicated in other organisational processes. Emphasis has been placed on the calculative procedures which give rise to 'the budget' and its subsequent comparison with actual performance, but not on the organisational processes through which budgetary pressures and demands emanate, and as a result of which budgeting achieves its organisational significance. Hardly any consideration has been given in traditional accounting sources to either the competing political processes within organisations which provide the bases for deliberations about an uncertain future, or those processes for organisational evaluation and review which provide the context within which budgetary comparisons are considered and used. Furthermore, in emphasising the calculative and procedural aspects of budgeting, attention has not been given to the ways in which budgeting and other instruments of financial control themselves have shaped the structure and operation of the modern organisation. However, the organisational map of cost centres, profit centres, divisions and programme units, which underlies the structure of budgeting today, bears witness to the roles which mechanisms for financial planning and control have played in reconstituting and, indeed, creating what we now know as the modern organisation. In part, at least, the organisation is now defined in terms of the mechanisms which were introduced to further its control. Moreover, by facilitating the separation of planning and control from action, budgets and other mechanisms for financial control have played a key role in enabling the centralised managerial control of ever larger groupings of activities.

An organisational view of budgeting also highlights the social as well as economic and technical nature of budgetary outcomes, a fact that is well known to practitioners of the craft. 'The budget' is a reflection of the underlying political structure of the organisation, as well as economic constraints and opportunities and the technical procedures out of which it arose. It has a social as well as an economic significance, reflecting the outcomes of debates over organisational power and influence, the social location of uncertainties and constraints within the organisation, and the allocation of organisational resources.

Therefore, in the realm of accounting practice as distinct from that of the accounting textbook, it is difficult, if not impossible, to disentangle the organisational and the technical aspects of budgeting. Both shape each other. The technical components are designed to activate organisational processes, and can themselves help to shape participants' perceptions of the organisational domain. And budgeting, in turn, achieves its significance through those organisational processes which the techniques engender.

To further our understanding of the organisational nature of budgeting, we will consider the many and often conflicting purposes which it serves, the processes which give rise to the practice of budgeting, and the different ways in which budgetary information can be used. We conclude with some speculations on the possible relationships between financial practice and organisational performance.

Budgeting as a Multi-purpose Activity

Budgeting can serve a variety of roles and purposes, often simultaneously. Even several purposes can enter into the justification and implementation of a budgetary control system, as different managerial groups, or even individuals, emphasise different roles which it can serve. Those in the finance department, for instance, can have interests and needs in mind very different from those in production and marketing, let alone general management; and yet all might agree on the need for an extension of budgetary practice. And the purposes to which budgeting is put also can be very different from those which entered into its original justification. For, once installed, budgetary systems have some measure of autonomy. As the technical apparatus becomes inter-twined with the activities of a wider array of organisational participants, it can be used to further a diverse and often conflicting array of organisational and personal ends.

Such a view of budgeting in action suggests that it would be a difficult and rather futile activity to list, in isolation from the organisational context in which they operate, the purposes which budgets and other mechanisms for financial control have come to serve. They are so diverse, and often so idiosyncratic, that very little of general value would be gained from the exercise. Instead, we shall try to understand some of the ways in which the practice of budgeting and financial control can arise out of the interplay of organisational processes, paying particular attention to how they are implicated in the processes of decision making.

Different Approaches to Organisational Decision Making

Decision making in organisations takes place in the context of uncertainty or disagreement over both the objectives and consequences of action. Different participant groups, both within and outside the organisation, have different views of both the desirable and the achievable. Whilst those with financial inclinations, for example, might seek to establish the primacy of economic ends, those interested in the management of the organisation's technical resources might articulate concerns with either more immediate physical indicators of performance, or the organisation's longer-term innovative potential. These, in turn, might well be different from the interests emphasised by marketing and personnel management groups. For the organisation is rarely an assembly of the agreed. Debate and deliberation are almost inevitable features of organisational life. With different interests and perspectives coming together to constitute the organised endeavour, objectives, as such, are rarely pre-given, but rather emerge out of the interplay of organisational pressures, constraints and opportunities. At times there might be a temporary resolution with many, if not all, agreed on the primacy of particular overall concerns. Equally, there might be agreement over the aims of either particular organisational actions or the activities of particular organisational units. At other times, however, discord and debate might well be the only way of characterising the organisational mission.

Views over the consequences of particular organisational actions are subject to no less variation. Where there is considerable investment in past experience and where the environment for action is stable and known, relative certainty may prevail. Organisational participants may then be able to presume that particular sequences of actions are likely to result in certain patterns of consequences. On other occasions, however, the

Uncertainty over the objectives for action

		Relative certainty	Relative uncertainty
Uncertainty over the consequences of action	Relative certainty	COMPUTATION	BARGAINING
	Relative uncertainty	JUDGEMENT	INSPIRATION

Figure 11.1   *Uncertainty and Decision Making Processes*

consequences of action may be far from predictable. With either limited experience or a volatile and poorly understood environment, they are likely to be subject to disagreement and debate. A whole range of possible consequences will then have to be considered at some stage in the decision making process.

What are the consequences of acknowledging such a variety of uncertainties in decision making? If in any particular instance the objectives for action are clear and undisputed, and if the consequences of action can also be presumed to be known, decision making can then proceed in a computational manner, as illustrated in figure 11.1.[1] In such circumstances it is possible to compute whether the consequences of the action or set of actions being considered will, or will not, satisfy the objectives that have been unambiguously articulated beforehand. As the consequences of action become more uncertain, however, the potential for computation diminishes.

1.   The discussion of organisational decision making is based on J.D. Thompson and A. Tuden, Strategies, structures and processes of organisational decision, in J.D. Thompson *et al.* (eds), *Comparative Studies in Administration*, University of Pittsburgh Press 1959. See also J.D. Thompson, *Organisations in Action*, McGraw-Hill 1967. Further discussions of the subsequent extension of this decision making framework to take account of the organisational roles of information and control systems are given in M.J. Earl and A.G. Hopwood, From management information to information management (a paper presented at the IFIP TC8—WG 8.2 Working Conference on the Information Systems Environment, Bonn 1979; to be published in *Organisational Dynamics*) and A.G. Hopwood, Information systems and organisational reality, Occasional Paper No. 5, Thames Valley Regional Management Centre 1980.

Decisions then have to be made in a judgmental manner, with organisational participants subjectively appraising the array of possible consequences in the light of the agreed objective or objectives. Just as the introduction of uncertainty into the specification of the consequences of action results in a different approach to decision making, so does the acknowledgement of debate or uncertainty over the objectives themselves. If the consequences of action are presumed to be known, disagreement or uncertainty over objectives results in a political, rather than a computational, rationale for action, as organisational participants seek to further their own particular objectives. A range of interests in action are articulated in such circumstances and decision making, as a result, tends to be characterised by bargaining and compromise. And when even the consequences of action are in dispute, decision processes can be complex indeed, being rather positively characterised in figure 11.1 as of an inspirational nature! With so little known beforehand, rationales for action can emerge in the course of the decision making process itself.

Mechanisms for financial planning and control, like other information and control systems, invariably have been justified in terms of the contribution which they make to organisational decision making. In providing such rationales, the process of decision making has only rarely been considered in social terms, however. Emphasis has repeatedly been placed on the economic and the technical, rather than on the social and the political. If, in contrast, we do try to recognise, not only such a social context, but also the variety of approaches to decision making that can stem from the uncertainties that might be inherent in both the consequences of action and the objectives for action, what insights can we gain into the roles which such mechanisms serve? How, in other words, might interests in budgets and other financial procedures emerge out of organisational decision processes? And what different roles might they serve in the contexts of the computational, the judgmental, the political and the inspirational? To such questions let us now turn.

Accounting and Computational Practice

Given low uncertainty over both the consequences and the

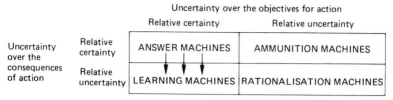

Figure 11.2 *Uncertainty, Decision Making and the Role of Information and Control Systems*

objectives of organisational action, we approach the management scientist's definition of certainty where algorithms, formulae and rules can be derived to solve problems by computation. Alternatively, this situation may represent what Herbert Simon[2] has called structured decision making, where the intelligence, design and choice phases are all specifiable and programmable. And in case you have not recognised it, this is also the organisational world presumed by many introductory management accounting textbooks!

In all cases a wide variety of management practices, including the mechanisms of financial planning and control, can serve as what in figure 11.2 are termed 'answer machine' aids to decision making. The techniques of budgeting and investment appraisal, for instance, can further the evaluation of proposed actions in the light of agreed financial objectives. By providing a way of comparing the achievable and the desirable, in a world of relative certainty, the computations introduce a powerful element of structure into the decision making process. Similarly, the practice of budgeting can facilitate the co-ordination and integration of organisational activities by computational means. Production and marketing operations can be synthesised, inventory policies evaluated and amended in the light of envisaged organisational circumstances, and the consequences for particular organisational resources, such as cash, calculated and evaluated.

Moreover, some, at least, of the certainties which enable the use of computational approaches can be created by managerial action, rather than having to be implicit within the organisational task. By a judicious management of inventory, for

2.   H.A. Simon, *The New Science of Management Decision*, Harper and Row 1960.

instance, production operations can sometimes be temporarily buffered from the uncertainties inherent in the market place. The impact of other uncertainties can be isolated by the availability of surplus capacity and resources. And internal organisational boundaries can be drawn so that the more certain spheres of organisational endeavour can be managed in partial isolation from their more uncertain context. In ways such as these, the organisational and the technical can together create a particular decision making environment. With organisational strategies creating pockets of activities with higher predictability and surer ends, computational approaches to decision making can function and flourish in otherwise alien terrains.

Accounting and Organisational Learning

In the context of judgmental decision making, such 'answer machine' approaches are no longer of such direct value. Acknowledging the uncertainties that are inherent in action requires that they be confronted rather than managed.

Of course, many of the procedures created to serve 'answer machine' roles are still used in judgmental contexts. Often, however, this is in spite of, rather than because of, the underlying uncertainties over the consequences of organisational action! So in circumstances which cry out for information to stimulate managerial learning and the exercise of judgement, we find routine financial evaluation and control systems which often assume the very certainties which cannot be found. Indeed, as is illustrated by the arrows in figure 11.2, such procedures have been subjected to enormous increases in technical sophistication as various experts have sought to extend the boundaries of computational practice. The articulation of forms of risk and probabilistic analysis in a budgetary context bears witness to such tendencies.

Often, however, computational procedures are used in a judgmental context, but in very different ways. Rather than directly facilitating the search for answers, they are used to explore problems and to probe into assumptions and the range of possible implications. Serving to stimulate the human mind, they can be used to analyse the analysable before organisational participants finally resort to judgement. In figure 11.2 such approaches are referred to as 'learning machines', in order to emphasise the potential for a more active interplay between the technical and the cognitive.

Sensitivity analyses involving the multiple use of computational procedures are of this type, as is the use of simulation models in budgeting and planning. In both cases the procedures can help organisational participants to appreciate the nature of the decision environment in which they are working. And the iterations to and from departments and organisational levels which characterise the practice of budgeting point to a similar interrelationship between the computational and the judgmental. Indeed, one of the most frequently quoted purposes of budgeting, that of encouraging an active concern with the future, focuses on the learning rather than the mere calculative potential of the process.[3] When seen in this way, the procedures of budgeting can serve to emphasise the need to investigate, albeit if thereafter to constrain, the financial and wider organisational implications of possible future activities. By iteration and deliberation, the discipline and structure which are implicit in the budgetary process can stimulate organisational participants to reflect on at least some of the implications of what they are proposing; to test out their assumptions and estimates, and ascertain whether the necessary resources are likely to be available to the organisation as a whole and its constituent parts.

Accounting and Political Processes

Whilst the roles served by the procedures of financial planning and control in computational and judgmental decision situations have been explicitly discussed in the official literature of accounting, those which are served when the objectives of action are themselves subject to debate have not. In their writings, at least, accountants have tended to assume that the objectives of organised endeavour are given. By now you are all familiar with those seemingly unproblematic

3. A stimulating discussion of the role of planning in organisational and social learning is given in D. Michael, *On Learning to Plan and Planning to Learn*, Jossey-Bass 1973.

assertions that the objectives of a firm are '. . . to maximise profits', '. . . to maximise cash flow', '. . . to maximise shareholder wealth', or whatever. Fortunately or unfortunately, such assertions represent gross abstractions from organisational practice, useful for some purposes perhaps, but of limited value when trying to understand rather than influence the ways in which organised endeavour emerges out of coalitions of interests and concerns. For when objectives are themselves uncertain and decisions characterised by bargaining and debate, financial planning and control practices can arise out of the political processes which permeate organisational life, serving as (in the terminology of figure 11.2) 'ammunition machines' to articulate and promote particular interested positions and values. Rather than being reflective of agreed ends, the mechanisms of financial control seek to articulate and further particular ends.

Indeed, budgeting and other mechanisms for financial control most likely achieved a great deal of their present organisational significance because of the roles which they came to play in furthering the centralised, financially orientated, control of large organisations, whether public or private. In this context, however, it should be stated that financial practices cannot be operated independently of other management practices. They both reinforce and, in turn, enable to operate those practices which establish particular patterns of organisational segmentation: the procedures which delineate management responsibilities, the methods for the regular reporting of performance, and the practices, formal or otherwise, for the evaluation of managerial performance.[4] Seen in such terms, mechanisms for financial control are but one component of the battery of control practices which enabled and assisted the birth of the modern organisation.

In such a constellation of management practices, budgeting and other mechanisms for financial control nevertheless have a

4.   For discussions of the organisational origins of management accounting and related practices see A. Chandler and H. Deams, Administrative co-ordination, allocation and monitoring: a comparative analysis of the emergence of accounting and organisation in the USA and Europe, *Accounting, Organisations and Society*, Vol. 4, Nos. 1 and 2, 1979.

number of vital roles to play. Out of the mass of organisational actions and their consequences, they can influence those which become relatively more visible and influential, particularly to senior management groups. And the visibility so established is invariably an asymmetric one: the powerful can observe the less powerful (but not vice versa), as a rather particular mode of surveillance is established. The centralised co-ordination of activities can thereby be facilitated. Equally, however, demands, requirements, pressures and influences can be more readily passed down through the organisation, particularly in the spheres of the financial and the economic, because of the disaggregative arithmetical properties of the accounting art. Budgeting and financial reporting practices together can provide the framework within which a measured and observed delegation of authority can take place. A pattern of expectations can be established, an organisational ethos articulated, and even motivations influenced, as the visibility which is created provides a basis for organisational rewards and sanctions. Moreover, by influencing the accepted language of negotiation and discourse, control and reporting systems can help to shape what is regarded as problematic, what can be deemed to be a credible solution and, perhaps most important of all, the criteria which ought to be used in the selection of a particular solution. Even the more ritualistic roles of budgeting are important in this context.[5] As one senior manager once commented: 'You will never understand the budgetary system in my company unless you realise that it is like a rosary bead: it quite simply makes sure that every manager says profit, cost, cash, working capital, etc. at least a thousand times a year!'

Accounting and the Rationalisation of Organisational Action

However, financial reporting practices are used not only to influence what is to be. Although the realms of the computational, the judgmental and the political can be important, in all organisations they are complemented by the inspirational,

5. An interesting discussion of the ritualistic and mythical roles of accounting is given in T. Gambling, Magic, accounting and morale, *Accounting, Organisations and Society*, Vol. 2, No. 2, 1977.

where actions arise out of the uncertainties of both aims and consequences. And even that particular variety of decision making provides a basis for roles which the mechanisms of financial planning and control can serve. In such circumstances, the roles are related to the justification and legitimation of what has been decided upon. In the terminology of figure 11.2, financial practices serve as 'rationalisation machines' in such a context.

The widespread use of capital budgeting procedures, for instance, has resulted in the availability of justification devices for proposals which have gained early commitment and support, as well as simply providing information (prior to decision making) on those proposals which remain problematic to the end.[6] Having decided on action, organisational participants can consciously or otherwise manage the calculations which are used for its more official evaluation. Similarly, budgets and plans can be built around what is to be. Particularly in the context of large, complex and highly innovative decisions, organisational knowledge of the preconditions for action can be widely dispersed and plans can serve to provide a more general, albeit retrospectively created, rationale. Even quite complex procedures for evaluation and control can arise out of the need to marshall support for action. The emergent apparatus of social cost—benefit analysis served such purposes in the nineteenth century,[7] let alone today, and many more recent innovations in control system design have originated from the pressures to maintain an organisation's autonomy for action in the face of external pressures and influences.[8]

6.   Further insights into the retrospective interpretation of action are given in K. Weick, *The Social Psychology of Organising*, 2nd edn, Addison-Wesley 1979.
7.   G. Pringle, The early development of cost—benefit analysis, *Journal of Agricultural Economics*, January 1978, pp. 63—71. For a further discussion of the role of accounting in the rationalisation of action see S. Burchell, C. Clubb, A.G. Hopwood, J. Hughes and J. Nahapiet, The roles of accounting in organisations and society, *Accounting, Organisations and Society*, Vol. 4, No. 4, 1979.
8.   See J. Meyer and B. Rowan, The structure of educational organisations, in M.W. Meyer *et al.* (eds), *Environments and Organisations*, Jossey-Bass 1978.

Pressures for the practices of financial planning and control therefore arise in many ways. Whilst accounting textbooks continue to emphasise those which reflect a particular computational rationality, other rationales are equally influential in organisational life. For, faced with the uncertainties and complexities of organised action, information is a vital resource. It can serve to constrain and influence in a political context, facilitate the exercise of judgement, and legitimise what has been done, as well as what might be. All such roles, including the computational, have provided organisational bases for the development of the technical practice of budgeting and financial control and, of equal importance, all continue to influence the use which is made of that practice, regardless of its specific organisational origins. Indeed, many of the complexities and dilemmas which characterise budgeting in action stem from the very diversity of the uses which have been, and are, made of it.

Budgeting and Organisational Action

With such diverse origins and uses, it is hardly surprising that the organisational practice of budgeting and financial control is complex, grounded as it is in the intricacies of organisational processes and politics. Unfortunately, however, all too little is systematically known about the organisational functioning of budgeting and other control practices. Whilst a wealth of experiential insights are potentially available, comparatively few attempts have been made to probe into the underlying organisational processes, the ways in which control practices do and do not interrelate with other management practices, and their significance for organisational performance.[9] Much

9. Some rich and interesting insights into the practice of budgeting in public organisations are given in A. Wildavsky, *The Politics of the Budgetary Process*, 2nd edn, Little, Brown 1974; A. Wildavsky, Policy analysis is what information systems are not, *Accounting, Organisations and Society*, Vol. 3, No. 1, 1978; and H. Heclo and A. Wildavsky, *The Private Government of Public Money*, Macmillan 1974. The last reference is based on British experience, whilst the others are based on US practice. Unfortunately there

of what is known contrasts with the rather stark computational and procedural rationality that has been codified in and propogated by accounting texts. Compared with the economic analytics of the latter, ongoing practice has been seen to be often characterised by bargaining, controversy and debate, and by a rather loose, indeed ill-defined and shifting, relationship with many other management practices; with its consequences being dependent upon the wider organisational processes in which it is embedded and which determine how it is used.

The Strategies of Budgeting

Assembling a budget for a large organisation is a massive as well as contentious endeavour. The persons engaged in the process have, of necessity, to use strategies to reduce both the uncertainty of the endeavour and the sheer burden of calculation, as well as to promote particular interests and aims. As a result the process is often an incremental activity. Emphasis is placed on the deviations which might be made from the firmer historical base of either past budgets or past performance. And because of, rather than in spite of, the complexity of the task, budgeting is an activity which is invariably characterised by the use of the simplest rules of thumb.

However, although such approaches reduce the burden of calculation and breadth of debate, these benefits are gained at the expense of focusing the remaining discussion on the areas of particular uncertainty and controversy, namely the changes from one year to the next. 'Is an increase justified?' 'And what of the over-spending on last year's budget?' 'Should this year's budget be the same or higher?' Careful analysis can, of course, provide some assistance, but since the basic problem involves the extrapolation of an uncertain past into an uncertain future, analysis alone cannot solve the problem. Lobbying, exhortation and an array of bargaining and simplifying strategies come into play.

---

are no similar descriptions of business practice, although the interested reader might consult the descriptive studies of capital budgeting reported in J. Bower, *Managing the Resource Allocation Process*, Graduate School of Business Administration, Harvard University 1970.

Where proposed activities are beyond the comprehension of budget officers and senior managers, the final decision may well depend on their impressions of factors which, although relatively minor, are nevertheless within the bounds of their own experience. Financial procedures themselves can also contribute to such simplifying processes, as they are used to force the debate along more predictable lines. Budgetary decisions can also be made within the context of a predetermined amount of resources which are to be allocated. 'How much can we afford?' then becomes more important than the objectives which might be attained, and organisational norms develop to guide the priority to be given to individual requests. A multitude of other similar simplifying strategies may be used; but in the end, if all else fails, the 'big meat-axe' approach (as it was called by one senior manager) may be used to 'just arbitrarily, without logic, dictate a cut of $x\%$ across the board'.[10]

Such strategies are a response, not only to the uncertainties and complexities which are inherent in the budgetary process, but also to the fact that budget demands reflect individual and group ambitions. Intertwining the logic of both economics and politics, the demands are strategies in an intensely serious game. The ability to estimate 'what will go' is a vital skill. Managers seek out facts and opinions, in order to arrive at an estimate of what they should ask for in the light of what they can expect to get and then, with due 'padding' to allow for anticipated cuts, they seek to market their budgetary demands. The support of others is actively canvassed and demands are packaged in the most appealing way. Tangible results can be given undue weight and complex activities described in either the simplest or the most complex of terms — but not the more understandable mean! Emphasis can be placed on the qualitative rather than the measurable advantages, the forthcoming rather than the current results, and the procedures to be gone through rather than the outcomes to be achieved. Points can be stretched a little, but never so far as can be

10.   C.C. Schwarz, The behavioural aspects of accounting data for performance evaluations at industrial nucleonics, in T.J. Burns (ed.), *The Behavioural Aspects of Accounting Data for Performance Evaluation*, College of Administrative Science, The Ohio State University 1970, p. 101.

tested. If some cuts are seen to be inevitable, essential or popular activities can be pruned first, in anticipation of their subsequent restoration. It can even be pleaded that the smallest of cuts could damage an entire programme of activities. For new activities it is often beneficial to emphasise their relationship to the old, and sometimes it is best to demonstrate that they can either 'pay for themselves' or that it is a case of 'spending a bit now to save a lot later'.

The practice of budgeting provides a forum for organisational debate. It can influence what are regarded as viable organisational strategies, and the techniques of budgeting themselves can be used more actively to influence and constrain the political processes which constitute organisational life. In the last resort, however, the technical components of both budgeting and other mechanisms of financial control are only a part of a wider organisational process — a process which combines the technical and the economic with the human and the political.

Using Budgetary Information

Very different approaches can be used to disseminate budgetary and other financial information through the organisation. Attempts can be made to ensure its widespread availability, or it can reside in the hands of a few. Many can participate in the processes from which it arises, or it can emanate from the higher realms of corporate authority. It can be integrated with other management practices, particularly those concerned with organisational evaluation and the provision of recognition and reward, or it can remain a rather detached endeavour, only loosely related to other aspects of organisational functioning. Because of such options, the practices of financial control have few automatic and obvious consequences. If there are consequences, they stem from the ways in which the financial controls intertwine with other organisational processes and from the managerial contexts which influence if, and how, they are used.

In the area of performance evaluation, for instance, comparisons of budgeted and actual performance can be used in very different ways. Even in large organisations noted for the sophistication and rigour of their financial planning and control practices, the data provided by them may have little influence on managerial concerns, if they are seen as being the almost exclusive province of specialist financial experts who are detached from the mainstream of management practice. At the other extreme, a great deal of managerial emphasis can be placed on the data.[11] For instance, data may be taken at their face value and used to influence the distribution of organisational recognition and rewards. Such use, however, can result in explicit concern with the data as such, rather than with the underlying organisational transactions which they (imperfectly) reflect. In such ways perceptions of the intra-organisational boundaries which are implicit within the budgetary framework can be intensified, lateral as well as hierarchical conflicts thereby engendered, and the budgets and accounts subjected to 'padding' and manipulation. In other contexts, however, the data can be used in more problem oriented ways, not being emphasised in their own right but evaluated, questioned and used alongside other pertinent information, both formal and informal.

An appreciation of the different ways in which financial planning and control practices are used in organisations must therefore be based on an understanding of the human and social contexts out of which their use arises. Technical understandings alone are not sufficient. The interpretation and use of the information provided by financial practices, although influenced by the technical characteristics of those practices, is also the outcome of personal and social processes which are sustained by the meanings, beliefs, pressures and purposes that are brought to bear by both organisational participants and external agents. It can be ultimately intertwined with the use of managerial power. External pressures and demands can create particular rationales for the economic and the financial. And in striving to facilitate the decision making process, its use can be influenced by the ways in which organisational participants clarify and define the problematic, the possible and the desirable. In placing the information in their own wider contexts, managers and employees provide

11.   For a more comprehensive discussion see A.G. Hopwood, *An Accounting System and Managerial Behaviour*, Saxon House 1973.

the information with a personal and organisational significance. In this way the information can be, and is, used in a variety of ways — and with a variety of consequences.

Some Thoughts on the Consequences of Financial Control Practices

Budgeting and other practices of financial planning and control have been shown to have a complex relationship to organisational functioning. Although invariably introduced in the name of economic efficiency, their origins and functioning have been seen to have as much to do with political and social, as with economic, rationality. Whilst they can, and do, facilitate economic decision making, they can also be used to introduce a particular political order, reinforce patterns of organisational power and segmentation, and provide for the legitimacy and understanding of the organisational past as well as playing a role in the creation of the organisational future. Once introduced into an organisation, the use which is made of financial practices, and thereby the consequences which they have, is shaped by the ways in which they interrelate with other complex organisational processes. Capable of being influenced by a wide variety of pressures, practices and beliefs, they can have a range of possible consequences, only some of which would be deemed to be compatible with the furtherance of economic performance.

In fact, we know very little about the organisational consequences of the practices of financial planning and control. A great deal of their ultimate utility has been taken on faith, despite the all-too-evident differences in investment in them made by different, but apparently equally successful, organisations. Rather than probing into the ways in which they operate and the consequences which they have, analysts have been content to emphasise the adequacy of the economic logic inherent in their construction and technical design. However, as we have seen, the technical can have an ambiguous relationship with the organisational; and the ultimate consequences of even economic rationales can be determined in the spheres of the social and the political as well as the economic — interrelationships which are only partially understood at the organisational level.

Perhaps in the light of these observations it should not be surprising that what evidence is available, which is not very much, points to the rather equivocal relationship between organisational performance and the practices of financial planning and control.[12] On the positive side, there are some insights into the processes through which they can facilitate organisational choice and action by helping to shape patterns of organisational visibility, influencing thereby perceptions of both the problematic and the possible and reinforcing certain sequences of actions and constraining others. Some other evidence is potentially more questioning, however. In part, this might reflect very different approaches to the organisational dissemination of the practices: at least on occasions, even potentially favourable consequences might not be exploited. And on other occasions, the evidence no doubt reflects the fact that poorly performing organisations tend to be the ones which systematically increase their investment in the practices of financial control as they seek, possibly with uncertain effect, to re-establish a particular economic order — a phenomenon which has been termed 'newly poor behaviour'. However, the evidence which remains is still consistent with the possibility that particularly heavy emphases on the rigours of financial planning and control can hinder, rather than facilitate, the achievement of economic ends. For organisations are complex artifacts, the survival and development of which are dependent on the mutual satisfaction of numerous and often conflicting demands, both internal and external to the organisation itself. To focus on any one, without due care, might result in the neglect of others, on which (paradoxically) the achievement of the focal concern can, in turn, depend.

If for no other reason, the equivocality of such findings

12. A very brief discussion of some of the evidence is given in A.G. Hopwood, Criteria of corporate effectiveness, in M. Brodie and R. Bennett (eds), *Perspectives on Managerial Effectiveness*, Thames Valley Regional Management Centre 1979, pp. 81—96.

points to the need for an organisational, as well as technical, appreciation of the financial craft.

Conclusion

In seeking to demonstrate both the breadth and potential of an organisational and behavioural understanding of the practices of financial planning and control, consideration has been given to how interests in such practices can arise out of organisational processes; and how those processes, in turn, can shape the use which is made of the practices and the consequences which they might have. Our explorations accordingly have taken us into realms that remain implicit within accounting texts. Almost inevitably, many problems have been raised rather than answered. Indeed, even conflicting tendencies have been acknowledged. For rather than focusing on detailed understandings and research findings, emphasis has been placed on illuminating the range of issues where an organisational appreciation can provide not only new, but useful, insights. All too obviously, the arena for such a discussion is enormous, both in scope and potential. Many issues of importance have not been discussed, or have received only fleeting mention. Hopefully, however, those issues which have been considered will stimulate you to think and read about those which have not.[13]

13.   A more comprehensive introduction to the area is provided by A.G. Hopwood, *Accounting and Human Behaviour*, Prentice-Hall 1974.

12

Financial Planning and Control in Large Companies

CYRIL TOMKINS

Professor of Business Finance,
University of Bath

Introduction

The selection of formal quantitative measurements is usually a key part of designing control systems for large organisations. Segments of the business may be assessed mainly upon the basis of one main indicator, such as profit or rate of return on investment (ROI), or by a consideration of multiple measures where each one is supposed to signal a different aspect of performance. It will be argued later in this chapter that control systems of modern large and complex corporations must normally be based on multiple measures of performance and, indeed, often incorporate non-financial as well as financial indicators. Moreover, it is proposed that there is no universal 'golden rule' which determines the type of control system to be used (simple or multiple index, financial or non-financial factors, etc). Accordingly, the best that one can do when writing normatively about control systems is to develop a clear methodology showing how the appropriate system for an organisation can be found, rather than what it should be. In other words, the appropriate financial control system is likely to be unique for each large organisation.

This is not to say that there are no general features common to different companies. Indeed some writers, currently following similar developments in the literature on organisation analysis, profess to be seeking a 'contingency theory of financial control systems'. Such writers believe that organisations can be classified in different ways and that members of each will exhibit similar financial control system characteristics. There is no doubt that, at a general level, some success will be achieved in this direction; however, it is this writer's belief (but it is not a proven point) that very limited progress will be made with this approach beyond the identification of *very general* 'contingent features'. To offer specific advice to individual organisations, one must be aware of the particular circumstances facing the organisation, the type of people in it and its specific environment. Of course, other organisations will have some features similar to those of the organisation being advised, but, especially with large companies, the particular *blend* of 'contingent factors' may well be unique to each organisation, requiring unique features in the control system.

Despite these introductory words and the promise that a case will be made later in this chapter for corporate financial controllers widening their notions of controllership to include non-financial factors, there are still problems associated with traditional primary financial measures that warrant attention. Moreover, formal financial measures of performance are still dominant indicators of company and sub-unit performance and almost certainly will remain a very important element of any wider scheme of evaluation which may be developed. This is understandable, for even where clear non-financial goals are set, there should always be a careful consideration of the financial costs or profits foregone in order to achieve the non-financial goals. Consequently, we shall turn first to a consideration of traditional financial measures.

Divisionalisation of Companies

As corporate groups grew larger and more complex, ways were sought to divide them up so that much of the decision making could be delegated, while overall control and co-ordination of the enterprise could be maintained. This led to many groups dividing themselves up into divisions, where each division was responsible for a particular group of products or a geographical region. In the main, the large UK controlled companies that 'divisionalised' formed divisions for each country or continent and formed product group divisions within the international divisions. Later, many companies formed more complex structures with (for example) the same product groups being the responsibility of one manager world-wide, while the country operating divisions were maintained. This meant that a product group manager in a country or continent could have responsibilities to both the international divisional manager and the world-wide product group manager. However, let us continue with the more traditional divisional structure for the time being.

Although it is a simplification of how divisions are operated, they can be described as either profit centres or investment centres. All types of divisions will be responsibile for revenues as well as costs, so that performance can be assessed by profits earned. However, some types of divisions have wider dis-cretion over the amount of investment to be undertaken and in those cases, obviously, assessment of financial performance by profit alone is inadequate: one needs to relate the profit earned to the investment used to generate that profit. The discussion will begin with profit centres and later deal with investment centres.

Profit Centres

Profit centres will be defined here as segments of a business which are primarily assessed on the basis of the amount of profit they earn and which have considerable discretion in framing their own production, cost and revenue policies. It will be appropriate, therefore, to consider first the strengths and weaknesses of the accounting profit measure as a means of segment performance evaluation.

The profit measure is so familiar that readers may think its strengths are obvious. However, there is so much criticism of

accounting profit in the recent performance evaluation literature, that it is worthwhile being explicit about its strengths.

To begin with, a profit measure is relatively comprehensive
in the sense of summarising a variety of activities in one figure.
It is not totally comprehensive, because conventional accounting methodologies do not measure all aspects of performance
which affect a company's future. Most notable, perhaps, is
the state of human labour and executive force. Some debate
has taken place, mostly in the academic circles, about whether
'human assets' should be valued and placed in the balance
sheet and their 'depreciation', positive or negative, included
in the profit calculation. However, only one or two companies
have attempted to do this. Nevertheless, while a profit measure
is obviously not completely comprehensive, it is relatively
comprehensive compared to other possible measures.

Next, a profit measure is easily decomposable into determinants of profitability. While a profit centre may be evaluated
primarily by the profit figure itself, this does not mean that
the division will not have to explain variations in profit by
reference to causal factors and support such reasons with
figures. In addition, the division will itself wish to control
activities during an operational period and need to be able to
estimate how variations in sub-activies will affect profit. Consequently, there is a basic need for information about individual activities which can be aggregated to provide an overall
measure of performance. The profit measure which emerges
from the detailed accounting system provides a means of
making systematic investigations into divisional activities
when the need arises. One may contrast this attribute of
accounting profit with the increase in wealth received by
shareholders in each period. The latter is the dividend received
during the period, plus the increase in share price. While conceptually this may be a better measure of shareholders' gain,
there is no way of directly unscrambling that overall measure
in a way that is operationally useful for controlling segments
of the business.

The accounting profit measure is also relatively objective
and it can be audited. If subordinates feel they are being
assessed on the basis of a performance measure, they may
wish to be assured that their evaluators are using a measure

which does not depend on too many subjective factors. Of course, because the profit measure is not fully comprehensive, some judgement will have to be used in evaluating the significance of a change in profit performance. But while the profit measure is not perfect, it does make a fairly creditable attempt at incorporating those factors which can be captured with a fair degree of objectivity.

Furthermore, the word 'profit' has through time gained a prestige attachment. To say that a manager is 'profit responsible' indicates that he has more independence and greater responsibilities than a cost centre manager. This is almost a truism, because evaluation by segment profit measures was introduced in order to allow greater subordinate independence. However, it is often argued that to make a person 'profit responsible' does now carry connotations of prestige and, hence, perhaps the use of that term itself may be a good motivator.

Irrespective of its strengths, the accounting profit measure does have weaknesses. First, as readers will know, the measure contains allocations over time in respect of various types of costs and, perhaps, revenues as well. Moreover, the measure focuses on the short run; it is not a very good indicator of the future well-being of the organisation. Also, like any formal measure, it may encourage managers to pay more attention to measured performance rather than actual performance; and this, in turn, may lead to managers manipulating activities, or even the measures themselves, in order to improve the reported performance — even though they know that their action is not in the long-run interests of the whole organisation. However, this criticism applies to *any* measure of performance, not just profit, and very few companies would accept that performance need not be measured at all. Finally, perhaps the most important of the weaknesses is that the conventional accounting profit figures do not fully incorporate the notion of opportunity costs. In other words, the profit measure may show that performance has improved, but it does not give any indication whether much better profit opportunities have been missed.

In conclusion, then, the profit measure does have defects and has been severely criticised. But it must be recognised that it has stood the test of time and so must have something significant to commend it. It has such obvious strengths that it cannot be completely discarded from consideration as a main tool of divisional evaluation, unless our society changes much more dramatically than even the current processes suggest. It is interesting to note that the USSR also uses profit for segment evaluation purposes. The objective of systems designers should be to recognise the weaknesses of the profit measure and allow for them by other means, and not to reject a very useful measure.

The Profit Measure

There are possibly four different aspects of the profit measure which could be used for divisional performance evaluation purposes:

Contribution margin

Direct divisional profit

Profit before taxes

Net profit

Contribution margin is the gross margin (sales less cost of sales), less variable divisional expenses. Some companies use this notion of surplus, but they confuse the role of contribution margin and the nature of profit centre control. Contribution margin is an approximate guide to the amount by which profits may be increased by changing the level of production. It does not include all the cost elements which the divisional manager may control or influence. Many fixed costs are controllable at divisional level and hence contribution margin is not a good index of the divisional manager's performance or of the profitability of the division itself.

Direct divisional profit is contribution margin, less cost which can be directly traced to the division whether controllable or not. This measure of profit may be criticised because, according to the conventional literature, a divisional manager's performance should only be evaluated in terms of the things over which he has control. Recently some academics have questioned this, arguing (approximately) that in most divisionalised companies there will be some activities, costs or revenues which will never be wholly under one person's control; and that by incorporating those elements into the evaluation measures of each of two or several persons who do have joint control, one is encouraging collaboration in the control process. Moreover, manager collaboration and the inclusion of non-controllable costs in segment reports may have the advantage of encouraging risk pooling throughout the organisation.[1] These ideas are rather novel in the management accounting literature, which still tends to emphasise that only those costs which are controllable by a manager should be included in his assessment. A deviation from the 'accepted theory' has not yet been fully explored, but it may indicate that the defect of not making the profit figure relate only to costs and revenues controllable by the divisional manager may not be too serious.

In terms of assessing the division's contribution to the whole group's profitability, direct divisional profit is weak, because it includes no charge for corporate costs. Some argue that direct divisional profit cannot therefore be compared with the published data of other companies in the same industry. However, in this writer's experience few companies place substantial reliance on external comparisons of this sort in assessing short-term divisional performance and so once again there is room to question the practical validity of such an argument.

Profit before taxes is calculated after all the group's pre-tax costs have been allocated or assigned directly to the divisions. Given the argument above, that it may be desirable to allocate costs which are not controllable by divisions, this measure of performance may be satisfactory in terms of assessing divisional manager performance. It is difficult to decide the issue in isolation from an actual application, although many texts are

1.   For further discussion see J.S. Demski, Uncertainty and evaluation based on controllable performance, *Journal of Accounting Research*, Autumn 1976.

dogmatic on the point. A change in allocated central group costs may make it appear that a divisional manager has a worse performance than before, when it is no fault of his, and so allocating such costs *may* lead to disputes and disaffection with the system — or at least lengthy debates about the allocations. However, some debate may be desirable and may even even act as an 'inverse control' on Head Office costs. This is a point put to the writer quite often in discussions with corporate controllers. Moreover, as discussed below, much will depend upon how the profit measure is used in the evaluation process. It is a mistake to think that it can be used only in one way and to focus on the profit figure to the exclusion of all else, even though the profit figure may be of prime importance. It appears from empirical studies that most domestic groups use profit before taxes as a formal measure of divisional performance, whereas multi-nationals use *net profit* (i.e. profit after taxes) as an index of achievement for their international divisions. The latter enables the divisional manager's ability to generate profit to be appraised net of the taxes appropriate to his own environment, which he should take into account to some extent in his decision making. Such a measure may be less than clear-cut for performance appraisal, if the international group head office plays a key role in balancing tax liabilities world-wide. However, for measuring performance of divisions within a country, the before tax measure will invariably be superior, because tax will almost certainly be dealt with at Head Office level. Whether using pre- or post-tax measures of profit, most groups usually make some allocations of central costs, but not necessarily all of them.

Transfer Pricing

A major problem of divisional profit measurement arises where there is a significant volume of trading undertaken between divisions. The question then arises as to what price should be used to record the purchases of the goods in the books of one division and the sale in the books of the others. Practices vary, with some companies using market price or approximations to it, while others use a calculated price based on various forms of cost, with or without additions for profit, etc.

Microeconomic theory has been used to show that if one wishes to get both the selling and buying division acting optimally in the sense of maximising their own and total group profits, the current transfer price should be the market price if there is a highly competitive market existing for the transferred goods. There is, in fact, some evidence to show that companies in such a situation tend to act in accordance with this rule.[2] However, microeconomics is not so satisfactory in terms of advising a *practical* rule where such a competitive intermediate product market does not exist.

Theorists have shown that autonomous group profit-maximising behaviour should be motivated by setting the transfer price equal to the marginal cost of production *at the optimal output level.* This is based on the simple notion that a division will go on producing up to full capacity, so long as the extra (marginal) revenue on each item sold is greater than the marginal cost of producing that item. If the division has a choice of selling to another division of the same group or to some organisation outside the group, the profit-maximising behaviour is to produce and sell to both markets until the marginal revenue in each market is equal to the marginal production cost at the optimal output level. This is in accordance with the basic neo-classical price discrimination model of microeconomics. However, while these conclusions are correct within the usual assumptions specified in such types of microeconomic analysis, there are practical difficulties in implementation.

Companies can usually only approximate marginal cost by use of the accounting notion of variable cost. Consequently, fixing a transfer price at variable cost, which is assumed constant for all levels of production, results in the producing division, at best, breaking-even in terms of the marginal profitability on the internal transfers. This is hardly likely to provide a strong motivation to sell internally within the

2.   See C.R. Tomkins, *Financial Planning in Divisionalised Companies,* Haymarket 1973.

group, even if it is in the group's interest. However, there are ways of dealing with this problem.

The trouble with using neo-classical economic theory to deduce practical rules of thumb is that the theory attempts to be too precise and aims to achieve *optimal* behaviour. In reality, companies are happy to achieve satisfactory profits rather than maximum profits. Indeed, given the uncertainties of real-world operation, different attitudes towards risks, and limited information quality and quantity, the notion of maximum profits loses most of its significance. Consequently, a tranfer price based on variable cost, plus a percentage-on-cost for profit and fixed costs, may not cause too great a departure from an apparent theoretical optimum − in other words it may motivate *satisfactory* performance. If it is decided that such transfer prices are preventing the group from achieving a trading arrangement which is deemed to be satisfactory, a two-part transfer pricing arrangement might be employed. The receiving division would pay the selling division a lump sum once a year for production capacity received and a transfer price based upon variable cost plus a small profit margin. However, not many companies deem it necessary to go to such lengths.

The above rules still need modification if a division is operating at full capacity. Then other divisions should pay at least the marginal revenue received from other organisations and this would normally be above the variable cost of production. A first stage in reviewing transfer price policy should therefore be to assess whether the producing division is likely to be at full capacity. If it is, prices should be fixed for the year on the basis of full capacity usage, taking into account both internal and external opportunities; and if it transpires that spare capacity becomes unexpectedly available, the producing division should advertise cut-price sales to both external and within-group customers. If full capacity is not expected, the previous proposals based on cost (single full-cost tranfer price or lump sum − 'variable cost plus' transfer price) alone will probably be sufficient to achieve a satisfactory level of internal trading.

There are various other proposals for transfer pricing schemes involving the use of different prices for buying and selling divisions and other arrangements, but space restriction prevents a full discussion of transfer pricing here and, in any case, most companies use one or other of the fairly straight-forward methods already described. There is just one fairly widely used practice not described above, and that is not to set a transfer price centrally at all, but to leave divisions free to negotiate with each other. Some claim this encourages inter-divisional co-operation and awareness of the other division's problems, and helps to increase total group profit-ability awareness. This seems consistent with the idea ex-pressed above that the inclusion of non-controllable costs in a divisional profit statement may induce inter-divisional co-operation. Obviously, if transfer prices are negotiated, they cannot be completely under the control of either divisional manager. Strangely, writers in management accounting do not argue that internally traded goods should be excluded from divisional profit statements when prices are negotiated, even though most do argue for exclusion of uncontrollable items. There is a considerable scope for refining our concepts of what is meant by 'controllable'. For many transactions, there is no simple dichotomy between controllable and un-controllable; and perhaps more attention should be paid to the notion of the degree of power to influence decisions in deciding what to include in segment profit statements used to evaluate managers of those corporate segments.

How the Profit Concept can be Used

Before leaving profit centres, it is important to ensure that the reader is not left with the impression that evaluation by a profit index must necessarily be a rigid process and, therefore, subject to all the defects in the measure specified earlier. It is quite likely that the Wimbledon champion this year would beat the author at tennis, even if the author had the best quality gut racquet whereas the professional had cheap nylon stringing. There is an art in using tools and the better craftsmen can often make good use of tools which are far from perfect.

While there may be a variety of styles in which the profit

measure may be used for divisional performance evaluation, for current purposes it is sufficient to distinguish two broadly different styles, each of which is associated with a different style of management. Even though top management may have decided to delegate decision making, there are different ways in which it can do so. First, a system of 'tight delegation' may be used, whereby divisional targets are set. Such an approach depends upon a management philosophy that divisional managers work best when they are required to meet short-term goals. Top management can assist divisional managers in solving many short-term problems and evaluate them to a large extent on the basis of personal contact, discussing revisions of targets at relatively frequent intervals and analysing reasons for under- or over-attainment. Under such a management approach, clear profit objectives would be set and any dysfunctional consequences of this apparently rigid approach would be overcome by the frequent contact between divisional and top management. Such an arrangement may strike the reader as odd. If divisionalisation was intended to provide autonomy to divisions in order to delegate certain senior management functions, it may seem contradictory for top management to set short-run targets and require frequent contact and discussion of progress. However, such an assumption really derives from the difficulty of expressing in a few words the subtleties of managerial processes. It *is* possible to leave prime responsibility for decison making with divisional managers, while still using top management as a sounding board for ideas and getting their views as to how new developments affect the group as a whole. *Apparently* rigid profit targets should not be taken as a naive use of such a measure, devoid of the benefits of informal communication and discussion.

The alternative extreme of management style is 'loose delegation'. The underlying philosophy of this approach can be summed up as follows. The best way to get results is to allow competent divisional managers to operate without constant interference from Head Office. Once again performance can be evaluated by profit measurement, but divisional managers will be informed that it is not their duty to adhere rigidly to profit plans, if circumstances change from those envisaged when the plan was constructed. In other words, *legitimate* failure will be permitted and the profit plan is a guide to action, not a specific target.

If used with common sense, sensitivity and flexibility, the notion of profit centres can therefore be a real aid to top management, through enabling delegation while at the same time maintaining overall control. The defects of profit measurement can be counteracted by sensible management practices. However, it sometimes appears that many companies do not take steps to avoid dysfunctional consequences of evaluating performance by profit measurement. One needs to be perpetually aware of the measure's defects and this should be explicitly recognised in the prescibed corporate management system.

Investment Centres

Earlier in this chapter it was stated that the major alternative to the profit centre concept in organising divisional companies was the investment centre. The latter implies that the divisional manager has discretion over investment as well as production, marketing, etc. In investment centres, the manager has therefore to be evaluated on the basis of how well he uses the volume of investment he decides to employ and returns must be related to the volume invested.

Much of the financial control literature on divisionalised companies stresses that most large companies have decision rules that specify that capital projects involving outlays in excess of a specified sum must be referred to Head Office for approval. Some writers therefore conclude that the investment centre is more of an academic construct, which is not met in practice, and that divisional performance can be measured by profit alone. If one could conclude such, it is odd that the majority of companies in both the USA and UK use a rate of return on investment as their main (but not only) divisional manager evaluation measure.

The reason for this apparent contradiction is probably that writers advocating the use of the profit measure alone, without reference to its investment base, are taking specified

capital budgeting rules far too literally and missing the richness
of investment decision processes. To begin with, minor projects
will probably never be referred to Head Office anyway, except
in terms of a declaration that £x will be spent on minor works.
Second, even production decisions affect the level of working
capital involved and so divisional managers do have discretion
for increasing or decreasing some part of investment. However,
the power of divisional managers over investment levels goes
far beyond this.

It needs to be remembered why divisionalised structures
are introduced in the first place. It is essential because top
management simply does not have the time, expertise or
knowledge to manage different products and markets in detail.
Top management's concern is with questions of balance in
the group's direction and broad strategy. In terms of investment, top management will normally decide *broadly* how
investment resources are to be allocated across divisions, but,
with the exception perhaps of major shifts in operations such
as entry into completely new markets or technologies or
major mergers of the conglomerate type, the majority of the
initiative for new investment will come from the divisions
themselves. Divisional managers need to be motivated to
search for new investment opportunities and evaluated upon
their success in so doing. The investment for the year may be
finally approved by top management, but that does not mean
that divisional performance in seeking out investment opportunities need not be evaluated.

The power and influence of divisional managers over
investment decisions becomes even more obvious when one
considers the time scale of major new investments. Recent
work in the UK indicates that some industries require 8—10
years investment lead time, with an average over British
industry of about 2½ years.[3] Throughout this period, there
will be regular reviews of the project and discussion of it at
various levels. It would be extremely odd if managers as
senior as main divisional executives did not have considerable

3.   Investment lead times in British manufacturing industry; a report
      of the CBI Working Party, CBI 1978.

sway over the investment decision. To think otherwise is to be not very familiar with the complexities and subtleties of organisational practices in most large organisations. Evidence has been provided to show that the Head Office plays a very restricted role in investment identification and selection in diversified companies.[4]

On the basis of the previous paragraphs, one may conclude that it is entirely proper for top management to want to evaluate divisions and their managers on the basis of relating profits earned to the investment needed to generate such profits. However, this does not necessarily mean that the use of the familiar accounting measure of rate of return on investment is the best way of doing it.

Measurement Difficulties with the Rate of Return on Investment (ROI)

There are a lot of measurement problems associated with this measure. Space does not permit an exhaustive treatment, but one could take each asset and liability type in the conventional balance sheet and ask what is the appropriate valuation base and, indeed, should the item even be included.

The most generally accepted basis seems to be that only assets and liabilities controllable at the divisional level should be included in the investment base. This would usually mean that most, or all, cash (except a cash float) would be excluded, as cash will be managed at Head Office level (except for certain types of multi-nationals). Trade debtors and creditors would be included, although there are some subtle points relating to debtors, such as: who is responsible for increases in debtors — is it Head Office through lax collection procedures (if debts are collected centrally), or the division through taking on lower 'quality' customers? Companies do not usually worry about such niceties and include net working capital plus fixed assets as shown in the divisional balance sheet.

4.   R.W. Ackerman, Influence of integration and diversity on the investment process, *Administration Science Quarterly*, September 1970, pp. 341–51.

Fixed assets are invariably included, but arguments arise as to whether the base should be gross or net of depreciation. Most European companies seem to use fixed assets after deduction of accumulated depreciation, but a number of USA companies prefer the gross-of-depreciation basis.

The argument about depreciation occurs because a division not investing a constant amount each year will show an increasing ROI over time, simply because assets are being depreciated. This assumes, of cource, that profits do not fall proportionately with the net asset valuation for balance sheet purposes. Generally speaking, the gross basis seems preferable, as investment at divisional level is usually 'lumpy' over time. However, there is also the argument that the ROI measure must be seen by divisional managers as being credible. If they see that the measures used to evaluate them are inconsistent with the measures by which the whole group and top management are evaluated, suspicions and doubts will be raised about the 'fairness' and reliability of the accounting measures which, they feel, are never fully understood by general managers anyway. The *logic* of such an argument has little to commend it; managers could be educated and, as stated when discussing profit centres, evaluation and communication will rarely depend upon formal statements alone. Nevertheless, several practising managers in large corporations have told the author that this *is* a real problem.

Whether one includes fixed assets gross or net of depreciation, there is still the question of whether one should use historic or 'inflation adjusted' values. It seems clear that in investigating time trends of ROI, some adjustment should be made for inflation. Many companies use replacement cost values to cover this point, but there is so much other literature on this matter that it will be left aside here.

Of growing practical importance is the question of leasing. With about 25% of externally financed investment in UK machinery, vehicles and equipment now financed by leasing, one can no longer dismiss it as a minor factor. Most companies still do not capitalise leased assets and so, on the assumption that depreciation plus interest approximately equals lease repayments, leasing inflates the ROI performance measure. For internal control purposes, it seems clear that divisions should be asked to capitalise leased assets.

There does not seem to be a need, however, for divisions to capitalise future liabilities to make lease payments. Head Office, not the division, invariably deals with financial structure and so divisional ROI is usually based on the net assets, irrespective of how they are financed.

Throughout the above discussion of the difficulties associated with ROI measures, it will be noticed that the resolution of difficulties again turned upon trying to identify whether the division did, or did not, exercise control over various activities. Given the questions raised under profit centres about whether there might not be real advantages in moving away from controllability as a criterion for determining evaluation methods, the same questions can logically be raised here — especially given the greater need for recognition of corporate inter-dependencies and risk in investment decisions. However, one can simply conclude at this stage that research is needed in this area and it may transpire that the conventional 'controllability criterion' *is* desirable — but it should not be taken as a foregone conclusion.

Other Difficulties with the ROI

Some other weaknesses of the ROI measure follow from the weaknesses associated with the profit measure, as discussed above. The measure involves arbitrary accounting allocations, has a short-run emphasis, and does not necessarily provide a good indicator of the future. In addition, it has other problems. To begin with, it may motivate managers to restrict growth. If projects are ranked by size of return on investment, an instruction to maximise ROI would suggest that only the highest ranked ROI project should be accepted when, of course, the division should undertake investment up to the point where the marginal rate of return equals the marginal cost of investment funds.

However, while theoretically likely to motivate restricted growth, the extent to which it does so will depend upon the way in which the measure is used (i.e. how tightly or loosely) and what other evaluation methods, formal or otherwise, are used along with ROI. Some writers advocate the use of the Residual Income concept to overcome that problem. Residual

income, which is defined as net profit less interest charged on
the total asset base of the division, provides an absolute measure
of performance and is not expressed as a percentage of investment. Again, space limitations prevent a full discussion of
the attributes of the residual income concept; however, both
it and the ROI measure suffer from inconsistency with the
discounted cash flow (DCF) methods of evaluating investment projects.[5]

Both ROI and residual income run the risk of seriously
misleading management in one other respect. If management
uses the *change* in ROI or residual income over time to
indicate whether performance is improved or not, this can
indirectly motivate divisional managers to include sunk costs
in their investment appraisal procedures. Specific examples
can be devised,[6] but the general point is as follows. By now
the reader will appreciate that past costs are irrelevant for
decisions[7] and, accordingly, only future incremental cash
flows should be included in investment appraisal. However,
if performance is based on the *change* in recorded performance, it is conceptually easy to see that situations must arise
where investment projects which are not worthwhile, based
on an evaluation of future incremental cash flows, do, nevertheless, increase accounting ROI or residual income compared
to the previous period. Divisional managers who are evaluated
significantly by ROI or residual income may place emphasis
on the change in their reported performance. Hence, indirectly,
past performance and sunk costs enter their analysis.

It is very difficult to see how significant the last point is in
practice. To begin with, investment decisions are not taken
on the basis of the DCF calculation alone. Such are the complexities of major investment decisions, that the usual concepts
of return (DCF basis or otherwise) and risk found in finance
and accounting texts are quite inadequate as an information
base for decision making. The uncertainties of the business
world are often so great (and they appear to be increasing
even more), that cash projections supplemented by simple

5.   For a full discussion of this point see C.R. Tomkins 1973 (foot-
     note 2), pp. 109–128.
6.   For such examples see C.R. Tompkins 1973 (footnote 2).
7.   This point was discussed in Chapter 6.

risk measures can only serve as *one* indicator of likely returns. The concept of return needs to be enriched and expressed in a variety of ways, including the use of non-financial indicators of profitability. Similarly, risks can no longer be thought of only in terms of cash flow variability (if they ever were by practitioners), but should be considered in terms of various discontinuities of events and their impact upon a whole range of financial parameters. In this case, any inconsistencies between ROI/residual income and DCF models may become of less relevance. However, resolution of such an issue can only be achieved empirically; it would also be a very complex piece of research.

Fitting Financial Planning and Control to a Specific Company

The previous section of this chapter indicated that there is a need for a wider set of indicators for both planning and control than the single notions of profits and ROI, and these appropriate indicators may well need to be different for each company. Moreover, it was stated earlier that companies may employ a variety of management styles. It should also be recognised that many large organisations are changing from a purely divisionalised structure to more sophisticated structures involving segments, with differing degrees of autonomy and horizontal and other forms of co-ordinating mechanisms, of both formal and non-formal type, as well as the vertical chain of command found in purely divisionalised organisations. These developments may indicate that the existing financial control literature on *divisionalised* companies is becoming rapidly 'dated'. It is still relevant, insofar as profit-centre and investment-centre notions are used within more sophisticated organisations, but it is by no means sufficient. So what is needed in terms of planning and monitoring variables? That can only be answered by examining each organisation's structure and decision processes.

The first step in answering such a question would seem to be to map a corporation's current methods for undertaking strategic planning, programming and resource allocation, and planning and control in each segment of the business. This in itself will yield relevant material for examining important questions: How many cycles should there be in each decision stage? In which way should information flow (up, down, across)? How much iteration should take place between interested parties before each decision stage is complete? How much time should it take? Exactly who should be involved and with what?

Having mapped the decision processes, it will be necessary to study the degree of *decentralisation* in the group as a whole and in each segment of the organisation. It is a mistake to think of divisionalised companies as being very decentralised — 'divisionalised' means that *top management* has merely delegated certain responsibilities to divisional *top management*. Within organisations which are divisionalised, there can be a variety of different degrees of decentralisation. The whole organisation should be examined for *differentiation*. It is obvious that a division in a developing country, given ten years to develop and build a market, should be evaluated by measures and perhaps methods (management style) different from a well-established division in the UK. But differentiation need not be so extreme in order to indicate the need for intra-group variety in terms of evaluation measures and management over-sight.

Observing the differing degrees of decentralisation and differentiation in the segmentation will give rise to recognition of *key variables* for use in planning and control — these variables may well be different for each business segment or level. Key variables are the key pieces of information upon which most attention can be focused in order to sharpen planning and control. These key variables will be of two types: key result areas and key success factors. Key result areas are those activities in which success is critical in order to achieve segment and total group goals. These may be long-term and stable in nature, or change from year to year. Key success factors are the items/activities upon which one must operate to achieve success in key result areas. Quite often, it may not be obvious which key success factors are leading to the specific success in some key areas. Then one must develop a research approach in order to identify the causal chain between the two types of key variables.

The above description is very general, but there is a growing literature in this field, much of it closely linked to developments in organisation theory and behaviour.[8] But, while the description is general, the end results of such a process are clear. For each business segment, one should identify a relatively small set of key success factors (KSF's) and key result areas (KRA's). Notions of profit and return on investment will inevitably figure prominently in KRA's of well-established organisation segments in developed countries, but they will be supplemented with other KRA's and KSF's acting as 'early warning devices' of impending likely change in KRA's.

It is no longer good enough to think of differences in control systems according to whether companies are divisionalised or non-divisionalised, or to think in terms of a neat dichotomy between profit centres and investment centres, or to think just of centralised or decentralised organisations. Such dichotomies are far too naive. It is time to recognise the variety and complexity both within and between organisations, and the differing mixes of formal and informal processses which can all lead to efficient control. It is time to develop efficient and systematic approaches for discovering the particular brand of complexity and formality/informality needed for the control systems of any *specific* organisation. It is time to develop more variety in accounting methods to obtain a better match between formal reports and organisational structure and decision processes. Who said, not long ago, that the possibilities for fruitful research in the management accounting field were very limited?

8.   An introduction to these ideas may be found in J. Dermer, *Management Planning and Control Systems*, Irwin 1977 (for a general textbook elaboration of this area); and R.T. Stein and E. Leja, Impact models as a method for planning change, *Sloan Management Review*, Spring 1977 (a general model for planning organisational change which, in the writer's opinion, can be used as a guideline for evaluating and changing financial control systems).

13

History of Accounting for Decisions

R H PARKER

Professor of Accountancy,
University of Exeter

Introduction

In 1617 the Berkshire farmer Robert Loder wrote in his account book:

> It were my best course to sow halfe my lande with wheat for in this year if I had done so I judge I had gotton ... xviij d or ther aboutes; besides I judge that for the carying of my wheat to Marquet I may reckon it to stand me in but little more then my manes labour that goeth with my horses and in selling it, because my charge in keping my horses is never the more or less (so long as I keep vj horses and a Teame) for they would be els idle in the stable: and the beannes or pese which they bring home at many times is more worth than my manes labour comes to, and sometimes lesse and sometimes nothing perhaps.

Nearly two centuries later in 1805–7, in the course of an *ex ante* comparison of the cost of coal gas as against candles to light the cotton mill of Phillips and Lee in Manchester, it was noted that:

> The cost of attendance upon candles would be as much, if not more, than upon the gas apparatus; so that in forming the comparison, nothing need be stated upon that score on either side.

A charge of £550 was made for 'the interest of capital sunk, and wear and tear of apparatus'. Loder also had made a charge for 'the use of my stocke [i.e. capital] which lay as dead'.

These two examples suggest that intelligent businessmen at an early date were aware intuitively of the notions of avoidable cost and opportunity cost, and of the irrelevance of costs which are the same under all alternatives.

But the examples are taken from practice, not from textbooks. There is no trace of such ideas in the literature of the time. When they did appear, which was not until the last three decades of the nineteenth century, they were to be found not in books on cost accounting, but in books on political economy. Moreover, although the last three decades of the nineteenth century were marked not only by a costing renaissance but also by the development of neo-classical economics, the interaction between cost accountants and economists was slight. The authors of the leading textbooks on cost accounting and economics, Emile Garcke and John Manger Fells, whose work *Factory Accounts* first appeared in 1887, and Alfred Marshall, whose *Principles of Economics* was first published three years later in 1890, quoted each other, but not on matters of central importance; and they made no attempt to reconcile their opposing viewpoints.

Garcke and Fells' text, excellent in many ways though it was, made only a small contribution to accounting for decisions. In it, they argued that all manufacturing costs fluctuated with the cost of labour and the price of material, and should therefore be allocated to products, whereas 'establishment expenses' (by which they meant administrative and selling costs) were, in the aggregate, more or less constant, and should not be so allocated because that would 'have the effect of disproportionately reducing the cost of each, with every increase, and the reverse with every diminution of business'. Such views did, of course, show some appreciation of the important distinction between fixed and variable costs.

In general, economists were not interested in accounting, because they believed, as Edward Cannan of the London School of Economics expressed it in his presidential address to the British Association for the Advancement of Science in 1902, that the practical usefulness of economic theory was not in private business but in politics.

W.J. Ashley, Professor of Commerce at the University of Birmingham, was not at all typical when he urged in an article in *The Economic Journal* in 1908 the enlargement of economics to include 'business economics', which frankly took for its point of view the interest of the individual businessman or business concern. The problem of cost accounts, he argued, was not how to get certain figures, but what figures to try to get, and how to combine them. Cost accounting could not, therefore, be left entirely to accountants.

Economic Concepts

But it was indeed so left and it was Stanley Jevons, first of the English neo-classical economists, not Garcke and Fells or their colleagues, who in a famous passage pointed out the irrelevance of past costs:

> A great undertaking like the Great Western Railway, or the Thames Tunnel, may embody a vast amount of labour, but its value depends entirely upon the number of persons who find it useful. If no use could be found for the Great Eastern steam ship, its value would be nil, except for the utility of some of its materials. On the other hand, a successful undertaking, which happens to possess great utility, may have a value for a time, at least, far exceeding what has been spent upon it, as in the case of the Atlantic cable. The fact is, that *labour once spent has no influence on the future value of any article:* it is gone and lost for ever. In commerce, bygones are for ever bygones; and we are always starting clear at each moment, judging the values of things with a view to future utility. (*The Theory of Political Economy*, London: Macmillan 1871; italics in the original)

It is worth noting that Jevons wrote it was in *commerce* (not in *economics* as it is usually misquoted) that bygones were for ever bygones. His examples were topical and well-chosen. Brunel's *Great Eastern* (launched 1858) was a disastrous failure; the successful Atlantic cable was laid by the *Great Eastern* in 1866. Garcke and Fells preferred Marx's view that machinery is 'congealed labour'. They quote Jevons on industrial partnership, but not on the theory of value.

By the turn of the century, 'marginalism' had triumphed in economics. In England its most avid exponent was Wicksteed, who in an address to the British Association explained that what a man will give for anything rather than go without it is determined by a comparison of the difference which he conceives its possession will make to him, compared with the difference that anything that he gives for it, or could have had instead of it, will or would make. The skill of a business manager consists in expanding and contracting his expenditure on the several factors of production so as to bring their differential significances to himself into coincidence with their market prices.

Meanwhile, Austrian and American economists were recognising and defining the concept of opportunity cost. 'To say that any kind of production involves cost', wrote von Wieser in 1889, 'simply implies that the economic means of production, which could doubtless have been usefully employed in other directions, are either used up in it, or are suspended during it'. 'As soon as we look more closely upon our varied resources and the individual activities of economic life', wrote Green in 1894, 'we discover that many of our good opportunities are limited in number and extent, so that before devoting the opportunity to a particular activity it behooves us to consider from what other uses we are thus withholding it. Such consideration gives rise to the concept of opportunity cost'. 'If', wrote Davenport in the same year, 'the choice lies between the production or purchase of two commodities, the value of one is measured by the sacrifice of going without the other'.

Accounting Practice

Early cost accounting practice, as developed by accountants and engineers, did not at all follow the ideas of Jevons and Wicksteed. Instead, the dominant ideas were that, firstly, cost accounting was mainly a matter of *ex post* recording rather than *ex ante* planning and, secondly, that all costs — fixed as well as variable — should be allocated to the product. The emphasis was thus on past allocations rather than future alternatives.

Cost accountants in fact convinced themselves that what was needed was the 'actual' cost of a manufactured product and increasingly concerned themselves with building up figures of total cost by means of overhead allocation. This philosophy was well expressed by Alexander Hamilton Church (an English electrical engineer who settled in the United States around the turn of the century) in his book *The Proper Distribution of Establishment Changes,* (New York: Engineering Magazine Co. 1916) (the italics are his):

> A production centre is, of course, either a machine or a bench at which a hand craftsman works. Each of these is in the position of a little shop carrying on one little special industry, paying rent for the floor space occupied, interest for the capital involved, depreciation for the wear and tear, and so on, *quite independently of what may be paid by other production centres* in the same shop. Then, in addition to this, there will be a separate debit representing those items of incidence which can only be treated as an average all-round charge ... whatever else is done, *every dollar of charges must be burdened into some item of work.*

The ideas of Hamilton Church became the established orthodoxy of cost accounting, although a few accountants stressed the importance of distinguishing between fixed and variable costs. Two Scottish chartered accountants to do so were John Mann and Harold Judd, whose names have survived in the name of a leading British accounting firm. Mann helped to develop the break-even chart. Judd gave in 1914 the example of the manager of a business who goes down to the Exchange one day and is offered a contract of 500 tons of iron at 100s per ton. Before going to the Exchange, he has been told by his accountant that the cost is running at 105s a ton. What the manager should do is to go back to his accountant and ask how the cost of 105s has been arrived at. The accountant may explain that direct materials and labour cost 80s and oncost (i.e. indirect costs) 25s. If the latter figure is dissected, it may show that 10s is fluctuating oncost and 15s fixed oncost. Now, asks Judd:

> If that man gets a price of 100s per ton, what is the result? He has covered his Direct Cost and his Fluctuating Oncost, and he has got 10s over to account of his 15s of Fixed Oncost. If the manager knew that much at the time he would have known that

in taking the contract at 100s he was getting a contribution of 10s a ton towards reduction of Oncost that is inevitably running on whether he gets work or not. The 'contribution to Oncost' is thus in reality 10s per ton, and not 20s per ton as first appeared; that is, he can without loss book orders down to 90s per ton, but anything below that is at an actual loss. With such information before him the manager knows how near he can sail to the wind without making undue leeway. (Fixed and fluctuating oncost, *Accountant's Magazine*, March 1914)

Why was it Hamilton Church's ideas which practising cost accountants preferred? One cannot be absolutely certain, but three reasons may be suggested. Firstly, cost accountants, whether from an engineering or an accounting background, did not often read economic theory (Garcke and Fells appear to have read it more than most) and when they did, they, like Cannan, did not expect to find anything of direct application to their own work. Secondly, a background of financial accounting, with its emphasis on past averages, was not conducive to a realisation of the importance of expected future increments. G. Charter Harrison, an Anglo-American accountant-engineer suggested in his book *Cost Accounting to Aid Production* (New York: Engineering Magazine Co. 1921) that the reason for the development of cost accounting along historical lines by professional accountants was that most of the work undertaken by them concerned past records and the investigation of past transactions. Thirdly, most accountants and engineers retained the idea, modified by the neo-classical economists, that value depends on cost. Economists had heavily qualified Adam Smith's contention that, if it costs twice the labour to kill a beaver as it costs to kill a deer, then a beaver will be worth two deer.

Cost Accounting after the First World War

The First World War greatly increased the need for cost accounts and both the UK Institute of Cost and Works Accountants and the US National Association of Cost Accountants (as they were then called) were established in 1919.

But it was not until 1923 that an economist took a hard

look at cost accounting. J. Maurice Clark's *Studies in the Economics of Overhead Costs* (University of Chicago Press 1923) was a major contribution. Cost accounting, wrote Clark, was still in its formative stage, but it already had a voluminous literature and at least one of the characteristics of a science — that of being inscrutable to the uninitiated. There were, he saw, great opportunities for the development of arbitrary and fictitious notions of cost, through the 'necessity' of apportioning items somehow, even if there was no scientific basis on which to do it. He coined the phrase 'different costs for different purposes' and pointed out that:

> If cost accounting sets out, determined to discover what the cost of everything is and convinced in advance that there is one figure which can be found and which will furnish exactly the informa- tion which is desired for every possible purpose, it will necessarily fail, because there is no such figure. If it finds a figure which is right for some purposes it must necessarily be wrong for others. (p. 234)

Clark's book was largely ignored by practising cost ac- countants and the mainstream practice and literature of the inter-war period reflects his ideas hardly at all. There were a few accounting academics, however, who understood the relevant economic theory and discussed how it could be applied to cost accounts. In the USA, W.J. Vatter re-examined cost accounting from a managerial viewpoint, as he put it, and stressed that the central idea of the concept of cost was that of giving up, parting with, or sacrificing, some thing or value to acquire some thing or value, but — '*There is no one cost* which will fit all purposes any more than there is a single wheel which will fit watches, motor trucks, and railway trains.' After a series of examples illustrating the practical importance of information concerning total-cost behaviour, differential costs, imputed costs, replacement costs, sunk and out-of- pocket costs, and opportunity cost, he concluded that the useful cost accountant,

> must be able and willing to secure the kind of data which manage- ment may require for the many and varied purposes cost data may serve. He must determine how total costs behave at various levels of production for the product. He must be able to determine differential costs where the situation demands their use. He must

know when to use imputed costs and replacement costs; he must understand the difference between sunk and out-of-pocket costs; and he must recognise the need for the use of such concepts in attacking special problems. The mere grinding out of figures according to a stereotyped plan is not cost accounting and should not be referred to as such.

The cost accountant is thus called upon not only to find costs, but to know what costs to use.

Similar ideas flourished in the UK at the London School of Economics. The London tradition in the theory of cost has been discussed by J.R. Gould. He concludes that the main contribution of the tradition to accounting for decisions was to direct attention away from the standard conventions of accounting practice and towards the choice between alternative business plans, and that it may have played an important role in 'releasing cost accounting from its historical shackles'. Brought together at the LSE in a way not then common elsewhere were economic theorists, academic accountants and administrative theorists. The line between accounting and applied economics was deliberately blurred by writers such as R.S. Edwards, R.H. Coase and W.T. Baxter.

The most important thing about costs, argued Edwards (who had practised as an accountant before turning to economics) in a paper on 'The Rationale of Cost Accounting' (1937), was the extent to which they changed with output. Most textbooks were still prone to emphasise that cost accounting analysed past costs, not future estimates, and did not make clear that data about the past were useful only in so far as they were a guide to future costs. It is, wrote Edwards,

> future variable cost which is important . . . cost accountants can ignore expenses which are completely unchangeable . . . depreciation and every other expense must be examined in order to establish the relationship between changes in cost and output variations.

Profitability should be tested by comparing increments to cost with increments to revenue, rather than by totals and averages. Accountants have spent too much effort in trying to arrive at total cost 'by building up complicated and delicate oncost structures which depend on arbitrary assumptions'. In tendering for orders, knowledge of market conditions was more important than estimates of total cost; methods of computing oncost varied so much that it would be dangerous to suppose that one's competitors had allowed roughly for the same oncost as oneself.

Edwards pursued the same theme in two other papers: 'Cost Accounting and Joint Production', which criticised the orthodox methods of allocating joint costs, and 'The Approach to Budgetary Control' (1938).

Ideas similar to those of Edwards were developed at greater length by his colleague R.H. Coase in a series of articles on 'Business Organisation and the Accountant' in *The Accountant* of 1938. Coase stressed that attention ought to be concentrated on the variations in costs or receipts which would result if a particular decision were taken; costs and receipts which would remain unchanged whatever decision were taken should be ignored.

He gave as an example a department store whose managers were discussing whether or not to close a particular department. A decision could not be reached, because there was no agreement on the allocation to be made for rent to the department. Coase pointed out that, since in this case the amount of rent to be paid would remain the same whether the department was closed or not, the question of rent allocation was irrelevant. All that was necessary was to discover what changes in costs and receipts would occur if the department were closed down, including those of any other departments affected.

This conclusion was attacked by Bigg (author of a student text on cost accounting first published in 1932), who was clearly thinking in terms of net profit per department and thought that Coase's methods were 'inequitable' to the other departments. Bigg's views are interesting because they show how a background of financial accounting and auditing can lead to ways of thought wholly unsuitable for management accounting. For purposes of external reporting, a reasonable case can be made for the use of total unit costs and obviously in auditing the ideas of fairness and equity are fundamental, but such ideas are just not relevant when the problem is to maximise the profits of the business as a whole. The relevant theory for this problem was in fact clearly stated by W.T. Baxter in an article ('A Note on the Allocation of Oncosts between Departments') in the same volume of *The Accountant*.

Baxter pointed out that the reasons for preparing departmental statements were (i) to find out whether each department was sufficiently profitable to justify its continuance, (ii) to find out whether the heads of the individual departments were avoiding unnecessary expense, and (iii) (in some cases) to find suitable selling prices for the individual articles in which the department dealt. There was no point in allocating any overhead expenses, which would remain undiminished even if a department were abandoned and over which departmental heads had no control. A manager should ask, not whether the sale price of an article exceeded its average 'cost' (which might vary enormously by altering the method of allocation), but whether the business was making more profit by selling that article at that price than it could by adopting any other policy.

It was not until the 1960s that a different-costs-for-different-purposes approach entered the textbooks. Probably the earliest were two American books still well-known to students: G. Shillinglaw's *Cost Accounting: Analysis and Control* (first published in 1961) and C.T. Horngren's *Cost Accounting: A Managerial Emphasis* (first published in 1962).

Investment Decisions

In order to evaluate an *investment* decision, it is necessary not only to forecast the relevant cash inflows (revenues) and outflows (costs), but also to allow for the time value of money. In other words, a discounted cash flow approach is required. This in turn requires both an understanding of compound interest and an ability to set out the cash inflows and outflows likely to result from a particular decision to invest.

Compound interest calculations are included in the writings of both Luca Pacioli (c. 1445—c. 1523) and Simon Stevin (1548—1620), two mathematicians well known to accounting historians for their contributions to the early literature of double entry bookkeeping. Stevin was also the second writer to publish interest tables (the first being Jean Trenchant in a book published at Lyons in 1558).

Setting out the cash implications of an investment is more difficult. It is not surprising that the earliest applications of discounted cash flow were to loans, where the cash outlays and receipts could be forecast with some certainty, and to life assurance, where probabilities could be calculated from historical evidence. The extension of discounted cash flow to investment in fixed assets came much later.

Stevin's book *Tables of Interest*, published in Antwerp in 1582, included 'a general rule for finding which is the most profitable of two or more conditions, and by how much it is more profitable than the other'. (Antwerp and Lyons were the two greatest financial centres of Western Europe in the sixteenth century.) Stevin's rule was the first exposition of what is now known as the 'net present value' criterion. He applied it, of course, only to financial investments.

Among the successors of Stevin were the actuarial scientists, who developed scientific life assurance in England in the eighteenth century. They included James Dodson FRS (c.1710–1757), 'Accountant and Teacher of the Mathematics', who not only, in his unpublished 'First Lecture on Insurances' (1756), made the first investigation into the principles of operation of a life assurance business and showed how premiums should be calculated, but also wrote in 1750 one of the very few early works on bookkeeping to deal with accounting for manufacturing operations.

It was not, however, until the nineteenth century that discounted cash flow criteria were applied to non-financial investments. This was probably the result, not only of the difficulties of forecasting the relevant cash flows, but also of the relatively small size of such investments. The coming of the railways changed this; their building entailed a massive capital outlay before any returns were received.

The problems of capital expenditure analysis were discussed at some length by railway economists and engineers. A.M. Wellington, for example, wrote as follows in his book *The Economic Theory of the Location of Railways* (2nd edn, 1887):

> The theory of the subject is simple: In Table 18 is given the present value or present justifiable expenditure to save $1 (or one unit of any other value) at the end of a given period at any given rate of interest; that is to say, the sum which, if placed at compound interest now, will produce $1 at the end of the specified period. This fact given, it logically follows, that if the value of a given betterment for a given immediate traffic be $1, the present value

of the same betterment for an equal traffic which is to exist only in the future will be that sum which at compound interest will produce $1 when the assumed traffic comes to exist. . .

All this is undeniably correct in theory . . . but the indications of Table 18 are of value only as fixing a maximum which should never be exceeded . . .
. . . while it may be taken as a practical certainty that the traffic of any ordinary railway not only will grow, but that it will grow at an average rate of something like 5 to 8 per cent per annum east of the Alleghenies, and 7 to 10 or 15 or even 20 per cent per year west of there, yet . . . the rate of this growth of traffic is excessively variable and uncertain — liable to cease altogether at any time for many years . . .

For this cause alone it is in general inexpedient to look forward more than at most five years for traffic to justify an increase of immediate expenditure . . .

It is interesting to note, not only Wellington's application of the net present value rule, but the way he copes with uncertainty by limiting the potential life of the project.

The political economists were also aware of the relevant concepts. The greatest contribution was made by the American economist Irving Fisher in his book *The Rate of Interest* (New York: Macmillan), first published in 1907 and extensively revised and reissued as *The Theory of Interest* (New York: Macmillan) in 1930. In these books, he sets out four ways of choosing between investment options and claims that they all give the same result. Out of all eligible options one should select:

(i) the one which has the maximum present value, reckoned at the market rate of interest (the principle of maximum present value);

(ii) the one whose advantages (returns) over any other outweigh, in present value, its disadvantages (costs), when both returns and costs are discounted at the market rate of interest (the principle of comparative advantage);

(iii) the one which, compared with any other option, yields a 'rate of return on sacrifice' or 'rate of return over cost' greater than the rate of interest (the principle of return over cost); or

(iv) where options differ by continuous gradations, the one

the difference of which from its nearest rival gives a rate
of return over cost equal to the rate of interest (the
marginal rate of return over cost).

In his *General Theory* (1936), Keynes confused Fisher's
rate of return over cost with his own 'marginal efficiency of
capital' or, as most accountants now term it, 'internal rate of
return'. When discounted cash flow methods started to become
familiar in the 1950s, it was Keynes's mis-interpretation
which became best known.

The accounting literature of the 1930s contained very few
references to making investment decisions. The net present
value method was, however, clearly described by the LSE
economist R.H. Coase in his series of articles in *The Accountant*
in 1938, to which we have already referred. His articles appear
to have had very little impact on accounting theory and even
less on accounting practice.

The 1950s saw a lively discussion in the economic and
financial literature of the problems of choosing among
mutually exclusive investments, of the possibility of multiple
rates of return and of capital rationing. In the 1960s DCF was
popularised in many books and courses.

Why did it take so long for the application of DCF criteria
to non-financial investments to gain acceptance? The blame
should perhaps be laid at the door of accountants. It is true
that Pacioli in the fifteenth century, Stevin in the sixteenth,
and Dodson in the eighteenth, all wrote on compound interest
and actuarial problems as well as on accounting; but the
accounting profession as it developed in the nineteenth
century concerned itself much more with historical recording
than with decision making. Nevertheless, it was accountants
in their role as financial experts who were in most cases
consulted on capital expenditure decisions. Since their
education did not include much economic theory, they
naturally turned, either to rates of return based on the
traditional financial statements, or to such simple and conservative techniques as the payback period. The relatively few
economists who took an interest in accounting, and who
made recommendations based on economic theory, were
ignored. Such was the fate of R.H. Coase's excellent series of
articles in *The Accountant* in 1938.

It was not until the 1950s that economists began to play an important part as advisers in business. In the same decade, accountants became more acquainted with economic ideas. In this new climate — whose coming in the United Kingdom was perhaps delayed a decade compared with the USA — the practical use of discounted cash flow criteria became not only possible but, we may say with the advantage of hindsight, inevitable.

Conclusions

It is clear that accountants cannot claim to be the originators of the relevant concepts for accounting for decisions. These concepts were first formulated by the neo-classical economists at the end of the nineteenth century. The impact of their ideas on accounting thought and practice was delayed for two reasons: the fact that they were not writing for, and consequently tended not to be read by, practising accountants; and also the historical bias which most accountants derived from the nature of their daily work.

Similarly, the contributions of Irving Fisher's *The Rate of Interest* (1907) and J.M. Clark's *Studies in the Economics of Overhead Costs* (1923) were not realised until long after their dates of publication.

It was only in the 1960s that it could be claimed with any justification that incremental and related concepts of cost, and the concept of discounting cash flows, had become a generally accepted part of the theory and practice of accounting for decisions.

References and Guide to Further Reading

This chapter has concentrated on only one aspect of the history of management accounting. A wider view is taken by D. Solomons in his chapter, The historical development of costing, in his book of readings, *Studies in Cost Analysis*, 2nd edn, Sweet and Maxwell 1968. Closer to the present chapter are, R.H. Parker, *Management Accounting: an Historical Perspective*, Part One, Macmillan 1969, and M.C. Wells, *Accounting for Common Costs*, Center for International Education and Research in Accounting, Urbana, Illinois, 1978.

The quotation of 1617 comes from G.E. Fussell (ed.), *Robert Loder's Farm Accounts 1610–1620*, Camden 3rd Series, vol. LIII, Royal Historical Society, London, 1936, pp. 137–8. The Phillips and Lee example is taken from, T.S. Peckston, *A Practical Treatise on Gas-Lighting*, 3rd edn, Hebert, London, 1841, pp. 99–100.

The first edition of E. Garcke and J.M. Fells, *Factory Accounts* was published in London by Crosby Lockwood and Son in 1887. The fourth edition of 1898 was reprinted by Arno Press, New York, in 1976. The reference to establishment expenses is on p. 73 of this edition. Jevons is quoted on p. 145 of the same edition and p. 197 of the sixth (1911). The reference to Marx is in the sixth edition (p. 93n), but not the fourth.

The addresses by Cannan and Wicksteed to the British Association are reprinted in R.L. Smyth (ed), *Essays in Economic Method*, Duckworth 1962.

The quotation from F. van Wieser is on p. 168 of his *Natural Value*, Macmillan, London, 1893. The German original was published in Vienna in 1889. D.I. Green's definition of opportunity cost is from his article, Pain-cost and opportunity-cost, *Quarterly Journal of Economics*, vol. 8, 1893–4. The quotation from H.J. Davenport is from his article, The formula of sacrifice, *Journal of Political Economy*, vol. 2, 1893–4.

Mann's contribution to the development of the break-even chart can be found in, Oncost or expenses, in G. Lisle (ed.), *Encyclopaedia of Accounting*, vol. 5, William Green and Sons, Edinburgh, 1903–07.

The quotations from Vatter are taken from Chapter 29 of the first and second editions of J.J.W. Neuner, *Cost Accounting: Principles and Practice*, 1939, 1942.

Gould's paper, Opportunity cost: the London tradition, is in H. Edey and B.S. Yamey (eds), *Debits, Credits, Finance and Profits*, Sweet and Maxwell 1974. The articles by Edwards, Coase and Baxter are most easily to be found in D. Solomons, *Studies in Costing*, Sweet and Maxwell 1952. Bigg's comments were published in *The Accountant*, vol. 99, 1938, pp. 539 and 795.

Stevin's book *Tafalen van Interest* (Tables of Interest) is reprinted with an English translation in D.J. Struik (ed.), *The Principal Works of Simon Stevin*, vol. IIA, Mathematics, C.V. Swets & Zeitlinger, Amsterdam, 1958. The career of Dodson is discussed in M.E. Ogborn, *Equitable Assurances*, Allen & Unwin 1962.

Sufficient reference to other works cited is given in the body of the text.

14

An Overview of Current Trends and Directions for the Future

ROBERT SCAPENS

Senior Lecturer in Accounting,
University of Manchester

The contributors to this book have discussed a number of topics in management accounting, reflecting the general nature of the subject area. In this chapter we shall attempt to provide an overview of the nature of management accounting and to identify the role of management accounting research. Some current trends in management accounting research will be reviewed and consideration will be given to a possible direction for future research.

The Nature of Management Accounting

It is not easy to find a definition of management accounting which is acceptable to both academics and practitioners. One approach is to suggest that management accounting is concerned with accounting for the needs of managers. But this raises further questions. What is accounting? What are the needs of managers? If we accept that accounting is concerned with the provision of information to meet the needs of users, we might be able to derive a working definition of management accounting by considering managers' needs for information.

It is conventionally argued that managers are concerned with a variety of business problems which can be categorised into two different, but interrelated, classes. The first class is concerned with the evaluation of future prospects and the allocation of resources (i.e. planning), while the second is concerned with the control and evaluation of the outcomes of previously formulated plans. We shall refer to these two aspects of the managerial function as planning and control, respectively. This dichotomy provides a convenient basis for discussion, but, as will be shown below, the distinction between planning and control is not at all clear in practice.

The planning phase involves selecting the course(s) of action to be pursued by the business in some future period — the products to be manufactured next month and the prices to be charged for them; the resources required in the next year; the plant and equipment to be used during the next five years; and so on. In order to select an appropriate course of action, managers must first perceive a need and identify the goals to be pursued and then identify the available alternatives, evaluate their likely outcomes, and select the most desirable. Management accounting is concerned with the evaluation of the likely outcomes and the methods (or models) which are available for selecting the optimal or most desirable outcomes. The perception of needs and identification of goals and available alternatives have not traditionally been regarded as part of management accounting, except insofar as they are suggested by the next phase of the management function, the control process.

Once plans have been formulated for a forthcoming period, the function of management is to ensure an appropriate conversion into actual results. This is achieved through a control process in which management accounting can play an important role. The management accounting system can be used to monitor the actual results against the plans. The variations from plan will indicate areas where management attention may be required. The variances could be due to internal factors, such as inefficient operations, or lack of appropriate coordination, which might be remedied by managerial action. However, they could be due to factors outside the manager's control — for instance, an unanticipated rise in the price of raw materials. Changes in external (environmental) factors may give rise to managerial action — for instance the substitution of alternative raw materials — or they may simply have to be accepted. In either case, these environmental changes should be reflected in any subsequent planning process. The higher raw material prices, for example, should be built into the plans for subsequent periods.

Thus, planning and control are interrelated. Plans will be formulated, and their implementation will be controlled. This control process will provide feedback for subsequent plans. In this way, managers will be able to learn about their performance and about the environment in which they operate. This problem-solving approach to management accounting has become generally accepted by academics and it is embodied in the standard textbooks.

Turning to management accounting in practice, it may be argued that the control function has had a major impact on the development of accounting methods. As indicated in Chapter 13, cost accounting developed primarily as a means of *ex post* recording, rather than *ex ante* planning. Furthermore, Chandler and Daems identified the need to coordinate and monitor (i.e. control) the activities of the various sections of large business entities as the primary influence on the development of cost accounting methods.[1] The need for information for resource allocation (i.e. planning) followed this initial development. Accordingly, many accounting methods have primarily a control emphasis. Information for planning is frequently derived from the application of such methods, and (as will be discussed below) it is not always clear what adjustments are made in order to obtain the relevant information for planning. *Ad hoc* adjustments may be made, but empirical evidence is limited.

The distinction between planning and control should be kept in mind. The emphasis of accounting for planning is forward-looking (for example, what are the alternative uses for the resources?), while accounting for control is a backward-looking exercise (how well have we done compared to the budget?). Unless this distinction is recognised by accountants

1. A.D. Chandler, Jr and H. Daems, Administrative coordination, allocation and monitoring: a comparative analysis of the emergence of accounting and organisation in the USA and Europe, *Accounting, Organisations and Society*, 1979, pp. 3—20.

and managers in practice, unwise decisions may be taken
as a result of evaluations based on control information.
Furthermore, academic researchers must also recognise the
implications of the distinction. For instance, a management
accounting system which is essentially backward-looking need
not necessarily imply the use of inappropriate information
for planning, provided the control data is suitably modified
by *ad hoc* procedures in order to generate relevant information
for planning. These modifications may not be prepared
formally by accountants; they could be made subjectively by
managers. For instance, researchers investigating pricing
decisions have observed that although accountants might
provide traditional cost-plus data (see Chapter 8), modifications
are often made to reflect the amounts that the market will
bear.

Recent research into the behavioural and organisational
implications of management accounting has provided new
insights. The management accounting system may be identified
as part of a political/bargaining process, which provides
legitimacy for actions within the organisation. It is suggested
in Chapter 11 that the role of accounting systems will vary
with the uncertainty surrounding the available alternatives
and the desired objectives. The traditional view of management
accounting (as reflected in the above discussion of the problem-
solving approach) is applicable mainly in situations of relative
certainty concerning both outcomes and objectives. In other
situations, Chapter 11 suggests that accounting systems
can serve a number of roles; a source of data for bargaining
processes, the means for learning from past experience and
even a means of rationalising decisions or compromises
which have already been reached. This view of management
accounting is not normally included in management accounting
textbooks, but it is likely to receive more attention in the
future.

The Development of Management Accounting Research

During the past decade research into management accounting
has proceeded along two almost separate paths: the development of quantitative techniques and the use of behavioural

analysis. The problem-solving approach has been extended by the incorporation of more complex mathematical models and techniques — in particular, operational research techniques have become an integral part of the management accounting literature. Mathematical models can describe the links between available alternatives and the likely outcomes, and various quantitative techniques are available to assist decision makers in selecting optimal actions. This problem-solving approach has been characterised by normative reasoning. The mathematical models and quantitative techniques are used to prescribe the course of action which *ought* to be adopted and the nature of the accounting information which *ought* to be provided to assist the decision taker.

In general, the behavioural and organisational analysis of management accounting has been descriptive (or empirical — according to the definition in Chapter 2). The role of management accounting in the organisational functioning of the business has been studied, as also have the effects on individual behaviour of using such accounting information. Whilst such analyses undoubtedly have prescriptive implications, this aspect of the approach needs more research. It is not entirely clear from this line of research to date, just how the accounting information should be produced in order best to fulfil its organisational roles.

An integration of the quantitative and behavioural aspects of management accounting would seem to be an essential task for future research. Developments of the quantitative implications of the behavioural and organisational analysis would represent a step in this direction (after all, accounting is generally acknowledged to involve, at least to some extent, quantitative data). In addition, new proposals for quantitative techniques should not ignore the insights gained from behavioural and organisational research. This approach should ensure that the proposed techniques are applicable for management accounting in practice. The general impression to be gained from any review of the quantitative aspects of management accounting currently appearing in the academic literature[2] is that theory is so far ahead of practice as to be of little

2.   For a review of quantitative models in management accounting

current use in the real world. This is a frequent criticism raised by practitioners, and it should not be dismissed lightly.

It seems to be generally accepted that management accounting practice will usually lag behind theory. It is argued that time is required for new techniques to be accepted and implemented by managers and accountants. However, the present time lag seems excessively long and only the relatively simple techniques appear to be adopted. If new techniques have the power that their advocates suggest, then one would expect managers in a competitive world to hire suitably qualified specialists to explain and implement the new techniques. Firms that did not do so would be placed at a competitive disadvantage. Nevertheless, many of the quantitative techniques developed five to ten years ago are not widely adopted, either in the United Kingdom or in the United States. It is very convenient to blame this on practitioners' lack of knowledge. But are there more fundamental reasons?[3] Large companies in the United States are increasingly employing accountants with substantial academic training. Accountants in such companies frequently have MBAs and even PhDs, and are quite familiar with the more complex quantitative models — models which they do not utilise in practice. The reasons for the non-acceptance of these models needs to be investigated. Below are some suggestions concerning the limitations of mathematical models and quantitative techniques in management accounting.

The Role of Quantitative Techniques

Even a casual examination of the quantitative techniques currently appearing in the academic literature might lead the

---

see R.S. Kaplan, Application of quantitative models in managerial accounting: a state of the art survey, in *Management Accounting — State of the Art*, Robert Beyer Lecture Series, University of Wisconsin Madison, 1977.

3. See C. West Churchman, Managerial acceptance of scientific recommendations, *California Management Review*, 1964 pp. 31–8, and also, D.J. Cooper, A social explanation for the avoidance of rigorous analysis in investment appraisal, *Accounting and Business Research*, Summer 1975, pp. 198–202.

reader to suspect that much of the analytical development may be more for academic respectability than to enhance the *usefulness* of the techniques. Simple techniques may be the most appropriate in practice. Certain writers have investigated the application of particular complex quantitative models, and come to the conclusion that when problems and costs of estimation and implementation are considered, simple models may be preferred by rational managers.[4] Does this imply that complex models should be avoided? To investigate this question, we shall consider the role of quantitative models in management accounting.

It is possible to distinguish two separate roles for management accounting models. First, they may be used by managers and/or accountants in practice *on a day-to-day basis*. These models assist the decision maker to arrive at particular decisions — for instance, linear programming models, the net present value rules for investment appraisal, stock control models, etc. We might include along with these models any rules which specify the inputs required for the decision maker's own (subjective) models. For the present discussion, the models will be called decision models, although they might be termed simply decision rules, or decision aids. Second, models are used by academics or consultants to analyse decision situations and to prescribe decision models. These models, which may be termed analytical models, include the valuation and allocation models used to identify criteria for investment appraisal, decision making and performance evaluation.

In distinguishing these two roles for models in management accounting we have identified two separate groups who might use models: the manager and the accountant in practice, who may be called *practitioners*, and the academic and consultant, who may be called *researchers*. It should be noted that managers and accountants form quite separate groups themselves — one group using, and the other preparing, accounting

---

4.   For example see G.L. Sundem, Evaluating simplified capital budgeting models using a time—state preference metric, *Accounting Review*, April 1974, pp. 306—20, and R.P. Magee, A simulation analysis of alternative cost variance investigation models, *Accounting Review*, July 1976, pp. 529—44.

information. For the present discussion, they are combined into a practitioner group, because they are both involved with management accounting information on a day-to-day basis and require decision models which can be applied in practice. The researcher, however, can step back from the pressures of practice to consider the relevance of the models used by the practitioner. Individual managers and accountants may move between the two groups. For instance, when taking day-to-day decisions a manager will be a member of the practitioner group, but when he is evaluating alternative decision models which he might use he could be included in the researcher group.

The classification of models as either decision models or analytical models implies that decision situations can be quantitatively modelled. This is unlikely to be true of all decision situations. Simon suggested a distinction between 'programmed' and 'non-programmed' decisions:

> Decisions are programmed to the extent that they are repetitive and routine, to the extent that a definite procedure has been worked out for handling them so that they don't have to be treated *de novo* each time they occur . . . Decisions are non-programmed to the extent that they are novel, unstructured, and consequential. There is no cut-and-dried method of handling the problem because it hasn't arisen before, or because its precise nature and structure are elusive or complex, or because it is so important that it deserves a custom-tailored treatment . . . By non-programmed I mean a response where the system has no specific procedure to deal with situations like the one at hand, but must fall back on whatever *general* capacity it has for intelligent, adaptive, problem-oriented action.[5]

To avoid confusion with methods of mathematical programming, the terms 'structured' and 'unstructured' will be used for programmed and non-programmed.[6] It should be recognised that Simon was not seeking to set up a simple dichotomy, but a whole continuum with highly structured decisions at one end and highly unstructured decisions at the

5. H.A. Simon, *The New Science of Management Decision*, Harper and Row 1966, pp. 5—6.
6. Similar terms are used by G.A. Gorry and M.S. Scott Moeton, A framework for management information systems, *Sloan Management Review*, Fall 1971, pp. 50—70.

other. Furthermore, the position of particular decisions on this continuum is not static; as new techniques become available, it may be possible to add structure to decisions which were previously unstructured. However, it will be convenient to use the terms structured and unstructured to categorise decision situations.

Combining these categories of decision situations with the dichotomy of practitioners and researchers gives the matrix shown in figure 14.1 We can investigate the role of simple and complex models by considering the cells in this matrix. Quantitative models which are applicable for structured decisions include operational research and other mathematical optimising techniques. An unstructured decision, such as an investment in research and development for which it is impossible to identify the potential outcomes, cannot be modelled in the same way. Some comments about the use of quantitative data for unstructured decisions will be made later.

Types of decision	Management Accounting	
	Practitioner	Researcher
Structured	Simple quantitative models	Complex quantitative models
Unstructured	Data bases Rules-of-thumb	Heuristics

Figure 14.1 *The Role of Quantitative Models*

In the meantime, consider the researcher's use of models for structured decisions. The quantitative techniques which may be used to model the potential costs and benefits arising from such decisions may be very complex. As the analytical models are used to prescribe particular decision models (or aids), they should include the costs and benefits of implementation. It may be that complexity will add to the academic respectability of these models. However, simplicity may be a desirable characteristic of the prescriptions derived from those models.

Complex analytical models need not imply complex decision models. For instance, it has been generally accepted that, in order to encourage managers to adopt profit maximising policies, the controllable elements of performance should be measured and rewarded. This may be regarded as a simple decision model for performance evaluation. If the controllable performance equals (or is better than) the budget, then performance is good and should be rewarded. Recently, Demski demonstrated (using a complex analytical model) that, in conditions of uncertainty, such a decision model would be sub-optimal.[7] He recommended a decision model which makes no distinction between controllable and non-controllable elements of performance. Despite the complex analytical model, the prescribed decision model is simple: measure all aspects of performance (controllable and non-controllable) and reward accordingly.

Simplicity may not be a virtue in analytical models. A strong case can probably be made for more complexity in such models, especially in the treatment of risk and uncertainty. For instance, what is the role of cost allocations, relevant costs, controllable costs, etc. in a world of uncertainty? Many of the techniques of management accounting, conventionally supported by academics, were developed without explicit considerations of risk. A re-assessment of such techniques using the recently developed methods of dealing with risk would be a useful piece of further research, which might indicate some of the reasons why particular methods are adopted in practice.

A further extension of analytical models should incorporate the costs and benefits of using the associated decision models (or aids) in practice. Such research will indicate whether the information costs associated with complex decision models are justified by the benefits obtained. More research is required to identify the estimation and implementation problems and costs associated with the proposed decision models.

At this point, a word of caution is necessary. When building analytical models, interpreting their results and prescribing decision models, it is important not to overestimate the role of quantitative information. Frequently, non-quantifiable

7.   J. Demski, Uncertainty and evaluation based on controllable performance, *Journal of Accounting Research*, Autumn 1976, pp. 230–45.

variables enter into business decisions and, accordingly, wholly quantitative models are unlikely to be complete. Here it is important to recognise the wider organisational aspects of the decision making process.

The models discussed above are applicable primarily to structured decisions. These models link the available alternatives and the resulting outcomes, in order to select the optimal course of action. Unstructured decisions lack an identifiable relationship between actions and outcomes and thus cannot be quantitatively modelled. Attempts to apply quantitative optimising techniques to such decisions will have little practical relevance. Some of the very complex techniques which are offered as decision models (i.e. for use by decision makers on a day-to-day basis) may be rejected in practice for this reason. Certain decisions which may have been previously unstructured may become structured as new mathematical forecasting and estimation techniques become available. However, where decisions are highly unstructured, attempts to apply techniques designed for structured decisions will be particularly unprofitable. Accounting researchers can serve a more useful role in this area by studying the nature of the unstructured decisions and their organisational context.

Unstructured decisions will generally have a quite substantial impact on the organisation and its participants. Examples of such decisions will include the introduction of new product lines, the development into new fields of production and the acquisition of interests in other companies. The implications of these decisions may be far-reaching and quite different for the various groups which comprise the organisation, and may be particularly uncertain. In such situations, the decision taker will not have encountered such decisions before and may be unable to specify possible outcomes or even the alternatives which are available. Researchers studying these decision situations have attempted to analyse the problem-solving processes or heuristics which might be adopted[8] This approach involves an understanding of human problem solving and the development of rules which the decision taker might adopt when confronted with an unstructured decision situation.

8.   See H.A. Simon 1966 (footnote 5), pp. 21–34.

Such rules might be quite simple (even rules-of-thumb), but would be designed to encourage practitioners to develop their own problem solving abilities. The management accounting system could assist the decision taker in this process by providing a source of data. Researchers should explore the heuristics of unstructured decision taking, with the object of designing appropriate data bases to assist decision takers in unstructured situations.

To conclude this discussion of the role of quantitative techniques, the importance of recognising the limitations of such techniques should be emphasised. Quantitative decision models can be extremely useful for structured decisions — but of little use for unstructured decisions. The researcher who does not recognise this may produce very elegant, but totally useless, models. A suggestion for further research into the role of opportunity costs for decision making is described below, to illustrate the type of research which is needed in management accounting. This research is primarily concerned with the use of quantitative techniques, but it should not ignore the insights which have been gained by the organisational and behavioural researchers.

An Illustrative Research Proposal

Chapter 13 described the history of accounting for decisions from 1617, when Robert Loder recognised the notions of avoidable costs and opportunity costs, to the 1960s, when the different-costs-for-different-purposes approach entered management (or cost) accounting textbooks. Chapter 6 described how relevant costs for a decision can be ascertained by asking the question: what difference will it make? Accordingly, relevant costs can be determined only in the context of the particular decision being taken. Inevitably, this gives rise to problems in the design of accounting systems. This may go some way to explain why accounting systems in practice are normally designed for control, rather than for the provision of information for decisions.

We can identify three aspects of the approach to costing for decisions normally discussed in the management accounting textbooks written by academics. First, past or sunk costs are irrelevant; relevant costs must reflect the possible alternative uses of available resources. Second, allocations of fixed costs are arbitrary and misleading. Third, when evaluating a particular alternative, foregone opportunities must be considered. These ideas are generally accepted by academic accountants and are normally taught to undergraduate students.

The extent to which this approach is used in practice is unclear at the present time. It is generally supposed that the techniques are not widely adopted, but there is a shortage of empirical evidence. An empirical examination of the routine (or formal) accounting systems which are found in practice will not be sufficient for this purpose. Organisational researchers have found that decision takers will have both formal and informal sources of information. The formal information will include routine reports prepared by the accountant. In addition, a decision maker may use information obtained informally (i.e. apart from the formal system, for example from casual observation, past experience and so on) to modify the formally obtained information.

The collection of comprehensive empirical evidence on the formal and informal uses of opportunity costs in practice would provide a sound basis for further research. In the absence of this empirical evidence, we will consider the possible implications and directions for further research, assuming that the above approach to costing for decisions is not generally used in practice. As was described in Chapter 13, the case for the opportunity cost approach has been argued by academics over the years. Accordingly, it is important to ask the question: why are opportunity costs apparently not used in practice?

Dillon and Nash examined the role of 'relevant costs' in a world of uncertainty.[9] They argued that when utility analysis is introduced to deal with uncertainty, apparently 'irrelevant' items (such as fixed costs) may become relevant as the decision maker will be concerned with changes in his total utility. An incremental approach may not be appropriate in an uncertain world; an evaluation of the total outcomes of the available

9. R.D. Dillon and J.F. Nash, The true relevance of relevant costs, *Accounting Review*, January 1978, pp. 11–17.

alternatives may be necessary. The arguments advanced by Dillon and Nash 'lead to the conclusion that the conventional incremental approach to decision making, in which costs are divided into relevant and irrelevant portions, needs to be used with caution under particular conditions, especially when large dollar amounts are involved and the decision involves uncertainty'.[10] The introduction of risk and uncertainty suggests a limitation of one aspect of costing for decisions — the use of relevant costs. An examination of the opportunity cost approach in an uncertain world is potentially interesting and necessary.

The role of overhead allocation is another issue which has received some attention recently. Zimmerman has suggested that overhead allocations might act as (i) a lump-sum tax which reduces the manager's consumption of perquisites and (ii) a proxy variable for difficult-to-observe opportunity costs.[11] The second of these two reasons for overhead allocation is reminiscent of a suggestion made by Baxter in 1938.[12] Baxter suggested that accountants should not rely on this proxy measure. Zimmerman, on the other hand, might argue that, as overheads are frequently allocated in practice, we should infer that the costs of obtaining more accurate measures of the difficult-to-observe opportunity costs must exceed the loss caused by using overhead allocations as a proxy measure.

Unfortunately, the strength of this argument cannot be evaluated at the present time, because of a lack of empirical evidence. New insights into the role of overhead allocation (and the use of opportunity costs generally) could be obtained by empirically investigating the various costs and benefits. A study of the effects of alternative costing approaches on the allocation of resources within firms could be very useful. Such a study might use simulation and/or empirical data and consider various decision situations. The survey of existing practice, suggested earlier, would be helpful in designing such

10. See footnote 9.
11. J.L. Zimmerman, The costs and benefits of cost allocations, *Accounting Review*, July 1979, pp. 504—21.
12. W.T. Baxter, A note on the allocation of oncosts between departments, *The Accountant*, 5 November 1938, pp. 633—6.

a study. The results of this research should give some indication of the costs and benefits of using the different-costs-for-different-purposes approach in practice.

The examination of alternative costing approaches suggested above starts from an acceptance of the underlying logic of the opportunity cost approach to costing for decisions, and seeks to examine the implementation problems. As was indicated in Chapter 13, the academically accepted approach was developed primarily by economists in the 1930s. Accordingly it is based on a neo-classical economic view of the organisation. The relevance of this view as a basis for designing management accounting information might be questioned. If accounting information is used in a political process within organisations, then a purely economic view (especially, a neo-classical economic view) is unlikely to provide an appropriate basis for the design of accounting systems.

In seeking to establish the reasons why particular costs are used by decision makers in practice, it may be necessary to look to behavioural and organisational research. The behavioural research should give some insights into the nature of personal choice, discussed in Chapter 3. This may indicate the limitations of a neo-classical economic approach to decisions — decision makers may seek to satisfice rather than maximise. Furthermore, the role of accounting in the functioning of an organisation may suggest that an economic emphasis is relatively unimportant. A consideration of the behavioural and organisational issues may suggest hypotheses to explain why particular methods are adopted in practice. Research studies could then be designed to test the validity of these hypotheses.

Thus, despite a general agreement among academics on relevant costs for decisions, more research is needed. The research areas suggested above can be summarised by the following questions to which answers are still required:

(i) What costs should be used by a rational decision maker acting under conditions of uncertainty?
(ii) What costs are used by decision makers in practice?
(iii) What are the effects on resource allocation of basing decisions on various measures of cost?

(iv) Are the academically accepted costing methods appropriate in the organisational context of management accounting?

Inevitably, the above list is not exhaustive. Nevertheless, it does suggest a direction in which future research might proceed. In the next section the issues to be studied by the proposed research will be extended to management accounting in general.

General Research Issues

The research proposal illustrated above indicates that even in an area in which there is substantial agreement between academic accountants, there is still a need for research. This research, however, should have a different emphasis from much of the work undertaken to date. Many management accounting researchers in the past have adopted a normative approach — they have sought to ascertain what methods ought to be used in practice. As recent research has had only a limited impact on practice, there is an urgent need for positive (or empirical) research to ascertain the reasons why particular methods are adopted by practitioners. Such research should lead to a better understanding of management accounting in practice and provide a base for *both* descriptive and prescriptive theories.

In some areas research has already been undertaken to collect systematic data on the methods used in practice, while in other areas the available evidence is either anecdotal or conjectural. More empirical research is needed to fill in the gaps in our knowledge of what actually happens in practice. What information is reported by the management accounting systems, either routinely or on special requests? What information do decision makers use for planning or control purposes? Care must be taken not to overlook the informal sources of information which may be available within organisations. Evidence concerning the formal management accounting system will be useful, but insufficient. Research effort must be directed to identifying what practices are *actually* adopted by accountants and managers — and not simply at enquiring what the chief accountant thinks should be happening!

A detailed awareness of existing practice will provide the basis for a *positive* analysis of management accounting. The object of such an analysis will be to identify and explain the determination of management accounting practice. The analysis can be undertaken at both the empirical and theoretical levels. The empirical work may involve the questioning and observation of practitioners, both accountants and managers, to identify the ways in which accounting information is used in the managerial process. Theoretical models may also be used to explain practice, as for instance Zimmerman explained the allocation of fixed costs referred to earlier. Initially, these theoretical models may be based on existing normative theories of behaviour — such as the economic theory of personal choice. But later it may become necessary to explore alternative behavioural approaches.

This research will have many facets in the various areas which are traditionally thought to encompass management accounting and some researchers will inevitably (and quite rightly) seek to redraw the boundaries of the subject. Accordingly, it would be impossible to describe, in anything except the most general terms, the nature of the research to be undertaken. However, some areas do seem quite clear.

Firstly, work needs to be done to investigate the problems of implementing the quantitative techniques which have been proposed in academic writings. In the development of these techniques, little attention was given to the problems of (i) estimating the necessary information in a world characterised by uncertainty, and (ii) the costs of data collection and analysis. Many of the more complex techniques handle risky situations through the use of probability estimates for the various outcomes. But in an uncertain world the nature of the outcomes may themselves be uncertain. For instance, a manager who decides to introduce a new product might find it impossible to identify and evaluate all the possible outcomes flowing from that decision. He introduces the product because he recognises that, unless he regularly markets new product lines, he will fall behind his competitors. In such a situation, the manager might be unable to provide meaningful data for the complex quantitative techniques. In addition, although the actual processing costs in terms of computer time may not be very large even for the most complex techniques, the costs of the managerial time required for making estimates and evaluating results may be large enough to discourage their use.

The second area is the study of the organisational context of management accounting. The role of management accounting in the organisation needs to be identified. The work completed to date in this area has done little more than raise a number of interesting questions. Developments of this line of research may help to clarify the purposes which management accounting can serve and to identify the characteristics of the techniques which are likely to be adopted in practice.

The third (but by no means the only other) development is likely to be in the study of individual decision making and information processing. The normative theories which have been used in management accounting research have been derived from neo-classical economics. These theories are likely to prove naive for models of management accounting practice. Organisational decision making may be rather more than a simple process of maximising the utility of some ownership group. Bargaining processes may form an important part of such models. Furthermore, little attention has been given in the study of management accounting to the role of information in decision making processes. Traditionally, it has been assumed that if information is provided (in almost any form!), it will be used. A branch of psychology dealing with human information processing may assist efforts to understand how information can be used by decision makers, and this may have implications for the design of management accounting systems.

The research suggestions outlined above are based partly on an extrapolation of trends which are beginning to appear in the literature and partly on a personal belief that a move towards a positive approach in management accounting research is essential to the development of the subject.

Conclusion

In this chapter we have attempted to obtain an overview of management accounting and to suggest the directions for further research. The coverage has been general and the research suggestions wide. However, the chapter was not intended to be comprehensive. Its purpose was to describe the relationship between theory and practice, and to illustrate the nature of the research issues which have to be resolved.

It was generally believed a few years ago that the major problems in management accounting had been solved in the 1960s and little research remained to be done. I hope that this chapter has convinced the reader that much still needs to be done and, indeed, that we are approaching a new era of development in the study of management accounting.

Index